Wagner's 'Ring' and its Symbols

By the same author

★

THE INTERPRETATION OF EARLY MUSIC

WAGNER'S 'RING'
AND ITS SYMBOLS

The Music and the Myth

———————— ❊ ————————

ROBERT
DONINGTON

FABER AND FABER
24 Russell Square
London

First published in mcmlxiii
by Faber and Faber Limited
24 Russell Square, London, W.C.1
Second impression mcmlxiii
Printed in Great Britain
by Ebenezer Baylis and Son, Limited
The Trinity Press, Worcester, and London

To

JOHN LAYARD

in gratitude and affection

Contents

———————— ❈ ————————

9

Contents

Contents

Contents

FAMILY TREES IN THE 'RING'

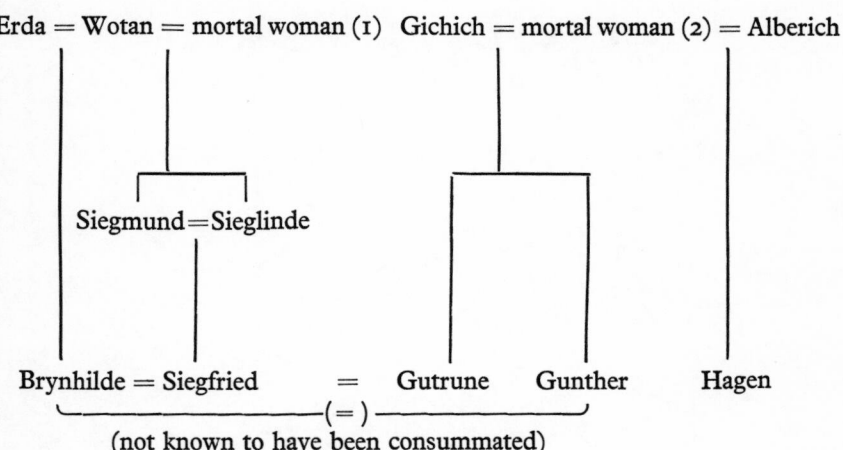

Erda = Wotan = mortal woman (1)   Gichich = mortal woman (2) = Alberich

Siegmund=Sieglinde

Brynhilde = Siegfried   =   Gutrune   Gunther   Hagen
(not known to have been consummated)

Wagner's treatment of these relationships differs considerably from his Norse originals, which are themselves very inconsistent. In the *Ring*, the following further indications of relationship occur: Fricka is Wotan's lawful spouse; Mime is Alberich's brother; the lesser gods and goddesses call each other brother and sister (with the exception of Loge); Fafner and Fasolt, the giants, are brothers; the Rhinemaidens are sisters; all the lesser Valkyries are Brynhilde's sisters, and like her, offspring of Wotan and Erda; the Norns are daughters of Erda but not of Wotan.

CHAPTER I

Myth and Music

———— ❈ ————

SYMBOLS AT WORK

This book is an approach to Wagner by way of his symbols. The subject of these symbols is in no way remote or mysterious. The subject is everyday reality.

We communicate through symbols of an elementary kind whenever we exchange glances, show our feelings on our faces and in our voices, or make instinctive or deliberate gestures. Wagner attached considerable artistic importance to this elementary symbolism of facial expression, vocal inflexion and bodily gesture; he discussed it with the same seriousness as the more highly developed images which constitute his poetry and his music. There is no difference in principle. There is no special secret about the symbols which are incorporated in a work of art. They are merely one variety of a method of communication with which we are all familiar. We are so familiar with it that we take it for granted. We use it all the time, but we are hardly aware that we are using it.

Poetry, unlike music, is conveyed in words; poetry uses verbal descriptions. These descriptions may work on our feelings very much as music does. But the descriptions themselves are not descriptions of our feelings; they are descriptions of scenes or actions which call up our feelings by the indirect but powerful workings of association. True poetic images, like true musical images, are always of this suggestive character. Poetry, so long as it remains poetry, never explains; it simply presents images, trusting these images to do their own work on our imagination. The images work because they are symbolic. They are not merely symbolic on a deliberate level; they are symbolic already of their own accord. True poetic creation is a primarily intuitive affair.

Our recognition of poetic and other symbols at the receiving end is likewise intuitive. Lovers, for example, may fall back on well-worn images, which once were poetry, when they have feelings to express which so far from being too remote or mysterious for mere ordinary words are too intimate and immediate; and so long as they remain in love, they have no difficulty in understanding one another. Falling in love is a perfectly definite experience; yet it is not an experience which words can describe directly in any adequate manner. Nor can music depict it literally; but it can depict the underlying mood. It is in this sense, and not in any more direct or literal sense, that the content of music is like the content of poetry in having mainly to do with feelings. In music as in poetry, the same kind of feelings call up the same kind of images; and what is more, the same kind of images meet with the same kind of recognition.

Not only in poetry, music and the other arts, but throughout our human experience, we show this strange capacity for producing and recognizing symbolic images: strange not in the sense of striking us as such when we are exercising it, but only in the sense of remaining something of a scientific puzzle. We are bound to admit that the cuckoo does not learn his call from his fond parents, since his fond parents were not around to learn it from; he can only produce and recognize it through inherited behaviour patterns. Human beings also inherit behaviour patterns. We have, moreover, the further advantage of an environment which is rich in the symbols characteristic of our species. So characteristic are they, indeed, that from one point of view it might be possible to define our species in terms of its symbols. What with our intuitions, which appear to be in some respects innate, and what with our traditions, which despite some wastage are vast and cumulative, we certainly grow up with a working knowledge of symbols. It may or may not matter whether we have much if any rational understanding of their meaning or even of their existence. It undoubtedly matters whether we can accept them intuitively enough for them to do their work.

SYMBOLS COMMON TO OUR SPECIES

It is one of the most impressive facts about our human species how widely we share our symbolic images in common. Throughout myths and folklore, throughout rituals and doctrines, throughout every branch of art, and throughout the dreams, the fantasies and the waking visions of both ordinary and extraordinary people, we meet, at all times and places, recurrences not only of the same material but of the same images for that material. It is only details of a comparatively minor importance, matters of idiom rather than of substance, which seem to vary to any great extent with variations of period, topography, natural and cultural setting, stylistic fashion and other factors whose influence might have been expected to be more radical than is in fact the case. Opinions still differ as to how this unmistakable similarity came to exist; for the moment, I am only concerned to note that it does exist, but I shall mention a suggested explanation in the next section but one.

The images themselves have always made their own immensely powerful impression by being accepted intuitively. It would be hard to exaggerate the value to mankind of this intuitive receptivity to the traditional symbols, great and small, which do so much to make our species what it is. But it is just as human a disposition to look behind our traditions inquisitively as it is to build them up; and this disposition to look for rational explanations where traditional explanations have previously served can also have its value. It is, indeed, an inescapable condition of our long journey from animal innocence into a human state of greater self-awareness.

Our rational awareness of our symbolic images has been put on to a new footing by a combination of recent researches in three fields of which the respective experts have so far achieved very little direct collaboration, but always with the most strikingly illuminating results in so far as they do achieve it. These fields are mythology, anthropology and depth psychology, in not one of which can we take a perspective view without some complementary insight into the other two. With regard to the latest of the three to be opened up, that is to say depth psychology, the pioneer was Freud, who already both learnt and taught something in the other two, though as an amateur, whereas his partial successor Jung became relatively professional in mythology and at least well equipped to keep abreast in anthropology. Very few professional mythologists and anthropologists could yet say as much in depth psychology. Yet direct collaboration has made a start, and there has been a much greater amount of general cross-fertilization and dissemination of ideas. Most of this has proved uncommonly fruitful.

The idea of applying some such combined approach to Wagner, with the addition of a further and most essential line of approach (developed both in my text and still more intensively in my Musical Appendix) directly by way of his music, had been shaping itself in my mind for some years before it abruptly exploded into the first draft of the present book over a period of seven weeks. Thereafter, of course, the hard work began. The most urgent necessity was to follow up what Wagner himself had said about the very numerous and striking symbols which make his *Ring* so interesting a study from my present point of view. It was also obvious

B

that I should have to learn a great deal more about the mythological sources where Wagner found most of these symbols in a traditional condition. All this was duly done, and resulted in a second and longer draft of which the fate will be mentioned in due course. It was not the last.

WAGNER'S ATTITUDE TO HIS SYMBOLS

With regard to Wagner's attitude, three points arise: first, that he had a very great deal to say about the symbols; second, that what he had to say is inconsistent and even self-contradictory in a way in which his actual use of the symbols is most emphatically not; third, that he became very well aware of this discrepancy, and had the artist's good sense to back his intuitive practice as against his theoretical rationalizations.

Wagner, in short, made many attempts at a rational explanation of his *Ring*; and very penetrating they often are. But they varied so much that he came to realize that his symbols were more truly communicative of their own accord than the best of his explanations. His friend Roeckel once attempted an explanation which Wagner was at great pains to correct in a long and famous letter (25 Jan. 1854). In this letter he himself made the fascinating and I think fully justified assertion that his under-lying subject is 'the depicting of reality': of life as it really is, than which no subject can be of more general human interest. We all at some time and in some form must have asked ourselves this most searching of questions: what is life really all about? And we must all know more of the answer than we can put into words. What we know wells up in us in the shape of symbols.

The *Ring* contains a great part of Wagner's answer. But he is very properly doubtful as to how much of this he or anyone else could explain in words. He makes (same letter) the pointed remark: 'I see afresh how much there is, from the very nature of my poetical intention, which can only be made understandable by the music.' He writes: 'I believe it was a sound instinct which set me on my guard against an undue enthusi-asm for making things clear, for I have come to the firm conclusion that to make my intention too obvious would get in the way of a genuine understanding; in drama and in art generally, the way to make an effect is not by arguing an opinion but by putting forward something in-stinctive.' Rubbing it in, he adds: 'Such mistakes are of course only possible in the case of a reader who substitutes his own ideas for those of the poet, while the simple-minded reader, perhaps without consciously realizing it, takes the matter in more easily, just as it is.'

Writing to the same friend (23 Aug. 1856) Wagner describes, as he already had to Liszt (25 Nov. 1850), the perennial conflict between his powers of reasoning and of intuition: between his 'consciously or rationally formed ideas' and 'the exquisite unconsciousness of artistic creation'. For 'how can an artist expect that what he has felt intuitively should be perfectly understood by other people, since he himself feels in the presence of his work, if it is genuine art, that he is faced by a riddle about which he too may have illusions, just as another person may?' Indeed 'we can form no abstract idea of a thing unless we have already taken it in as a living intuition'.

It is because we respond intuitively to Wagner's symbols in the opera-house that his audience continues to be so large and popular. Even a mistaken abstract idea of what a symbol means can at the worst only lessen our response. It cannot prevent us from responding if we have it in us to do so. It cannot force a false response out of us, nor enable an artist to force a false meaning on to a symbol. Certainly a symbol can develop in use; certainly it can be made to serve good or bad causes; certainly it can die from prolonged misunderstanding or neglect. But so long as it remains alive in substance and not just in form, a symbol wields an uncanny power of its own. As some outer or inner image brings a symbol into our awareness, with or without our rational assent something happens to us. A symbol in the full sense of the word is something more than the image which carries it. The impact of a symbol is not just a perception. It is an event. It does something to us.

The main sense given by the *Oxford English Dictionary* to the word symbol is 'something that stands for, represents or denotes something else . . . especially a material object representing or taken to represent something immaterial or abstract'; a secondary sense is merely equivalent to a sign, a figure or a mark. In this book, I shall keep within the first of these definitions, but with rather more emphasis on the literal rendering, which is something 'brought together'. A symbolical image only works as a symbol for us in so far as we have an answering potentiality to bring together with it. We have, however, more such potentialities in common than may superficially appear; for we have a considerable capacity for suppressing responses well within the range of our potentialities; while our awareness of those which we do not suppress varies to an astonishing degree.

A symbol in the sense intended here is not an arbitrary contrivance or a convenient substitute for words, as a slogan, a trade-mark or an emblem may be. A symbol has a rightness and inevitability which we can recognize, and of which we can elaborate the imagery in various artistic and other ways, but which we cannot counterfeit. We can project an inner meaning on to an outer object, thus making a personal symbol of it; when enough people and generations have done this, the symbol is a collective one; but nothing can make an object carry a symbolical meaning which is incongruous. It is only a certain intrinsic similarity and correspondence between the object or image on the one side and the inner experience or realization on the other side which can give rise to a symbol.

What a symbol can do when it impinges on us is to bring to a sharp and effectual focus an experience or realization previously latent in us as a potentiality. The result is a concentration of energy which may alter the balance of inner forces so substantially as to amount to a change in the personality: a change to which both symbol and personality contribute. It is one of the most important facts about symbolism that the personality is capable of growing by means of the symbols it assimilates.

When we go to Wagner's *Ring*, we invite his symbols to make their own direct and irrational impact on us through what he so rightly calls a 'living intuition'. It still remains open to us, however, to amplify them rationally by drawing comparisons which set them in a wider context, so as to find out rather more about what it is to which we are intuitively responding. In my attempt to do this here, I shall try to tell the story of the *Ring* with some of the spontaneous excitement in which we experience it in the opera-house; I shall bring in aspects of Wagner's own life-story which may throw light on his symbols; I shall have something to say about the symbols in the music as well as in the myth. My general approach will be on the lines opened up by the work of Jung.

SYMBOLS AS ARCHETYPAL IMAGES

That different interpreters of Wagner, and Wagner himself at different times, should have offered different explanations of the *Ring* is not surprising. Like other experiences which have roots in the unconscious, a work of art contains more meanings than an onion has skins. We can get to the centre of an onion, but we cannot get to the centre of a work of art. There is always another meaning underneath. An explanation which is true and adequate on one level may be more or less irrelevant on another level. But even when they appear to be mutually contradictory, these layers of meaning never really cancel each other out. They may show opposite facets of the same truth; but our life is full of opposites, and one of the services which art performs for us is to suggest that they may not be so irreconcilable as they often appear.

The underlying mood of a work as complex as Wagner's *Ring* is neither delight nor pain but an extraordinarily poignant compound of the two. The poignancy comes from our feeling that this really is what life is like, in all the fullness of its bitter-sweet intensity. A work complex enough to take us as far as that is certain to contain paradoxes. There is not one important symbol in the *Ring* of which we shall not find that the significance is ultimately ambiguous. A large part of our attention will be given to looking for the factors which make sense of this ambiguity.

That a paradox makes sense is the whole point of its being a paradox. It is only our rational attention that has to be turned somewhat cumbersomely from one layer of meaning to another. Our intuition gets to work without the least discomfort on as many layers at once as lie within reach of our own potentialities. It does not disturb our intuition to find that the same symbol carries meanings which if taken separately would appear to be incompatible. Our intuition does not take them separately.

If our potentialities were basically different, we could never respond intuitively, as we do, in much the same way to the same work of art. Our basic potentialities are shared in common. Perhaps the clearest confirmation of this is to be seen in the world-wide and age-old distribution already mentioned of symbolic images which, though endlessly varied in style and detail, are plainly variations on the same underlying themes.

It has been shown by anthropologists that this similarity is associated with a vast process of cultural diffusion. But it is elementary psychology that cultural influences are only taken up where some answering potentiality awaits them. There is, moreover, both anthropological and psychological evidence for the spontaneous recurrence of the same underlying themes where neither conscious imitation nor unconscious recollection appears to have been possible. Jung, for example, has repeatedly drawn attention to modern dreams and fantasies which recapitulate traditional symbols, often with uncanny exactness, in circumstances precluding even a buried memory of the existing sources (as when these were unpublished or otherwise inaccessible at the time).

The explanation to which Jung was led empirically during his work of deepening and expanding Freud's crucial discoveries is that we have an innate disposition to throw up the same kind of images for the same kind of themes. These themes are not all equally important or widespread; but they have the common characteristic of being more than merely individual. They have in some way crystallized out from the age-old experience of our race. They have a collective rather than an exclusively personal significance. One of the terms which Jung applied to such collective themes when their roots lie deep in racial experience is 'archetypal'. The most important of them appear to be fundamental to our human living, and therefore universal in their incidence.

The science of biology gives us no present reason to suppose that mental images can be inherited. But behaviour patterns can be inherited, including a predisposition not only to throw up but also to recognize and respond to symbolical imagery without even the necessity of knowing that it is symbolical (just as the cuckoo's call, though a symbol, is not a conscious symbol). We recognize the experience of our race as successive generations have distilled it through myth and ritual, art and folk-lore, none of which would retain their fascination as they do if their underlying subjects were merely fanciful. Their underlying subjects are, in fact, ourselves, and those unseen forces which surely we must all, however comprehendingly or uncomprehendingly, and under whatever attempted explanation if any, somehow sense at work within ourselves. Wagner, like most artists, was very aware of being worked through by something bigger than his conscious self. In one form or another the experience is a very general one.

It is to describe these forces working like an unseen magnetic field to induce a collective alignment into our individual lives that Jung has revived the ancient term 'archetype'. Though we know the archetypes only from their effects, what we know tallies with the intuitive appreciation of them revealed in sacred writings, art, ritual, mythology and other traditional sources. Such tradition is of inestimable value. Yet even independently of tradition, traditional images make their autonomous appearance. We may regard them as a means of communication by which the archetypes make their presence felt.

SYMBOLS REGARDED AS FUNCTIONS OF PSYCHIC CONSCIOUSNESS

One rather significant problem of description may be mentioned here. We can have a very full experience of the *Ring* without being conscious, in the rational sense, of the enhanced understanding of life which Wagner's symbols are conveying to us in some deeper layer of receptiveness. Yet we are certainly conscious of having the experience and of being profoundly moved by it. How are we to describe this work which the symbols are doing on us, in one sense consciously, in another sense not?

The word 'unconscious' seems inappropriate. I am not at all sure that 'unconscious symbol' is not a contradiction in terms. It is by impinging on our awareness that an image can play the part of a symbol for us. But this awareness, though it cannot be in the total sense unconscious, need not be in the ordinary sense conscious. We are conscious of the symbols. We may not be, in the rational sense, conscious of their meaning, though their meaning is working on us through our intuition.

This difficulty of description is one which arises in many other connections besides the artistic imagery with which we are here concerned. A term has recently been introduced by John Layard to meet the not uncommon situations in which it occurs. In preference to the term 'unconscious' (which is too wide and too inaccurate for this purpose) or the term 'creative unconscious' sometimes favoured (which is too vague and still not very accurate) Layard uses his new term 'psychic consciousness', as an opposite to 'ego consciousness', when he wants to emphasize the dynamic aspect of our deeper psychic processes: that is to say, processes deep enough in the psyche not to lie directly within the awareness of our conscious ego; yet not so deep that we cannot have a most vivid indirect awareness of what is going on.

What emerges into psychic consciousness is no longer altogether unknown to us; though it may be unknown rationally, it is in effect known intuitively. As this intuitive knowledge rises nearer to the surface, it may also become accessible to rational consideration, which in its turn will not be without its impact on our deeper layers. In such ways as this, our consciousness can play the most delicate game of ball with the unconscious, and indeed is continually doing so. Now the unconscious will score a point, and now the conscious, but what matters most is that the game itself shall be going along reasonably well. It may perhaps not be stretching this metaphor too far if we regard psychic consciousness, from one point of view, as providing the field of play, or from another point of view, as being the game. In other words, psychic consciousness may sometimes be thought of as a region of the psyche, and sometimes as an activity of the psyche. Like all such terms, it must not be taken in a more fixed sense than the exceedingly fluid and elusive reality to which it applies.

With regard to the psyche itself, at any rate in its deeper processes, we have to make up our minds to the fact that it is essentially autonomous. Like T. S. Eliot's 'Rum Tum Tugger the Curious Cat', it will do what it do do and there's no doing anything about it; fortunately for us, since at such levels ego would not know what was the best thing to do. However, though we can do nothing to control the autonomous psyche, we can do a great deal towards getting into relation with it. The part of ourselves of which we are directly conscious, and to which psychologists give this name of ego, is the smaller part; but its importance is not small. Our conscious attitude can be as helpful to the psyche as the psyche is likely to be helpful to our conscious living if a co-operative relationship has developed.

The psyche responds to our attention and perception whether brought to it by going to the opera or any other artistic pursuit, by going to church, by analysing our dreams, or merely by following its hints out through the ordinary vicissitudes of personal relationship and working life. It responds by uncovering a purpose for us which not only transcends personal wishes formed in ego consciousness, but may fulfil them in unexpected ways such as the ego by itself could neither have anticipated nor achieved. Very many people live well tuned into their own underlying purpose without needing much if any directly conscious awareness of it. But the psyche is greatly encouraged by all forms of awareness of its activities, and it is part of the value of the arts that they draw our attention inwards to the psyche, whether or not we could give any such account of our experience in rational terms.[1]

Wagner must have had more than a glimpse of this side of art when in his *Opera and Drama* (1851) and elsewhere he described it as a function of the artist 'to bring the unconscious part of human nature into consciousness within society'. The artist can do this through our innate capacity to recognize his images, perhaps in very much the sense Plato had in mind when he wrote that learning is a kind of recognition. The same images were also used by Wagner to convey certain consciously allegorical allusions to political, social and economic realities of the outer world. These allusions have rightly interested his interpreters, but my

---

[1] John Layard, 'On Psychic Consciousness,' *Eranos-Jahrbuch*, Vol. XXVII, 1960, esp. pp. 277–78, and p. 342; I understand that Layard is now (1962) elaborating this theme in a larger work. For statements by C. G. Jung of his views as cited here, see my Bibl.; for an excellent short account, see Frieda Fordham, *Introduction to Jung's Psychology*, London (Pelican), 1953. For the archetypes, see Jolande Jacobi, *Complex, Archetype, Symbol*, tr. R. Manheim, London, 1959, and Michael Fordham, *New Developments in Analytical Psychology*, London, 1957, Ch. I, 'Biological Theory and the Concept of Archetypes', and Ch. III, 'Reflections on Image and Symbol'. For the views of Sigmund Freud, see especially his *Totem and Taboo*, tr. A. A. Brill, London, 1919, (Pelican) 1938.

concern here will be mainly with that complementary world in which our inner experiences arise. It is my working assumption that whenever Wagner uses a traditional symbol, this symbol has, for its primary meaning, the root meaning it has traditionally included in myth, ritual, doctrine, folk-lore, the arts, dreams, fantasies and visions. There may well be other important meanings, but the primary meaning is as the symbol itself conveys it.

With regard to this inner aspect, I am profoundly indebted to John Layard for his grasp of psychic structure, including the concept of 'psychic consciousness' already mentioned, the meaning of 'death' as a symbol of transformation, the term 'split shadow' later employed, the symbolic significance of 'incest' and other matters. Much of my general attitude derives from our many conversations, not specifically about the *Ring*, but ranging from anthropology and primitive religion to current problems of psychology. Layard has been good enough to read through early stages of my manuscript and to give me advice from which it greatly benefited. I must absolve him from any responsibility for the book itself, but I should like to put my gratitude on record here.

I have also discussed this aspect of the book with Mrs. Patricia Dale-Green, and I am grateful to her for many valuable suggestions.

SYMBOLS AS INNER EXPERIENCE

The term inner experience is not meant in any esoteric sense. Our educational institutions have at the moment a certain tendency to disparage anything which cannot be more or less objectively measured. But subjective reality is not as a matter of experience less real than objective reality. The relationship between the two remains a philosophical and scientific enigma, but there is as good evidence for the existence of the one as there is for the existence of the other, and the relationship comes increasingly to seem intimate beyond all our previous scientific conceptions. There have always been philosophers capable of this inclusive view; but then there are some philosophers, and some scientists, who seem capable of anything. Some philosophers have taken matter as an exclusively mental phenomenon and some scientists have taken mind as an exclusively material phenomenon. Perhaps mind and matter are ultimately one, but as we experience them they are different, and we cannot give a complete account of Beethoven in terms of measurable electricity.

As a matter of experience, our inner world includes perceptions, sensations, judgments and feelings, all of which are inner events, whatever their relationship to the outer world. The values we set on things and the beauty or ugliness we ascribe to them are inner events, as Hume meant when he said that 'beauty is no quality in things themselves: it exists merely in the mind which contemplates them'. Mental events cannot merely be reduced to a function of matter. Psychology is not a branch of neurology. The interaction, however, is growing clearer all the time. Many disorders such as asthma, ulcers and cancer are already known or believed to be psycho-somatic, originating in the psyche though operating in the body. We call a man an introvert if he is more inclined to notice the inner aspects of reality, and we call him an extrovert if he is more inclined to notice the outer aspects. But as a matter of experience, both inner and outer reality are important. Indeed, the most potent dynamism in our ordinary living is experienced as working on us from the inside. We sometimes call it the life-force, or more technically, libido.

When a psychotic believes that he is Napoleon I, we can disprove this as a fact of the outer world, but not as a fact of the inner world, where it is real enough to have him desperately in its power. It is real as a symbol, and to help him we have not to deny his symbol but to try to find out what it means. The irrational beliefs of sane men in religion and metaphysics are also symbols whose reality it is naïve to deny, since they certainly have power and they certainly mean something. No inner fact means literally what it would mean as an outer fact. We are continually confusing the two kinds of reality; but in so far as we can sort them out, they do not contradict one another. They are complementary. Material facts can be measured. Symbols have to be understood and valued. The evidence on the conscious and unconscious workings of symbolism now accumulated in case-histories and general studies is extensive and deserves the greatest scientific respect. Symbols are imponderables, but imponderables are real.

THE MUSICAL SYMBOLS

A musical motive is a symbolic image, and like other such images may, on one level, be thought of as an act of self-portraiture on the part of something archetypal. It occurs to the composer because an archetype, or a group of archetypes, is active in his psyche. It is this basically spontaneous activity which if all goes well will result, aided by a great deal of more or less conscious shaping, in a composition.

When Elgar said that he had only to stretch out his hand to take what music he needed from the air around him, he was using a suggestive metaphor. The music is not waiting in the air outside; but it is waiting in the psyche, in the sense that the archetypes are always waiting for an opportunity to get themselves clothed in images. There has only been one Elgar, and only one Wagner: no one else can repeat (though many have tried) another man's personal vision. Those who can collaborate with the archetypes in producing works of art do so at first hand rather than by imitating. But many who cannot produce images of genius can recognize them when they are of so general an appeal as Wagner's. All who enjoy his music, and some who do not, receive an intuitive impression of what his motives mean.

When composers use similar motives, we need not assume imitation, even inadvertently. It is, on the whole, remarkable what inexhaustible diversity composers find, seeing that their compositions are all variations on fundamental material which we have no cause for thinking to be very extensive. But only a very little satisfactory research had been done until recently into the significance not of the divergencies but of the similarities in the basic images of music. Deryck Cooke has now opened up the subject with a matter-of-fact lucidity and straightforwardness in admirable contrast to the involved approaches of previous writers, none of whom quite succeeded in arriving at Cooke's starting-point.[1]

The leading motives by which Wagner so often reveals the unspoken thought behind the words, the unavowed intention behind the actions or the hidden personality behind the plausible exterior are images having a certain relative completeness in themselves. But they are also capable of symphonic development and of contrapuntal combination. They are not finite, but organic, and in many cases their power of growth is as striking as the distinctness with which their essential character persists through both development and combination. Like the archetypes portrayed in them, they are essentially fluid. So freely do they inter-react that a great part of the musical texture comes close to fulfilling Wagner's ideal of a seamless tapestry.

In my text, I refer to the motives by number, sometimes adding a descriptive label, more often not. Fundamentally, Wagner's motives speak for themselves. This is a general truth with regard to music, being what lies behind Mendelssohn's much quoted and very perceptive remark to the effect that the meanings conveyed by music are not too indefinite to be put into words but too definite. Nevertheless, Wagner's music does strike us as going to exceptional lengths in the directness of its expression. When we come to examine it, the formal virtues are there, but in so

[1] Deryck Cooke, *The Language of Music*, London, 1959.

flexible a condition that they seem to be almost dissolved in the irresistible flow of feeling. Wagner's music cannot be resisted; it can only be accepted or rejected. It has an immediacy rare even for this most immediate of the arts.

This directness of expression, this immediacy of feeling, this fluidity of form coupled with definiteness of content were factors even more important than the originality of the melodic line, the novelty of the harmony and the enrichment of the orchestration in making Wagner a composer hardly anyone of his generation interested in music at all was able to ignore. There were many who disliked him; and even when we set aside the excellent personal grounds he so often gave them for doing so, there remains a hard core of aesthetic distaste and disparagement. He was a figure of controversy all over Europe: itself a tribute to the forcefulness with which he impinged on the contemporary scene. To a very large extent he remains a figure of controversy even now, and it is not hard to see why.

The quality in Wagner's music which attracts his admirers is the same quality which repels his detractors. It is not merely that the emotion it expresses is overwhelmingly human: this is equally true of Beethoven, and in the noblest sense. There are noble elements in Wagner's music; yet noble is not the word I should choose in which to sum it up. Wagner's music is not only very human, but human in a very earthy way. Against this earthiness there is set a capacity for exaltation not only of the senses but of the spirit too. In other words, Wagner touches the depths and he touches the heights. He covers the span of human experience with an impartial zest and relish which is at the very least Rabelaisian, and which those who admire him as much as I do would call Faustian.

Like Faust, Wagner was driven on to experience the best and the worst in himself until he really knew what it is like to be a human being, with a thoroughness few mortals either need or could achieve. All this experience was brought into and worked out through his music-dramas. Unfortunately for Wagner as a person, but fortunately for his art, he had a temperament which compelled him, often enough, to live out his worst and blindest side in his dealings with the outer world of men and women, but his best and most insightful side in his dealings with the inner world of visionary creativeness: i.e. in his work. Not equally, however, in all his work. Whatever his *reason* touched, he illuminated, but fitfully, with a smoky glow, as he himself once realized in a rare yet somehow characteristic moment of lucidity when he described his prose-writings as a poison that he had somehow to get out of his system (letter to the King of

Saxony, May 1856). Whatever his *intuition* decided for him in the matter of his art, on the other hand, tended to be decided with real wisdom and inspiration.

Many people are virtually unable to live out their darker side except in their dreams and fantasies. This may help to keep them out of tangible troubles, but often at a high cost in half-hearted living. Wagner brought interminable troubles down on to his own head, but he lived with a whole-hearted intensity which is inseparably bound up with the intensity of his work. Because he was not the man to put much conscious check or unconscious inhibition on his own disposition to behave badly, he was correspondingly uninhibited in his composing. That is the nature of inhibition. It is all too often the case that if we form the unconscious habit of inhibiting our less desirable characteristics, our more desirable characteristics somehow get included in the ban. It is quite a different matter in so far as the control is genuinely conscious.

Brahms is the familiar contrast to Wagner in this respect. A few songs and late piano pieces, the clarinet quintet and certain other glimpses of his underlying warmth of feeling show how different a composer he might have been if he could have escaped more successfully from his own inhibitedness. This is not to disparage his fine achievements; but the one quality we least find there is the uninhibited flow which attracts to Wagner those whom it temperamentally suits, while repelling those whom it does not.

Wagner had an uncanny power of sending a musical phrase straight inside us, so that we instantly light up with a perfect incandescence of response and recognition. Brahms' violin sonata in A major is called the 'Meistersinger' on the grounds that its opening phrase resembles the opening of Walther's prize-song. So it does; but the temperature is lower. That is one difference (partly due to the appoggiatura on Wagner's fourth note, which is lacking in Brahms). Another difference is that Brahms quickly settles down to a well-constructed piece of musical architecture; but Wagner goes straight on with an impassioned flood of feeling.

It is not that Wagner lacked discipline or control; but he had an impassioned genius. So strongly does his music release the corresponding emotions in ourselves that it can be exceedingly distasteful or actually dangerous to some temperaments and in some states of mind. People who find this so, or who have a saving premonition that it might be so in their case, are justifiably prone to defend themselves either by forming a powerful dislike for Wagner's music or by subjectively filtering down its effect on themselves into an innocuous insignificance. People, on the other hand, who have no objection to being swept off their feet by a current of tremendous strength and vitality are rewarded by a singularly rich experience. Both good and evil are found in it, but reconciled after the healing manner of art, and indeed treated with an uncommon degree of intuitive understanding.

The very situations which Wagner seemed unable to handle with any sense of balance in the outer world, he handled with certainty in the depths of his intuition as an artist. He lived out the worst in himself and worked out the best in himself; he was a fumbler in the world and a genius in his art. The same intemperance which served him badly in his outer life served him well in his inner life. That seems to be a not unusual way with genius. It is unrealistic to regret the reverse side of Wagner's intemperance while welcoming its obverse side. They are opposite sides of the same coin.

For all its romantic vehemence, Wagner's music is mostly so definite and, in its own intuitive way, so self-explanatory that we shall more often find ourselves calling on the music to help in explaining the text than on the text to help in explaining the music. Every musical resemblance and relationship between two motives, whether consciously or unconsciously produced or a little of each, has a meaning for us in so far as we can get in touch with it. To help in bringing this out, the motives are here grouped in order of resemblance rather than of first appearance, as will be seen in my Musical Appendix. The numbers in my text refer to this grouping. My Musical Appendix itself contains the results of my own careful investigation into the similarities and correspondencies among the motives, and I hope that readers interested in the music will make full use of it, both by turning up the examples from the numbers in the text, and by working through the Musical Appendix separately.

As I had heard that Cooke had also a book on the *Ring* in preparation, I consulted him, and he delighted me by sending not only everything he then had in draft, but some fifty pages of detailed criticisms of my typescript. I accepted most of these, and started on a second revision, in course of which I found myself stimulated into some further re-thinking on my own account. At one point it seemed worth trying to produce between us and use in common what has so lamentably been lacking hitherto, an agreed list of motives in the *Ring* which would have some chance of being accepted as standard: the order being that of first appearance in the score. But while this list, on which we broadly agreed, will form an important element in his book, it became evident that it would be too long for mine, since I am not attempting a musical analysis of the richness of detail to which he has carried his. This detail will put our musical understanding of the *Ring* on a decidedly new footing. I am very much in sympathy with his approach though it is so very different from mine (being, as I think, more extroverted); and I believe our readers will find our two books complementary to one another. Meanwhile, I am indebted to him for a most unusual degree of help and encouragement.

This second revision was substantially my book as it now appears.

THE DRAMATIC SYMBOLS

Wagner's stage directions specify a number of visual symbols which in keeping with modern taste it has become usual to suggest impressionistically and in the main by lighting effects. Some of these effects are beautiful and appropriate; but the danger of them is that a symbol may fail to make its proper impact if it is not seen to be solidly present. Wagner repeatedly insists in his *Religion and Art* (1880) and elsewhere on the 'figurative value of the mythological symbols' in so far as 'the artist succeeds in revealing their deep and hidden truth'; for 'the incomparable thing about myth is that it is true for all time, and its content, however compressed, is inexhaustible throughout the ages'. Each new age will interpret the deep and hidden truth afresh, and is right to do so, but not to the extent of leaving out such essential symbols, for example, as the walls of Hunding's hut in Act I of the *Valkyrie*. On the whole, fairly solid and realistic stage scenery and properties seem to me extremely desirable in Wagner, not only because they were part of his original intention and are thus somehow more congruous with his style, but also because they give more substantiality to the symbolism than a virtually empty stage.

Again, while it is perfectly possible to enjoy the *Ring* with no intellectual benefit from the words, the speeches are so long, so boring if no word is understood (what speech is not?) yet so full of mythological and poetic symbols of absorbing interest and importance to the drama if properly appreciated, that some preparatory work on the text is really much more necessary than it is on the music. Words in an opera are often hard to catch, especially in a foreign language, but it is remarkably helpful to read the text through shortly beforehand, where necessary in two languages, one's own and the composer's. It is also helpful to make some study of what the words mean, since this is not only what they say.

Wagner's head sources for the text of the *Ring* were the poetic (Elder) and prose (Younger) Icelandic Eddas, together with the subsequent

Sagas largely based on them.[1] There is no consistent story or mythology to be extracted from these; but they are all the more symbolically suggestive on that account. No system of mutually consistent images could evoke the basic realities as this shifting panorama does. Our experience of the archetypes themselves is always fluctuating and often paradoxical. Their images condense and disperse in the psyche like eddies in a column of smoke, forming and re-forming, merging and remerging as the underlying archetypes mark this, that and the other myth or legend with some imprint of their own unseen essence. No wonder the myths and the legends, the gods and the heroes also intermingle; they would not be faithful images if they were static and systematic. They must always have intermingled; and since to some extent the individual recapitulates both the psychic and the physical stages of our racial development, not even the most primordial of these mythological manifestations has lost its relevance.

From this rich treasury Wagner took what he wanted and adapted it and added to it as he wanted. The art of myth-making is not dead; we find the age-old archetypes under some very odd disguises in the film-plots, the space-fiction or the detective stories of our time, but we find them, and on the whole, the naïver the plot the thinner the disguise. Wagner, however, like Goethe in writing *Faust*, gave himself the advantage of deliberately assimilating a body of traditional imagery before settling down to write a poem which besides being individual and contemporary achieved some of the timeless quality which he noticed in the traditional myths themselves.

WAGNER'S CHARACTERS AS SYMBOLS

Wagner's characters in the *Ring* are so alive that we have no difficulty in accepting them as individuals who love and hate, struggle and triumph, suffer and die with all the fascination for us of vivid personalities; and this straightforward aspect of them is exceedingly important. But like everything else in the drama, they are symbols too. As symbols, they are

---

[1] Ernest Newman, *Life of Wagner*, London, Vol. II, 1937, quotes Wagner as stating that he had consulted: *Der Nibelunge Noth und Klage*, ed. Lachmann; *Zu den Nibelungen*, etc., by Lachmann; Grimm's *Mythologie*; the *Eddas*; the *Volsunga-Saga*, in Hagen's version; the *Wilkina und Niflunga-Saga*, in Hagen's version; *Das deutsche Heldenbuch*, ed. Hagen, re-ed. Simrock; *Die deutsche Heldensaga*, by Wm. Grimm; More's writings on the German Sagas; the *Heimskringla*, tr. Mohnike.

parts of one another, so that in *Valkyrie*, Act II, Scene 2, for example, Brynhilde describes herself as Wotan's will. They are parts of Wagner, as to a very large extent he knew; and they are parts of us, since Wagner's basic conflicts are the same as ours, and his characters are such as we can recognize among our own characteristics.

In this very real sense, the *Ring* is interesting to you and me because it is about you and me. Its characters combine to add up to a further, unseen character who is not on the list of the cast, though present in every drama that has ever been written. This unseen character is the product of all the seen characters sensed as the diverse characteristics contributing to a composite portrait. Wagner's characters, besides all the other levels on which they simultaneously operate, are contrasted attributes each bringing some quality of its own to this composite portrait.

It is a living portrait which shows character in motion; and the drama consists, as usual, in the development of character through a series of testing circumstances and actions. The development is closely linked with Wagner's own development, and the character has obvious elements of Wagner's character. The underlying subject of the *Ring*, however, is not literally Wagner's nature nor yours nor mine. It is human nature.

The portrait is not literally a portrait of Wagner or you or me. An artist never speaks only for himself or any other individual; he also speaks for our collective experience. He is like a man taken blindfold to some hidden treasure-house of intuition from which he returns with precious insights, but with little awareness of their origin or even necessarily of their interpretation,[1] and with little ability to apply the obvious lessons to his own private life (all of which is seen with considerable force in the case of Wagner). These insights, in short, are archetypal rather than individual. They are true for you and me, but they are true because we share with other people the human characteristics of our kind.

We have each of us a psyche; but that psyche is not confined within our separate personalities. It merges into the human psyche. A work of art of the calibre of the *Ring* is not so much a portrait of 'a psyche' as a portrait of 'the psyche'. It is a study of life from the psyche's point of view. It is an answer, but an inside answer to the perennial question: what is life all about?

It is not *only* an inside answer. We must never forget that the *Ring* goes on meaning many things to many people at one and the same time. My own tendency is introverted, and I have most to contribute from this

---

[1] Philip Metman, 'Around and Beyond the Confines of Art', Guild of Pastoral Psychology Lecture No. 67, London, 1950.

angle; but the many meanings are all in their degree important, and the many levels are all active at once.

The levels to which our main attention will be directed in this book are the levels on which the psyche itself is the ultimate hero of the *Ring*.

CHAPTER II

Prelude to Rhinegold

———————— ✵ ————————

THE BEGINNING OF THE WORLD
AS A SYMBOL FOR OUR OWN BEGINNING

The *Ring* opens quietly, but with an effect which in the context of harmonized music is apparently unique. For a very long passage there is not only no modulation but no change of chord. A chord of E flat major builds up: first the tonic sounds in the abysmal depths; next a fifth is added; then an arpeggio movement on the complete triad, calm but swelling, an embryonic motive (1) which becomes partly stepwise to give us the first genuinely melodic motive (2). But still the chord does not change. We become increasingly aware of the modulation which is not happening. A sense of timelessness sets in.

This sense of having somehow drifted out of time is increased as the curtain goes up. We see, not the surface, but the underwater bottom of the Rhine. It is most important that there should be some cunning arrangement of scenery and lighting to make us feel, and not merely learn from our programme notes, that we are indeed underwater. Moving ripples can be projected, and perhaps play on streamers at the back kept in wavy motion by a concealed fan. We must be shown the great river in perpetual flow, as we are already hearing it in the orchestra. This underwater symbolism is the crucial beginning to the drama.

'Mark my new poem well,' wrote Wagner to Liszt (11 Feb. 1853); 'it holds the world's beginning, and its destruction.' The primordial chaos at the world's beginning is regularly depicted in creation myths as a waste of waters from which the first self-generated gods emerged as they established some foothold of solid matter, some bubble of air to keep the waters at bay. We read in Wagner's stage directions of water thinning to a fine mist below, so as to leave a space the height of a man. He must have forgotten this later when he makes his Rhinemaidens swim low and his Alberich climb high; and indeed in the original Sagas

35

Alberich himself is half a water-creature. In any case, no mythical creature, terrestrial or otherwise, has any difficulty in breathing underwater if the symbolism requires it.

Before very long we are going to be shown another regular feature of creation myths: the coming of light into the darkness of the waters. When that had happened, and there were beings who could give the animals their names, so that they fell into recognizable species in place of the mere fluctuating monstrosities of primordial chaos, order came into the world.

This is not a valid account of the origins of species. But it is a valid account of the origins of consciousness.[1] For consciousness, nothing exists until we know that it exists, and nothing has order until we know that it has order. Creation myths are important to a primitive mentality not so much for their ostensible explanation of physical nature as for their intuitive explanation of the nature of the psyche. Cosmologies are one way of answering the old, urgent questions: what is life all about, and in particular, what manner of creature are we human beings? The macrocosm fascinates us very largely because of our intuition that we comprise a microcosm in some manner corresponding to it. The origins of consciousness in the race are in some degree recapitulated by the origins of consciousness in the individual. We have each of us started in pre-conscious infancy and grown to a measure of consciousness. The story of creation in this aspect is our own story writ large.

It might, perhaps, not have occurred to anyone but Wagner to start an operatic libretto with the beginning of the world and to end with its destruction. We should be wrong to conclude that the subject is of no personal interest to us; on the contrary, it concerns us in the most direct way possible. We may well conclude that only a partial megalomaniac could have undertaken such a subject at all.

In the outside world, Wagner's element of megalomania was in conflict with the reality principle: his attempt, for example, to control Bavarian politics by cajoling and bullying his patron King Ludwig would strike us as quite farcical if the consequences to Wagner himself had not been so very nearly disastrous. In the inside world, Wagner's powers were as great as he conceived them to be; for his artistic judgement was as sure as his personal judgement was erratic. Such a confusion between inner and outer reality occurs to all of us, but too much of it leads to the borders of insanity or beyond. Not that Wagner was insane; but there were times

[1] Erich Neumann, tr. R. F. C. Hull, *The Origins and History of Consciousness*, London, 1954.

when he could hardly have tried his contemporaries more sorely if he had been. His megalomania was a burden to them and still more to himself; but there can be very little doubt that we owe to it Wagner's ability to carry through so prodigious a feat of concentrated insight and creativeness.

A vast theme, yet bearing intimately on our ordinary lives, and worked out with a sensitive and imaginative eye for detail: this is what we owe to the combination of Wagner's megalomania and genius. It is misleading to look at these two elements apart. It is just that combination and none other which we must accept as Wagner's greatness. No mere coincidence can account for his having given so repeatedly the wrong answers in the outside world and the right answers in the inside world. The two facts must be related to one another. There must be some law of compensation which is generally applicable and which in a case so extreme as this should not be ignored if we want to understand the symbolism arising from it.

From the very extremeness of the contradictions in Wagner's character we might expect his intuition to be particularly well equipped to express the contradictoriness of life's inherent opposites by means of his artistic symbols. I think his work shows that he was so, and I also think it shows that he had more success in reconciling these opposites by means of his artistic symbols than his outward biography could in itself suggest. He paid for it bitterly in trouble and distress, as artists so often seem to have to do; he got little enough personal peace in reward for it; but he gave the fruits of it to the world in a measure commensurate to the price he paid himself, as well as the price he exacted from his long-suffering contemporaries. The price and the success were indivisible.

THE STATE OF NATURE
AND THE FALL FROM INNOCENCE

The state depicted at the start of *Rhinegold* has always been described, correctly, as the state of nature. The opposite implied by the state of nature is the human state. Between the two there lies a development which is the subject of a class of myth leading directly on, as for example in Genesis, from creation myths. This development is presented as the fall of man from pristine innocence.

Broadly speaking, the state of nature is the state in which we think of the animals, though not of mankind, as still being. We think of the animals as still being innocent in virtue of their not possessing our two-

37

edged human attribute of consciousness. We humans first became different from the other animals when we first grew aware of ourselves as something distinct from our environment. To be able to formulate even with momentary self-awareness 'this here is me, and that over there is'—*e.g.*—'mother' represents an achievement so revolutionary in the animal kingdom that only men, so far as we know, have become capable of it. To this day our power to distinguish ourselves from the rest of the world and the other inhabitants of it remains both partial and intermittent. But in so far as we have it, the consequences are manifold.

Among these consequences is our sense of time. Unconscious experience, like eternity, is timeless, in just such a sense as the prelude to *Rhinegold* suggests. It is only for a conscious ego that there can be a yesterday to hold remembered regrets and satisfactions or a tomorrow to cast hopes and fears like shadows in front of it. In the same way, it was only through gaining a measure of consciousness that we took up our human burden and opportunity of responsibility. We have responsibility in so far as we are no longer wholly governed by nature through the workings of unconscious instinct. We have some partial freedom of choice. Having choice, we are liable to inner conflict such as the animals are spared.

Choice and conflict are inseparable partners. The rewards of growing consciousness are incalculable; but so are the pains, and indeed the man-made dangers. Our myths have always tended to present these pains and dangers as the punishment for a previous transgression. Genesis describes this transgression as having 'eaten of the tree of the knowledge of good and evil', which implies self-knowledge, i.e. consciousness. The description is a valid one; but why a transgression? What makes us feel guilty at having become partially conscious beings?

So mixed are the blessings of consciousness that it is perhaps not surprising that they sometimes feel more like a punishment. There is genuine loss as well as genuine gain in having become severed from the animal's unquestioning unity with nature's purpose. This loss may well be regarded as the price though not literally as the punishment of our growth towards individual consciousness. It was Goethe who said that while nature cares nothing for individuals, her purpose for man seems to be that he shall develop his individuality. Every good mother wants her child to defy her in the end by becoming a responsible individual in his own right. Nevertheless we feel guilty at defying mother nature.

We have evidence in other myths for this hidden or half-hidden sense of guilt at stealing the forbidden fruits of consciousness. Prometheus was punished by the gods for stealing the light and warmth of their celestial fire. There are myths, as there are dreams and fantasies, of killing the parents, castrating the father or otherwise rebelling, and thereupon being threatened, exiled, imprisoned, devoured or castrated by parental representatives in the shape of dangerous beasts, monsters or ogres.

Such creatures have a primary tendency to serve as symbols for our fear of mother nature in her devouring capacity. Nature is nothing if not ambivalent in her effect on us who are her children. She gives life, but takes it away in death. She feeds us, but she overwhelms us with disasters. She delights us, but she deceives us. She is generous, but she is thoroughly unreliable. Since the human mothers who nurture us have inevitably something of the same ambivalence and ultimate unreliability, and cannot simply see us safely through life as the infantile part of us would sorely like them to, we form inwardly just such an ambivalent mother-image, more archetypal than personal, yet coloured by both varieties of experience. The negative aspects of this mother-image are frequently projected on to dangerous creatures both actual and mythical.

The force which is not nature but which we call spirit, and which is capable of transforming nature in the direction of consciousness, tends to become associated not so much with our mother-image as with our father-image. We may exalt this force as God the Father, but we fear it none the less. It too has a benevolent and a threatening aspect. In its avenging role, the spirit can put us to the torment. We may suffer from that cruel rigidity of conscience which Freud ascribed to the super-ego. Even when the spirit is tormenting us in our own best interests and for the sake of our own development, we still suffer. Since consciousness is an essentially patriarchal modification of nature's matriarchy, it is God or the gods whose vengeance is especially feared when Adam or Prometheus or other comparable culture heroes take on themselves the god-like attribute of the knowledge of good and evil. We also suffer unavoidably from guilty feelings due to our repressed incestuous longings for the actual mother, and expect to be punished for them by the father in the manner so conclusively revealed by Freud in his study of the Oedipus complex. We bring disasters, ranging from war downwards, on to our own heads in an unconscious attempt to seek relief from our nameless dread of future punishment—by making sure of it in advance. These and other negative aspects of the father-image are again frequently projected into the symbolism of dangerous creatures both actual and mythical.

More alarming still, because less differentiated, is the combined parent-image we may project on to such creatures when we have not even sorted out our fears to the extent of associating them with one or other of the two parental principles. I write 'parental principles' rather than 'parents' in order to emphasize that the part taken by our personal experience of father and mother is only a contributory factor. The towering stature and vast authority for good and ill of these inner images comes not from their personal but from their archetypal content.

Irrational and obscure though our fears may be of the vengeance any successful progress may somehow be felt to invite, they are a formidable obstacle, and one which the heroes of mythology have to overcome again and again in symbolic imagery. Many are the dragons and the ogres; many are the victories; but the contest can never be permanently won, because it represents an adventure which every individual has to repeat after his own fashion. No fear is more comprehensive than that fear of success itself which our guilty forebodings of vengeance may unconsciously impose on us. If the tacit assumptions of our upbringing have left us afraid and ashamed of instinct, and thus unduly out of touch with mother nature herself, it may begin to seem dangerous and wicked to be alive at all. So cautious may we unconsciously become that we virtually miss out on life. This is a condition for which castration is an appropriate symbol, and one which it may take real inner heroism to combat.[1]

The element of unconscious fear and guilt inherent in our emergence from the state of nature may well underlie that strain of restlessness seen negatively in our mutual destructiveness as a species, but also positively in our constructive energies and curiosity. For it is not only nature and the gods that we experience as ambivalent. The ambivalence runs through ourselves.

ACCEPTING THE OPPOSITES
OR ESCAPING THEM IN FANTASY

To be human is to experience life in the clash and turmoil of its unavoidable opposites. Wagner accepted this intuitively, which is why he was able to be so uninhibited as a composer. But we all temper our acceptance in some degree by escaping into unconscious fantasy. Wagner was no exception, as many pointers in his life and work reveal; and it is a measure of the profound integrity beneath his surface evasiveness that in his work,

[1] For this and the previous paragraphs, see Sigmund Freud, *passim*, but esp. *Totem and Taboo*, tr. A. A. Brill, London, 1919 (Pelican ed. 1938); C. G. Jung, *passim*, but esp. *Symbols of Transformation*, tr. R. F. C. Hull, London, 1956, p. 235, etc.; Erich Neumann, *Origins and History of Consciousness*, tr. R. F. C. Hull, London, 1954, esp. pp. 117 and 120 ff.

at any rate, he never ran away. On the contrary, he set out the problem by means of his artistic symbols with a clarity which shows how real it was for him, and how heroic was his own inner struggle with it.

Life's opposites include our capacity to be both good and evil, both happy and unhappy, both in delight and in torment of both mind and body; above all to be both alive and sure to die. The fear brought by growing more conscious of these facts, though not insuperable, is real. One of the ways in which to varying degrees we are strongly disposed to veil our fear instead of confronting it is by idealizing the state of nature, at the same time indulging in an unconscious fantasy of escaping back into some supposedly carefree enjoyment of that state: that is to say, into an Eden of blissful irresponsibility where mother nature may enfold us in her arms again, and instinct carry us as unthinkingly as an animal. But we are not only animals; we are men. Our illusion of escaping from the responsibility of consciousness takes many forms, but it remains an illusion. It is a dangerous illusion in so far as it keeps us in an infantile attitude to our problems and interferes with the growth of a more mature attitude.

Since this kind of fantasy centres around the unconscious longing to get back to the breast or even to the womb as the most irresponsible situations within our human experience, it is often most accurate to speak of mother-longings, or in some contexts of incest-longings (as in the *Valkyrie*). We must not be too naïve about the state of nature with which *Rhinegold* opens. The primal charm of it is real enough, but we must not overlook the potential seductiveness of the unconscious fantasies we are apt to weave around the theme of nature and innocence. It is to guard against this seductiveness that we find in Genesis the symbol of the angel with the flaming sword who bars the path back again to Eden. We shall do well to remember that theologically the Fall of Man has been called (as in the Latin rite for blessing the Easter candles) a *felix culpa*, a fortunate crime. It is fortunate precisely because it marks our departure from the state of nature.

THE RETURN TO NATURE IN REBIRTH SYMBOLISM

In addition to the negative possibilities of being swallowed up to which attention has just been drawn, the fantasy of returning to mother nature also holds the positive possibilities of going down symbolically into her womb not as a victim of seduction but as a candidate for rebirth. This is an experience which, while it cannot be produced to order, is encouraged by many rituals and doctrines; it seems, for example, to have been central to the Orphic Mysteries. In John iii, 3, Jesus says: 'Except a man be born again, he cannot see the kingdom of God . . . that which is born of the flesh is flesh, and that which is born of the Spirit is spirit.' The flesh relates to the state of nature, and the spirit relates to the transformation of nature by consciousness. This transformation is what made our species human, and recapitulations of it occur in every lifetime.

Rebirth imagery occurs spontaneously in dreams and fantasies, and is also a subject for art, though not always so openly as in the *Magic Flute* or as deliberately as in Michael Tippett's *Midsummer Marriage*. During the final gestation of the music of *Rhinegold*, Wagner had an experience described in his autobiography, *My Life*, where he relates the events of September 1853. He had a night of disturbing restlessness such as does commonly accompany the birth-pangs of an inwardly long-prepared creative achievement. Next day, after a strenuous but weary morning walk, and little lunch, he tried again to sleep. Instead, he fell into a strange waking stupor, in which he immediately had the sensation of being carried down into deep and swiftly-moving waters. 'The rushing of them presently appeared to me as the musical notes of the E flat major chord, from which arpeggios rose unceasingly, growing into melodic figures in continually increasing movement, yet never departing from the simple triadic tonality of the E flat major chord, which seemed by its persistence to be trying to impress on me that condition into which I had sunk as immeasurably significant. With the feeling that the waves were breaking high over my head, I woke in terror from my near-sleep. I realized at once that the orchestral introduction to *Rhinegold* as I had been carrying it about without being able to find it had come up inside me. I also knew at once that however things might turn out with me, the flow of life would never pour into me from the outside, but only from inside.'

Two things happened in this waking vision of Wagner's, and the probability is that they were closely connected. One was that the music for the beginning of *Rhinegold* welled up into consciousness. The other was that a piece of self-knowledge welled up: the knowledge that his own strength lay not in his tortuous dealings with the outer world but in his masterly dealings with the inner world. He could not keep this knowledge steadily in front of him, of course, since that is the kind of lesson which has to be learnt over and over again; but experiences of this kind, even in a dream, and still more in a waking vision, are milestones in any lifetime. They give such a sense of a new start and have such a rejuvenating effect that they are often expressed in the traditional images of rebirth.

Being submerged and swept away by a torrent of water is a rebirth image. The experience of symbolical rebirth does feel very like death and dissolution, and is just as terrifying as Wagner describes. Every conscious and unconscious support so laboriously acquired seems to be giving way. The habitual defences are down, the ingrained attitudes are of no avail, the ego is left helpless and must yield or suffer serious damage in the attempt to resist the irresistible. But the autonomous psyche which is exerting all this pressure is not in itself hostile. By going with it the ego may be brought out again into a greater strength and independence than before, from the very fact of having been stripped of some of its conscious pretensions, denuded of some of its unconscious assumptions, and made to feel the force of a purpose within the psyche incomparably stronger than itself. To feel thus stripped and denuded is to feel as naked as a new-born babe, but with some of the new-born babe's unspoilt potentialities. Such moments of renewal in the psyche can be of crucial importance, and though they are never final they never leave the personality quite as it was before.

It would be clear from Wagner's description, even if it were not self-evident in the opera-house, that the music of the prelude to *Rhinegold* with its surging arpeggios is another image for the same inner experience which the image of the surging water represents. In connection with its E flat major tonality, I happen to have noticed several coincidences which might possibly be significant. One is that the music of Elsa's dream in *Lohengrin* has E flat for dominant. Another is that Mahler's magnificent *Resurrection* symphony (No. 2) at last works its way through to E flat major as the faith in rebirth is finally built up out of the doubt and agony of the earlier movements. Another is that I have been told by a skilful music-therapist that the note E seems to possess particular emotional significance for the mentally disturbed children who come to her with Heaven knows what tortured, hidden hopes of a new start in life. At this I pricked up my ears, remembering a dream of my own in which I watched the actual birth of a baby to the accompaniment of a musical note so prolonged and vivid that when I woke I had the impulse to check the pitch of it against my piano. It was a somewhat flat E or sharp E flat. Allowing for the higher pitch prevailing in the second half of the nineteenth century, this is approximately the tonic of the opening of *Rhinegold*. I mention these facts without building on them.

My personal association to my dream was the music of the spheres.

43

This traditional and decidedly haunting image of the music of the spheres has probably to do with our intuitive perception that incomprehensible though they may often seem, the archetypes move with an order and a harmony of their own which we might surely hear if only we had the right kind of ears. 'For there is a musick', wrote Sir Thomas Browne, 'where ever there is a harmony, order or proportion.' And conversely: 'Even that vulgar and Tavern-Musick, which makes one man merry, another mad, strikes in me a deep fit of devotion, and a profound contemplation of the First Composer. There is something in it of Divinity more than the ear discovers: it is an Hieroglyphical and shadowed lesson of the whole World, and creatures of God; such a melody to the ear, as the whole World, well understood, would afford the understanding'.[1]

As a general image rather than as a specific planet, the sphere is one of the traditional symbols for the archetype of the 'self'. Different archetypes have been projected on to different planets, but the roundness of a sphere or a circle always carries a suggestion of this archetype of archetypes; and we shall presently find that this is true of the actual ring which provides Wagner's *Ring* with its title. The 'self' is what the ego commonly thinks it is but actually is not: the effective centre of the personality. As such it is the source from which the impulse to rebirth originates.

Of all the many levels of symbolism in the *Ring*, the level on which rebirth imagery appears may well be the most crucial. There are plenty of experiences in an ordinary life-story through which to keep in touch with it. We all run into times of stress and strain when our established attitudes seem to have to break up in preparation for the next stage. It is a painful process, and may be a dangerous one, whether or not it is partly expressed in physical illness. But our convalescence may be more than a mere recovery. We may gain new ground; indeed, if we do not, we are likely to lose ground. Our sense of renewal may be accompanied by some of the traditional symbols of rebirth. Such symbols are recognizable in the present underwater scene, and we shall find them developing through later stages of the *Ring* up to the climax at the end of *Götterdämmerung*.

---

[1] Sir Thomas Browne, *Religio Medici*, London, 1642, Everyman Ed., p. 79.

CHAPTER III

Rhinegold, Scene 1

———————— ❋ ————————

ALBERICH AND THE RHINEMAIDENS

As we hear the Rhine flooding so steadily along in the orchestra, and see it now that the curtain has gone up, we need no rational awareness that this flood of water is a symbol for the fluid unconscious from which rebirth is possible. It tells its own story to our intuition. Water is ubiquitous; water finds its own level; water flows freely in any direction, yet has no predetermined shape of its own; water takes the light and plays queer tricks with it; water is the breeding-ground of strange fishes. Three such now swim into sight (26) and though they are strange they are not unknown, with their flowing hair, their human bodies and their fishes' tails. We have known from early childhood of the breed of mermaids, who lure men down as Fricka will later tell us that our present trio of Rhinemaidens lure men down. They lure men, in fact, as our fantasies of mother nature may lure us away from real living into that supposedly blissful irresponsibility we can in reality only enjoy, if ever, as infants in the womb or at the breast, so that our longing takes the form of mother-longing and our fantasies may be of union with a haunting beauty who can assume the illusory role of mother. In short, with a mermaid.

Preluded at last by the very first modulatory accidentals in 162 bars (of a Wagner score!) Alberich comes stumbling in. He is stumbling because the rocks and mud are slippery and because he is traditionally an awkward mover. For we have plenty of traditional information as to what manner of creature Alberich is. By race he is a dwarf: that is to say, he is squat, broad for his small height, and what the world calls ugly. He is also very strong. Such people are occasionally born; but the race of dwarfs itself is a mythical race, which means that it has grown up in our imaginations as an image to carry our projections of something in ourselves. This something is evidently felt to be unacceptable, or we should not find so unprepossessing an image for it. Yet it must also strike us as compact and full of power.

Alberich has a decisive part to play in the events which follow. He is the chief villain, and there is not the slightest doubt that we are meant to take him as an evil character. But if that were all, the drama would be very unbalanced. There would be nothing to put in the scales against our natural sympathy for its heroes and heroines. As a matter of fact, there are several occasions when our sympathies are much more divided than a crudely melodramatic interpretation would explain. Actual evil can be very terrible. As a symbol, it is more ambivalent.

On the archetypal level, there are no unequivocal villains or heroes. There are only ambivalent forces capable of positive and negative effects. We are bound to experience them as good and evil, but the difference largely depends on how we are taking them. Wotan himself, in his role of chief hero, does not go on taking Alberich merely as an alien and an enemy. In *Siegfried*, Act I, Scene 2, Wotan refers to the dwarf by the customary title of 'black Alberich'. In the very next breath, he refers to *himself* as 'light Alberich'. He has come to see himself and his old enemy as the light and the dark aspects of a single force; and by Act II the pair of them have a conversation in which Wotan surprises Alberich very much by refusing to treat him as an enemy any more.

Whatever in us we reject from consciousness because rightly or wrongly we would feel it to be base or weak or otherwise unacceptable, we tend to project on to other people, so that we see them as villains, or on to some collective archetype of villainy, such as the devil, or such collective scapegoats as the Jews or the Russians or the Americans (according to the standpoint).

Jung's term for these unaccepted attributes and desires within ourselves is the shadow.[1] We not only want to do but succeed in doing a great many things unconsciously, at the prompting of the shadow, which we then accuse some colleague or acquaintance or spouse or politician in the wrong party or on the wrong side of the Iron Curtain of doing or wanting to do to us. In this way, the shadow really is often the villain of the piece. He needs to be opposed, and still more exposed. It is his invisibility which makes him so dangerous. He is dark; we cannot see him where he really is, in ourselves. Yet dark in the sense of unknown

[1] See my Bibl. s.v. Jung; also H. G. Baynes, *Mythology of the Soul*, London, 1940, pp. 91–104.

does not necessarily mean dark in the sense of hostile. The shadow holds part of our value too. The shadow is ambivalent.

In a crude melodrama, all the unacceptable qualities are naïvely concentrated in the villain, and the acceptable qualities in the hero. But the *Ring* is not a crude melodrama. Wagner tells us in some surprise that he felt on Alberich's side in the scene next to be described, though hating him throughout the rest of the story. We hate him too, and are right to do so. But beneath our hatred, we somehow sense the point of Alberich. Wagner, for all his antagonism, somehow retained his intuitive respect for the archetype, and has seen to it that we shall do the same.

The point of a dwarf is that his outward deformity expresses a positive as well as a negative symbolism. He is often a smith, as were lame Wieland, lame Vulcan (Hephaestus) and others. Loge the fire-god and Lucifer the 'firebearer' (whom Milton in spite of himself came very near making the real hero of *Paradise Lost*) are traditionally lame. The lameness symbolizes not only our projection of our own extreme ambivalence, but also our recognition of the fact that creative gifts such as smithing represents are usually associated with a certain unbalance or one-sidedness: Wagner's own case once more.

As a phallic symbol, again, a dwarf may stand not only for the unruly force of male sexuality but for Logos, the typically male principle of discriminating intelligence, as opposed to Eros, the typically female principle of unifying feeling. Sexuality is so close to the primal energy of life that Freud substantially identified the two in his concept of libido. Jung more accurately, as it now appears, regarded libido as primary, and sex as one of its various manifestations. In any case, body and spirit are so complementary that sexual symbols always include spiritual implications. To our primitive intuition, there is no activity which is not capable of being experienced as a sacrament.[1] It is for this reason, for example, that a fish is a familiar phallic symbol and intentionally so used in primitive art and ritual, yet is also one of the main theriomorphic symbols for Christ.[2] In the Prose Edda, Andvari (Alberich) is captured (for the sake of the treasure which he so characteristically guards) in the form of a fish.[3] Wagner presently describes him as captured in the form of a toad:

---

[1] Mircea Eliade, *Patterns in Comparative Religion*, tr. Rosemary Sheed, London, 1958, esp. p. 32.

[2] C. G. Jung, *Aion*, tr. R. F. C Hull, London, 1959, see index s.v. Fish; Erich Neumann, *Origins and History f Consciousness*, tr. R. F. C. Hull, London, 1954, p. 49.

[3] Snorri Sturluson, *The Prose Edda*, tr. A. G. Brodeur, London, 1929, p. 151.

47

i.e. an amphibian, and a traditional symbol not only for ambivalence but also (as in alchemy) for transformation and rebirth.[1]

THE RHINEMAIDENS AND THEIR GOLD

An ugly exterior is not necessarily a barrier to love; and no sooner has Alberich set eyes on the Rhinemaidens than he feels a love for them rising within him. But to them he is as ugly as he looks. Their reaction is more than unfavourable; it is contemptuously heartless. They make a cruel game of him, drawing him on only to rebuff him with galling mockery. He shows his spirit by growing increasingly angry.

So far we see only the not uncommon situation in which a man (or a woman) may offer something genuine, and in all good faith, but to the wrong recipient. Alberich and the Rhinemaidens are so incongruous one with another that the rebuff, though it might have been more kindly done, was to have been expected. But now a distraction occurs, as timely and relevant as it was unforeseen, which in the most literal sense throws new light on the scene. The rays of the rising sun strike down on to a lump of gold near the surface of the water. We had not noticed it before; but suddenly it is glowing out at us with uncanny radiance. The Rhine-maidens greet the lovely sight to the accompaniment of a shimmering motive (28), through which there pierces the vivid motive (44) of the gold itself. This last is on the notes of a triad, here major, but in later and more sinister contexts sometimes minor, or modified to a diminished seventh.

The Rhinemaidens break out into a glorious cry of 'Rhinegold, Rhinegold!' The music of this is a motive (31) which is particularly memorable and haunting, so that it has a most powerful effect on us whenever it reappears later in the *Ring*. It is very beautiful, but with a poignant and almost plaintive beauty easier to recognize than to describe. The beauty of the Rhinemaidens is very real. The delight they have to offer is nature's own, and the man who cannot delight in nature will never delight in anything. But the man who lets nature seduce him away from taking human responsibility for himself is heading not towards reality but towards illusion. All this is somehow combined in our image of a mermaid; and mermaids are what these enchanting Rhinemaidens are. Their music conveys to us the almost irresistible delight of their beauty, but also the nostalgia of its ultimate unattainability. That longing

[1] Patricia Dale-Green, *The Symbolism of the Toad: a study in Ambivalence*, Guild of Pastoral Psychology, Lecture 110, London [1960].

48

which at bottom derives from the infant's longing to be at one with mother is ultimately unassuageable. Yet it plays its part in all our maturer longings. Hence the extreme ambivalence, as usual, of the mermaid archetype.

One of the most famous lines in all poetry, and one well known to Wagner, is the line with which Goethe ended his *Faust*: 'das Ewig-weibliche zieht uns hinan', 'the eternal feminine draws us on'. This is not simply a description of sex-appeal, though it includes that. It is an intuitive vision of the indescribable force of which the whole of *Faust*, both the more extroverted Part I and the more introverted Part II, shows an example of the workings. For a man, certainly, and probably at bottom for a woman too, this force has an inalienable association with our experience of femininity, starting from mother and the mother-image. It is her creative femininity glowing through her beauty which draws a man towards an actual woman, as a beacon of light may draw a ship to the harbour. We desire her, as nature rightly intends that we should; but she also carries our projection of an inward search. She is not personally the beacon, though she does us the immeasurable service of transmitting it to us. The beacon is the archetype we see in and through her. It is the archetype of the eternal feminine, and not the mortal woman, which draws us on in the sense Goethe had in mind.

Thus when we see a beacon of light glowing out from behind the Rhinemaidens, with a radiance even brighter than their own, we should perhaps ask whether there is a level on which this light was always the ultimate object of Alberich's longing. Little though he has hitherto suspected it, there is something here which may be more genuinely worthy of his desire than the gorgeous creatures towards whom he has just been incongruously directing it. He is immediately riveted on the new spectacle. Compared with his own darkness, the Rhinemaidens are undoubtedly creatures of the light. But perhaps his deepest impulse was towards the light itself.

There is a further resemblance here to the underlying situation depicted in creation myths. Light penetrating the waters is an age-old symbol for the male spirit of consciousness fertilizing the female unconsciousness of mother nature. That happened to our race and it happens to each one of us, not once but repeatedly. It is a very deep but a very ordinary human experience.

Being deep, it is not seen directly, though it may be vividly symbolized in our dreams and elsewhere. Unseen developments fall within the influence of the shadow. Since Alberich is the primary representative of the shadow in the *Ring*, we must try hard to see just what he is up to here, and just what this gold means for him on which he is now casting such fascinated eyes.

MONEY SEEN AS THE ROOT OF ALL EVIL

The Rhinemaidens give us our most important piece of information about the gold. Though they would not satisfy Alberich's desire, they satisfy his curiosity, telling him that the man who steals their gold and makes a ring of it can use this ring to achieve the mastery of the world.

Mastery, whether of the outer world of men or the inner world of the psyche, depends ultimately on the disposition of one power, and one power alone: the libido which is the force of life itself. If enough libido pours into outward action, that action is likely to succeed. If it pours into inward development, such development is likely to occur. The two are not mutually exclusive, though the first tends to assume greater importance early in life, and the second later in life. The only psychic force more powerful than a surge of libido is another surge of libido of even greater intensity, whether in the outer world or within the same man. There are also resistances, both outer and inner, which may prove stronger than the libido attacking them. But that, again, may be because too much libido is inertly committed to defending them.

Among the many formidable means by which mastery can be imposed in the outer world, the possession of gold ranks high. An accumulation of gold implies that somebody's libido went into accumulating it. For a long time past, it has not even been necessary to accumulate gold itself. Gold used to hold the value; nowadays it is only necessary to record the value in a bank ledger. Money as attenuated as this is a symbol if ever there was one.

On the face of it, the gold on which the plot of the *Ring* turns, to a large extent functions in its historical capacity as a movable symbol of value, in the sense of money. This is what Wagner meant when he wrote in his letter to Liszt of 15 January 1854: 'I have carried it'—*Rhinegold*—'through and ended it at last in a real rage of despair! Was not I too the slave of the need for gold?' The letter, as so often, was a begging one. Wagner was in financial trouble again: he nearly always was, being a compulsive spender. But the root cause of compulsive spending is the need to satisfy an unconscious symbolism. The same need drove Wagner to hate Jews, and above all rich Jews, the traditional scapegoats for the evil power we tend to project on to money. But money is not itself an evil power; it is merely a power which will lend itself indifferently to good ends or bad. Wagner purported to think that gold could only be good when innocently admired for its beauty and put to no other purpose whatsoever: i.e. left to the Rhinemaidens to enjoy and admire. Nevertheless, in practice he saw another good use to which gold could be put. It could be put into his own pocket. It was.

No one who has followed Wagner's life-story, and in particular read a sufficient selection from his private letters, can doubt that in regard to money, women, ill-health and many other matters, Wagner showed himself a deeply neurotic man. But just as lameness and creativeness are associated in myth, so too are instability and genius in reality. They are so often the negative and the positive manifestations of the same driving intensity. Like so many men of genius, Wagner knew he was a driven man, in both senses. His tacit assumption that money is an evil, but not when given freely to himself, is symptomatic of a schizoid element in his character for which there is much further evidence, as there also is for a paranoid element. Most people if not all have some such tendencies, and this is no disparagement of Wagner's greatness. We have to take them into account, especially when considering his rational or rationalizing explanations of his own work, but in his work itself they increased rather than decreased the range and depth of his insight. He knew so many of our human problems from the inside, and while this did not avail him to mend his life, it availed him to create his characters in the round. In so many ways his art reaped what his life had sown.

Behind the naïve suggestion that the coveting of gold, and of the outward power wielded by gold, is the source of all evil, Wagner himself saw an implication of much deeper relevance: that material acquisitiveness (more truly, the neurotic insecurity of which acquisitiveness is one symptom) may drive out love, by which in this context he meant all the uniting force of sympathy and compassion as well as the mutual desire of men and women. Here too, however, we find that in practice he looked not so much for sympathy as for unquestioning acceptance of himself in all his vagaries; and that is a serious obstacle to genuine love. We find several passages in his letters such as that written to Liszt on 30 March 1853: 'I have come to my thirty-fifth year before realizing that *up to now I have not lived at all* . . . I have never yet enjoyed the true happiness of love.' It is quite questionable whether he ever did; not because he was not offered it, and not because he did not want it, but because his insecurity made him so avid for superhuman love that he could not altogether accept and reciprocate the ordinary human kind.

With a genius—and not only with a genius—the very thing which goes most wrong with his outer life may often go most right with his inner life, in the sense that the deeper levels of his work show an appreciation of the very truths and realities which most elude him in his personal life-story. Wagner's explanations of the *Ring* are obscured by his own private obsessions and the rationalizations into which they drove him. But the *Ring* itself is not. Without the driving force of his obsessions, the *Ring* might never have been created. And we must remember how frequently Wagner informs us that his conscious intentions in shaping the moral of his music-dramas were reversed in the outcome because when he was actually at work he was 'unconsciously guided by a wholly different, infinitely more profound intuition' (letter to Roeckel, 23 Aug., 1856). He first made Brynhilde draw the moral at the end of *Götterdämmerung* by an 'artificial' passage 'in which, having pointed out the evils of material possessions, she insists on love as the one salvation, without (unfortunately) describing just what the character of that love is'; then, as he explains with some pride, he changed this passage to conform with his latest rational view of the world under the influence of Schopenhauer (same letter). But ultimately he cut the passage out altogether, and left the *Ring* to impart its own moral.

The level on which the *Ring* is an allegory of the power of money seen as the root of all evil has been well explored by interpreters in sympathy with this point of view: brilliantly, for example, by Bernard Shaw in a one-sided study which does full justice to the economic issues but to very little else.[1] Gold as a traditional symbol is commonly associated with violent deeds of covetousness and rapine. Wagner was not perverting the traditional symbolism in depicting 'the power of evil, the true poison of love, under the similitude of the gold, stolen from nature and misused, the Nibelungen Ring' (letter to Roeckel, 25 Jan. 1854). But in using the outward allegory, he was also invoking the inward symbolism. Inwardly, 'gold' may certainly operate as a 'poison of love'. A very clear case of this is where a mother-bound man acts out his fantasies of infantile dependence by marrying a rich woman, and finds not merely his love but his very manhood drained away by his unconscious subservience to her. But on a symbolic level, gold has other associations of a very positive, not to say archetypal importance, as innumerable myths reveal; and these deeper associations are subliminally but effectually at work on us in the present situation.

---

[1] George Bernard Shaw, *The Perfect Wagnerite*, London, 1898.

THE FIRE UNDER THE WATER

There is one mythological association, sometimes amounting to an identification, of gold with fire.

We learn from the Prose Edda that gold 'gave forth light and illumined the hall like fire' for the sea-giant Aegir beneath the waters, and incidentally that Aegir had a daughter (in some versions a wife, perhaps originally a daughter-wife) called Ran, who seems to have been a mermaid, since she 'had that net wherein she was wont to catch all men who go upon the sea'; in consequence of which 'gold is now called' among other poetic synonyms 'Fire of Waters or of Rivers'.[1] There is a comparable reference to gold giving off light like fire under the water in connection with Beowulf's fight with the Mother Monster; indeed, this poetic synonym by which 'gold' is paraphrased as 'fire of waters' or 'of rivers' or 'of the sea' is widespread throughout the Icelandic Sagas, and is certainly no accident, as is confirmed by the fact that in modern life, dreams of a fire burning underwater are not uncommon. A beautiful and moving painting by a patient of a naked candle burning uncannily in the depths of the sea and attracting deep-sea fishes by its light is reproduced among other analytical material by Baynes.[2] All these are forms of the same archetypal imagery.

The general reference of such images is to a stirring in the deep unconscious as some new light of consciousness is lit; their particular piquancy arises from the familiar incompatibility of fire and water in ordinary outside circumstances, where fire burns but water quenches and candles do not stay alight in the depths of the sea. We have in this paradox a typical symbol of the reconciliation of opposites, by which is meant not suppressing one side of an unavoidable conflict into unconsciousness, but somehow learning to live with both sides. It is not possible to resolve a fundamental conflict which is inherent in life itself, but it is possible to pass out of the stress and turmoil of it into a measure of quiet acceptance. It is possible to integrate our awareness of the conflict into our personality as a whole. Whenever two previously warring components in the psyche are brought into some such effectual union with one another, a reconciliation is achieved which amounts to a transformation, however partial, of the character, and contributes towards maturing it. As we thus assimilate elements of our own dark or shadow side, we become to that extent more conscious and less at the mercy of unconscious impulse

[1] *The Prose Edda*, by Snorri Sturluson, tr. A. G. Brodeur, (New York, 1916) London, 1929, pp. 143 ff.
[2] H. G. Baynes, *Mythology of the Soul*, London, 1940, and 1949, p. 784.

We become more truly individuals and therefore more truly human. This gain in consciousness born like some third element from the union of the opposites is so precious that it is often referred to mythologically as gold or hidden treasure. It is always represented as difficult and dangerous to attain, and commonly as attained only by some desperate or even criminal act. That is where our sense of guilt comes in.

Gold is traditionally associated with the light of the sun and thus with consciousness, just as silver is associated with the moon and with that indirect illumination which is somehow reflected back from the unconscious (we may perhaps say, using Layard's term, in the form of psychic consciousness). Water is a primary necessity of life, so common that it is seldom valued until it runs scarce; but gold is never otherwise than scarce. Prized both for its beauty and for its incorruptibility, gold is royal and makes the crowns of kings, as silver makes the crowns of queens; royalty is itself an image for the integrated centre of the personality, called by Jung the 'self'. Gold is the colour of corn-seed and shares in the imagery of renewal and rejuvenation, of blood-sacrifices and fertility.[1] Gold, as the sun metal, is linked with the solar myth of death and rebirth through the perilous night-journey under the sea.[2] Gold was the substance of that most celebrated of all talismans (since Frazer's masterpiece), the golden bough which Aeneas had to discover and take as a passport to Hades and a present to Proserpine.[3] Gold was the ostensible aim of alchemy, of which the esoteric aim was the integration and individuation of the personality.[4] Through all these images and many others, the same fundamental experience is suggested and hinted at and circumscribed from every side, but never described outright, because like everything archetypal it is ultimately indescribable. We only know that it has to do with that slow, life-long growth in a man's character by which he draws away from the collective unconsciousness of mother nature and acquires an increasing awareness of his own individuality in its deepest sense, so much deeper than his ego alone.

The gold we are now watching in delight as the sun's rays light it up, so that it burns like a fire beneath the water, is not, however, the refined

[1] Erich Neumann, op. cit., p. 160, and *The Great Mother*, tr. R. Manheim, London, 1955, p. 199.

[2] C. G. Jung and C. Kerenyi, *Essays on a Science of Mythology*, New York, 1949, pp. 60 ff, and Erich Neumann, tr. R. F. C. Hull, *The Origins and History of Consciousness*, 1949, p. 160.

[3] Interestingly discussed, for our present purposes, by Maud Bodkin, *Archetypal Patterns in Poetry*, London, 1934, pp. 130 ff.

[4] C. G. Jung, tr. R. F. C. Hull, *Psychology and Alchemy*, London, 1953, esp. Part III.

and quintessential gold which is the hard-won culmination of the alchemical transformation. It is gold, but it is virgin gold; it is treasure, but it is latent treasure. It is like the true worth and purpose of a man before he has found what are these central values in his life, so that he is still at the mercy of other people's values. He still accepts their judgements and veers with their opinions. He over-rates and under-rates himself as they rate him. But in so far as he can find the individual worth we all have within us, he will become truly himself, he will have his own scale of values and his life will have its own meaning; not regardless of others, yet sufficiently independent. Can any metal be more precious to a man than his own worth?

In so far as gold is symbolically equated with fire, its primary reference is to the burning energy of life: i.e. libido. In so far as gold is symbolically equated with light, its primary reference is to the spread of consciousness. Here we have a lump of gold which is dark and invisible until the rays of the sun strike down through the water to light it up, whereupon the Rhinemaidens swim round it in delight rather as the deep-sea creatures swim round the candle in the painting by Baynes' patient referred to above. A creature from the deeper unconscious clambers up to join the Rhinemaidens, and to wonder what all this glory of light can mean. They tell him that it is a delight in itself, which does not interest him. They further tell him that it has worldly power to confer, which interests him very much. If the Rhinemaidens' gold is fundamentally a supply of libido which can be brought into awareness only after the light of consciousness has touched on it, and turned to effective use only after it has been moulded into a ring by comparatively conscious shaping, Alberich's interest is understandable; and so is ours.

ACCIDENTALLY ON PURPOSE?

When, in outside life, we make some seemingly unaccountable slip the effect of which is to undo all our conscious planning and ensure a directly contrary result, the reason is likely to be that an unconscious part of us does desire this contrary result, and takes very cunning steps to bring it about. It seems on the face of it unaccountable that the Rhinemaidens should let slip to Alberich not only that their gold is uncommonly well worth stealing, but also, as they add next, by exactly what means it is possible to steal it. Criminal negligence on their part, it would appear; but nothing happens negligently in a myth, and we have certainly to ask whether this is another of those crimes which, like the Fall itself, can only be called a *felix culpa*, a crime fortunate in its consequences. That, too, would have its counterpart in the outside world, since it very often happens that the slip which reverses all our conscious planning, though seemingly inadvertent, can be seen in retrospect to have been wiser than the plan itself. It is possible that nothing even in the outside world is ultimately inadvertent: least of all, slips of the tongue.

By a typical piece of unconscious self-deception, two of the Rhine-maidens (the third is more realistic and anxious) feel perfectly convinced that they are putting their gold in no danger. As they now point out, it can only be seized on the most terrible of conditions, or what seems to them the most terrible of conditions and is certainly no light one. The condition is forswearing love. They rightly perceive that Alberich is not insensitive to love; but it is suspiciously blind of them to overlook the obvious fact that he has been thrown by their own frustration of his love into a rage and despair unbearable enough to make him capable of anything.

On hearing, then, that if he deliberately and of his own free will renounces all that comfort, reassurance and delight for which at present he has only the bitterness of longing in vain, he can transform his frustra-tion into an unprecedented strength, he at once makes a virtue of that bitter necessity. We sometimes say 'the virtue went out of me', meaning that all the conviction and energy, that is to say all the libido, which we were pouring into a task have dried up as mysteriously as at first they flowed into it. When Alberich deliberately accepts frustration as his own individual destiny, the virtue, on the contrary, comes into him. He becomes a force to reckon with.

There is much that needs looking into here. We are confronted this time with something which really does look like an unmitigated crime: a crime for which, at most, we might claim the extenuating circumstances of extreme provocation. It is not as if Wagner supposed Alberich to be renouncing mere sexual satisfaction, or even fatherhood. On the contrary, Alberich is presently able to buy a mortal woman with gold (again gold used on the face of it for what is assumed to be a corrupt purpose); that is how he presently begets his formidable son, Hagen. What Wagner, according to his published account of the matter, supposed Alberich to be renouncing by the act of forswearing love was that very principle of sympathy and compassion by which Wagner, by no means mistakenly, believed the world to be knit together.

It seems almost impossible not to conclude that on one level Wagner was symbolizing here a profoundly unsettling intuition that without intending it, and above all without knowing it, he had himself largely shut out the genuinely mutual relationship of love. Over and over again he courted a woman in the sincere conviction of loving her, and of loving her beyond all ordinary love. But that was precisely the difficulty. He loved her with a love surcharged with unconscious mother-longing. She was to understand him perfectly; to serve him; if possible (and it often was) to assist him financially; to bear with him; to believe in him both in justifiable and in unjustifiable ways; to condone or even applaud his infidelities: in short, to be the perfect mother we none of us had, but all of us in some degree long for in the infantile part of our fantasies.

To an infant, mother is part of itself. To the mother-bound element in a grown man, the same illusion persists. But what is necessary for the infant is debilitating and isolating for the man. In so far as his sexual partner represents mother to him, and he is identified with mother, his partner cannot exist for him as a person in her own right; she is just part of himself. No wonder he expects her to think his thoughts and feel his feelings. There is no loneliness worse than the loneliness of a man for whom other people cannot really exist at all. No sane man is altogether in that condition; no man whatsoever is altogether free of it; but Wagner had rather too much of it not to suffer intermittently but acutely from the feeling of being doomed to loneliness.

Our mother-image is an aspect of our image of the eternal feminine. Since our first and quite our most intimate personal experience of woman is the mother who bore us, everything womanly that comes into our lives recalls her, little as we may realize the fact. Our experience of her and other women further interweaves with our intuitions of archetypal femininity. It is from all this in combination that our image of the eternal feminine takes shape. It is perfectly natural that we should see it projected on to the beloved person.

For a man, it is natural to see, in the women he meets, his own inner feminine side, of which he is not as a rule directly conscious. For a woman, it is her inner masculine side of which she is as a rule not directly conscious; it is bound up with her father-image, and it is natural for her to see it in the men she meets. Wagner was a man, and everything that was most mysterious and intuitive in his inner life had its centre in his half-conscious image of the eternal feminine. 'For what is love itself', he wrote to Roeckel (25 Jan. 1854) 'but the eternal feminine?' He was right in a way; but fundamentally our experience of the eternal feminine is something inside us and not outside us. It is fundamentally our own inner selves with which we need to make contact.

There are many levels on which a woman may exercise a fascination over a man. One of these levels, perhaps the deepest, is simply her resemblance to his own inner femininity, just as it is his resemblance to her inner masculinity which is perhaps his deepest fascination for her. All our relationships have a substratum of this sort of mutual projection. So far from precluding real love, this is the ordinary human condition for it. But if the projections fill up and go on filling up too much of the picture, they may not leave room for genuinely mutual love to develop as it should. The more obsessive the projections, the more constricted the reality. This is above all the case where the element of infantile mother-projection remains unduly large.

Wagner could only place the naïve hopes he did on women, and on men too, in so far as the infantile part of him remained both strong and unrecognized. 'Dear Mother' he used to call his benefactress Frau Julie Ritter (e.g. letter of 9 June 1850); to Liszt, who so often came to his rescue in financial and other ways, he wrote, 'I feel as safe with you as a child in its mother's lap' (11 July 1851). The fact that his infantile side was so effectually cut off from his mature side made it possible for him to beg, to scrounge, to womanize, to twist and to turn in ways he could hardly have brought himself to go through with if his right hand had been better able to know what his left hand was doing. It was just as well for him and for the world that this element of schizoid compartmentalization did intervene to protect his feelings in such matters; given his particular attributes, which were inseparable from his genius as is always the case, he could not very well have got through his disturbed but creative life's journey without a considerable capacity for self-deception. He could scarcely have stood being Wagner if he had been too mercilessly aware of all that Wagner was.

We must not suppose that the element of self-deception deprived his personal relationships of value. They were absolutely necessary to him; they included genuine feeling as well as heartless projection; they brought him distress and comfort, agony and delight, disillusionment and inspiration in about equal measure. But not till quite late in life was he able to work his way through even to the relative stability of his marriage to Cosima. Meanwhile, the element of mother-longing in his repeated experiences, though it was very far from excluding maturer elements, was enough of a barrier to make him feel that the reality of love was continually eluding him, as indeed it very largely was. That is why he went on through the outer world so desperately in search of it. He never really found out in his life, though he did in his work, that the search for mothering and the search for the eternal feminine are ultimately fruitful in proportion as they take an inward direction. This was the search on which Faust was successful only when he was able to journey in the depths of his own psyche 'to the mothers', by which Goethe symbolized the multi-form archetype of feminity.

Nevertheless, Wagner knew something about the eternal feminine rationally, and still more intuitively. Libido which is blocked from one channel will find another if it can. Wagner was blessed with abounding libido. His very difficulty in sustaining a genuinely reciprocal outward relationship diverted his energies the more intensively into his work. He was on better terms with his muse than with any actual woman. If he had realized this to the full, he might have spared himself much of his harrowing involvement with the fair sex in outer reality. But though he never quite realized that what he was ultimately in search of was not in the keeping of any woman, since he already had and could only have it in himself, he was aware of seeking solutions to his life's problems in his work. 'As I have never in my life tasted the true delight of love', he wrote to Liszt (16 Dec. 1854), 'I will set up a memorial to this most lovely of all dreams, in which from beginning to end this love shall be completely satisfied. I have planned out in my mind a *Tristan and Isolde*.'

Among the questions to which Wagner most needed to evolve an answer was this very question of what happens to a man when he is largely incapacitated by his own personality-difficulties from accepting the love he so badly needs and which would so gladly be given to him: the 'need which life denies me—the need of *love*', as he wrote to Robert Franz (25 Sept. 1852). But it was not life which denied love to him; it was himself. Knowing this intuitively though not rationally, he posed the question in his music dramas, and found the answer in a woman's willing self-sacrifice, in which he saw the hope of what he called redemption. This theme recurs like a refrain in his main works, and we shall try to see the positive as well as the negative meaning of it when we reach the end of *Götterdämmerung*.

We can already see Wagner posing the inevitable question here, this time by portraying a figure dark enough to reject love not partially but totally, and not unconsciously but deliberately. No mere human could do that, and Alberich is an archetypal figure if ever there was one. Being archetypal, he carries more than Wagner rationally conceived of him as carrying. Alberich is ambivalent, at bottom, as all archetypes are. He carries a value of his own, and we must try to uncover this value concealed behind his obvious and very real power of doing harm.

59

THE RENUNCIATION OF LOVE

We have already remarked on the most suspicious of the given facts as they appear at surface level. This is the fact that the Rhinemaidens themselves provide Alberich with the incentive and the information to rob them of their own gold. He has not knowingly pursued them in search of power; he has pursued them in search of love. The rejection of love actually comes, or at any rate starts, from their side, not from his. If one of them could have accepted him in love, he would have rejoiced in her like any other lover. If, while rejecting him, the three of them had kept the secret of their gold, he could only have retired discomforted. Instead, they do everything which is necessary to make it not merely possible but probable for him to take the proffered alternative.

What is the consequence? The consequence is everything that happens subsequently in the *Ring*. Unless we are prepared to write off these subsequent happenings as on balance a bad thing, we must at the very least give Alberich the credit for taking the bold step by which they were set in train. If it were not for Alberich, we should still be stuck fast in the prelude to *Rhinegold*, and the chord of E flat major would still be going on.

On the surface, this is just what the Rhinemaidens wanted. Yet it was their own indiscretion which gave Alberich his opportunity, just as it was their own unfeeling handling of his overtures which pushed him into taking it. That was surely no accident. It was as if nature herself, in the persons of her three watery beauties, lifted her skirt just enough to reveal that she has values worth wresting from her so as to turn them into something which is no longer nature, but culture. Regarded on this level, the symbolism once more suggests some perennial episode in the growth of conscious civilization, some working of the spirit on the raw facts of nature, some inward crisis such as the race underwent and the individual must recapitulate not once in a lifetime but many times over.

The immediate crisis to which the Rhinemaidens' revelations lead is Alberich's renunciation of love. It would be very wrong to underestimate the horror and terror of this renunciation as it is enacted before our eyes and ears. But considering it calmly and in retrospect, we may be able to put ourselves for a moment into Alberich's position. He has set his heart on something on the face of it legitimate which, for good or bad, he cannot have. This something is the comfort, the reassurance and the delight of love. But what sort of love is in question here? We must not forget that the Rhinemaidens are mermaids. A mermaid's embrace does not stand for human intercourse, with its mixture of projection and reality and its painful but rewarding struggle towards true mutual relationship. A mermaid's embrace stands for illusion, for seduction by infantile fantasies, for everything that Wagner most needed to grow free of if his search for true relationship and mature living was to prosper.

That being the case, what better favour can a mermaid show her suitor than by rejecting him? Her embrace is death; but her rejection is a challenge. If a man falls into self-pity and spends the rest of his life in search of the illusion which obstinately refuses to swallow him up, he will come to nothing. But if he can accept a measure of unsought frustration as the inevitable consequence of his own individuality (including all the neurotic tension which is at once the weakness and the strength of that individuality), then he may go on growing in stature and in character. He may grow to a point at which he is more capable of real love. If so, the mother-longings which used to pass for love with him will no longer be such a danger, and he can genuinely and thankfully receive the real thing. But before that can happen, he may actually or symbolically have to find the courage to renounce every appearance of love, not knowing whether its reality will come back to him in the end or not.

This might suggest a more positive interpretation of Alberich's renunciation of love, to set alongside the negative interpretation which has certainly to be put on it in the first place. Because the situation is not merely a human one but is also archetypal, both interpretations may be thought to carry part of the truth. If we only see one side, we are missing the essential ambivalence of the archetypal aspect. The archetypal aspect has to do with the paradox that we all need love, but cannot genuinely receive or give it except in so far as we can do without our infantile dependence on it. The situation is somewhat reminiscent of Abraham's acceptance of the Lord's command to sacrifice his son Isaac. He accepted it in horror and terror, not knowing why. Because he accepted it, he did not have to carry it out. But he could not know that in advance.

It may be easier to understand this paradox if we recall that the events here in question are primarily inner events which are being worked out on the level of archetypal symbolism. As far as I know, Wagner made no sustained attempt to curtail his amorous adventures in the outer world. Whether he did so or not is of no fundamental importance. What is of fundamental importance is that he made a lifelong intuitive attempt to grow inwardly independent of his own escapist fantasies. We may judge this by comparing Alberich with Parsifal, another legendary figure and Wagnerian character whose outstanding achievement was the renunciation of love—of a sort. The difference between the two characters, which is enormous, lies in the fact that Parsifal learnt in the course of his adventures to distinguish between love as seduction, which he needed to reject, and love as compassion, for which he showed his capacity by being able to heal Amfortas of the wound caused by seduction in the first place; whereas Alberich remained both literally and metaphorically pretty much in the dark. Yet to do as much as Alberich did, even in the dark, may represent real inner progress. On this level of interpretation, the essence of what Alberich renounced was not the love of woman. It was an undue dependence on the love of woman. He renounced the infantile fantasy of being mothered through life by one woman after another: a fantasy which all too many men act out to their own harm and that of the women who become involved with them. No wonder Alberich got the gold in return for his renunciation. The gold, on this level, stands for the true individuality which we all have within us but cannot possess in so far as we remain entangled in our unconscious longing to get back to 'paradise' as mother's boys or father's daughters.

Another comparison which may be suggested here is between Wagner and Beethoven. Their problems took different directions, but Beethoven's relationships with his fellow beings were still more agonizing than Wagner's, and love in the ordinary human sense played a sadly small part in his life. His deafness increased but did not originate his loneliness. One of the most moving of documents is his own account of the inner struggle through which he was able to accept the frustration of that deafness and that loneliness and find there the strength which his music distils for us as perhaps none other quite can. Love in the sense of compassion and understanding underwent the deepest of sea-changes in Beethoven, to emerge so triumphantly in his music.

The best of Wagner too went into his music, and into the poetry and drama allied to it. His inward understanding of life grew with his characters, and it is a long step from *Rhinegold* to *Parsifal*. In *Rhinegold* we have only Wagner's dark premonition that he would at some time and in some sense have to stand up to the power of love, as this premonition is put here into the mouth of Alberich the hated villain and representative of the shadow. By the time of *Parsifal* Wagner must have come rather nearer to a conscious discrimination, which he was therefore able to voice through the 'pure fool' Parsifal, the bright hero of that exceedingly mature opera of his old age. Yet there is certainly some connection between the two renunciations. We need to renounce, not the love of woman, but neurotic dependence on the love of woman.

A PROMETHEAN THEFT?

The music seems to bear out these suppositions. At the first mention of the power to be won by forging the gold into a ring, we hear the ring's own motive (8), a succession of thirds progressing by intervals of a third, first downwards and then up again. It is an eerily cornerless motive: rings have no corners. It will prove adaptable to an astonishing range of moods, produced by the slightest changes in its harmony and rhythm: no other motive in the *Ring* is quite so musically ambivalent, nor more readily combined with other motives. It turns about easily through chords of the ninth or the eleventh, major and minor, with or without a pedal bass to give a further twist to its harmonic orientation; it can sound very sinister in its characteristic form as dominant minor ninth with eleventh; it is more chromatic at some times than at others; but it is never quite on a simple triad such as defined the motive (44) of the virgin Rhinegold from which the ring is to be forged. These two are in different families of motives, confirming that the gold is in a different condition before and after the forging of it. On the other hand, the first statement of the ring motive grows smoothly enough out of the Rhinemaidens' music. The common element thus suggested is once more the quality of ambivalence. Who are unmanned by the Rhinemaidens' seduction? Those on whom they succeed in bestowing their insidious favours. Who learns from them how to turn the bitterness of frustration into a source of strength? Alberich whom they appear most to disfavour. What uses is the ring capable of being put to? That depends on the intentions of the user. The ring itself is neutral, powerful in use or misuse, ambivalent.

The Rhinemaidens tell Alberich the secret of their gold in the words: 'Only he that renounces the power of desire (*Minne*), only he that forgoes the delights of love (*Liebe*), only he gains the magic to enforce the gold into a ring.' This is sung to a motive (76) not harsh and forbidding, as might on the face of it be expected, but of a singularly sad, moving and resigned nobility. The acceptance of an unsought and undesired but ultimately creative destiny, simply because it is destiny and therefore real and inescapable, could not be more truthfully matched in the mood of the music. But the truth at which the music seems to be hinting is not the avowed truth as literally presented; it is the unavowed truth which Black Alberich, standing for both Wotan's and Wagner's shadow, has to accept because Light Alberich, Wotan himself with his greater nearness to Wagner's conscious thoughts, cannot yet accept it.

This truth is that a man may be condemned by his own nature to

63

great loneliness, and that in so far as this is the case he has the choice of unavailingly resenting the fact, which will undermine him, or of accepting it freely, which will harden and strengthen him as no amount of irresponsible (that is to say illusory) bliss could ever do. Alberich has certainly the courage to follow the implications of his nature to their lonely conclusion, and we respect him for it even while we hate and fear him in his new-found power. I cannot help being reminded of the enormous courage with which Wagner, whatever his surface protestations and self-pityings, at bottom faced up to the loneliness inherent in his own troubled character, and made it the means to his creative strength. For good as well as for bad, there was a great deal more of Alberich in Wagner's make-up than he could consciously have admitted. That is how he was able to understand him so well.

I must again repeat that the positive aspect of Alberich's crime is neither more nor less real than the negative aspect, whose importance is not in any doubt. We can, if we so wish, see Alberich in the Mephisto-phelean function of that force which continually wills evil but brings good to pass: for Mephistopheles, according to Goethe, actually knows himself to be 'part of that power which would Ever work evil, but engenders good'.[1] More radically still, we can view him simply as force: as libido at work in the psyche to bring about a change which may turn out well or badly according to how we manage to take it, but at any rate a change. Yet we are bound to come back to it: for dramatic purposes, he is an evil character. As he clambers up the rock now to snatch his dearly-bought gold, cursing and forswearing love as he reaches the top, his music refers poignantly enough to the 'renunciation' motive (76), yet with a harsh twist to it which it did not have before. The motive of the gold (44) is also twisted into the minor mode, and then on to an unsettling chord of the diminished seventh. We hear the evil unmistakably, but we hear a great deal besides that. We hear, I feel certain, a hint of pathos, which reminds us how unenviable a future Alberich, on his human side, has been driven by his own despair, or rather by his own destiny, into accepting. We hear, too, an undertone of pure ambiguity. We are in the very act of listening to an appalling blasphemy: 'So let love be accursed!' If that were meant at full face value, with nothing else implied, the music conveying it would have to be inexpressibly dreary, empty and at the same time final. It is nothing of the kind. It is full of significance, baleful indeed, but strangely moving, questing, and above all suggesting not an end but a beginning, which is exactly what it is. It is almost as if the

[1] Goethe, *Faust*, Part I, tr. P. Wayne, Harmondsworth, 1949, p. 75.

music were urging us to ask: can good come out of this terrible deed? This year? Next year? Sometime? Never?

We simply do not know. At all events, Alberich pulls the gold away from the rock readily enough, so it seems not impossible that he was meant to do so. Like Prometheus, he has dared a crime. But dare we once more call it a fortunate crime? We have absolutely no means of foretelling that as yet. We shall just have to wait and see.

CHAPTER IV

Rhinegold, Scene 2

——————— ❄ ———————

WOTAN AS AN IMAGE OF THE SELF

The scene dissolves in a swirl of blackening water which seems to sink, so that we are in effect carried upwards. The music, too, is a swirl of agitated notes, on which is superimposed first (68) a descending semitone on subdominant to dominant harmony; second (76) the 'renunciation' motive. The first is an elemental expression of grief which acquires many further important connotations as the *Ring* unfolds (we have already heard it during Alberich's despair at being frustrated by the Rhinemaidens); the second expresses a mood of extraordinary complexity and elusiveness, not to be defined by any single interpretation, but perhaps centring on the spirit of acceptance by means of which grief can become a creative experience. The prominence of a falling semitone in each of these motives connects them musically. Then comes the ring motive (8), ambivalent as always, but in a rather glowing version (8A; 8B) as it broadens into its near relative the Valhalla motive (63); the swirling resumes, but the waves are turning into clouds, through which we continue to rise until they thin to a fine mist; and as this clears we find ourselves on an open mountain height, where Wotan (Odin) and his consort Fricka (Frigga) lie asleep. The music moves into a full statement of that majestically sonorous and diatonic offshoot of the ring motive which comprises the Valhalla motive (63), the very embodiment of the power and glory of Wotan and all that Wotan represents.

Wotan represents, above all, godhead. His other attributes are secondary to this tremendous fact. Even his very important political implications as a carrier of wordly authority follow upon the divine authority which he carries in his own right. Wagner must have found in this commanding figure of Nordic mythology something which echoed among his own deepest intuitions. We all have our intuitions of godhead, whether or not we recognize it under this or any other name. It is one of Jung's best sayings that man cannot stand a meaningless existence. Everything which makes life meaningful for us is implied in what is here described as godhead.

There are several other gods and goddesses in the cast of the *Ring*, and indeed none of the characters is without some share of that mysterious quality which makes us call them numinous. Their numinous quality means that they represent archetypes. But Wotan is by common consent the chief god of the *Ring*, as he was of Nordic mythology. He represents godhead in its simplest essence. He is not, primarily, a god of war or of love or of any other specific attribute. He is the head of the gods, both as their ruler and as the head-source from which their divine essence flows.

In this capacity as head of the gods, Wotan is a symbol for that central principle of the psyche for which Jung has borrowed his term from the traditional Vedantic teachings of Indian metaphysics: the 'self'. Jung does not claim to be an exponent of this most complex and disciplined of traditions.[1] But the concept of the self is found wherever men have tried to give some description of their inner experience, and symbols for it are extremely numerous and diversified. We have no direct knowledge of the self, but we have a great deal of indirect knowledge, since its effects on us are continually felt, and both through tradition and through personal experience we are bound to take these effects into account under whatever explanation, if any, we may wish to put forward.

Life will offer some kind of a meaning to anyone in so far as he can find his way to becoming the individual who really is himself. This is not done by becoming egocentric, since ego is not, as it tends to seem, the centre of the personality. The centre of the personality is the self. Most people have the experience of being worked upon and worked through by something greater than themselves. That would be what Jung calls the self. We do not really know whether that which is greater is immanent or transcendent. If we call it God, we still do not know whether God exists only in the psyche of individuals, or independently of individuals. We only know for certain that the self exists.

The self means not only the central principle but the totality of the psyche. It includes our unconscious and also our conscious components. Now the workings of the self undoubtedly tend towards an increase of consciousness. As we grow more conscious of life's inherent opposites,

[1] An uncompromisingly concise and reliable introduction is René Guenon, *Man and his Becoming According to the Vedanta*, tr. R. C. Nicholson, London, 1945. Jung's treatment of the concept of the self is crucial in all his later writings, but see esp. C. G. Jung, *Psychology and Alchemy*, tr. R. F. C. Hull, London, 1953, pp. 170 ff.

we may manage to integrate them more into our personalities. This brings us nearer to being whole persons, rather than mere collections of fragmentary components. We can never reach that goal, but we can approach it. The self is the whole person, and its fundamental purpose for us seems to be that we should increase our effectual experience of the whole.

One of Jung's names for the growth of character thus produced is integration; another is individuation. This is because the more we can integrate our own fragmentary components, the more we can become individuals. Paradoxical as it may appear, we do not become individuals by clinging wilfully to the purposes we shape for ourselves in the conscious ego, but by letting these conscious purposes adapt themselves to the underlying purposes shaped for us by the self. The whole subtle interplay, if it is going reasonably well, is intuitive, inconspicuous, unselfconscious in the right sense and, also in the right sense, self-regulating. But under whatever outward manifestations, our experience of the self is what gives meaning to our lives.

Wotan's indefinable air of authority is due to the fact that we cannot help taking him for what he is: a god, and a supreme one. But he is only a supreme god in so far as he is an image for the self.

WOTAN AS A SKY-GOD AND A SAVIOUR GOD

Supreme gods are traditionally sky-gods. Wotan rides through the air on his eight-legged horse Sleipnir. He sends his two ravens flying daily across the world to bring him back the latest news. His daughter-companions are the Valkyries, who gallop through the storm-clouds and gather slain heroes to form his bodyguard. His dwelling is on the rocky heights to which we have now been brought, and which are mythologically related to the sky itself. The Greek equivalent is Olympus; but there are many such sacred mountains, and they are customarily regarded not only as heights but as centres. They are symbolically the central point at which earth meets heaven: the axis and the point of contact. Hence their peculiar sanctity, which derives from that of the sky itself.

The sky is sacred from its own obvious nature. Boundless, permanent, inaccessible, alternating uninterruptedly from night to day and from day to night, lit by sun, moon and stars, the sky tells its own story to our sense of awe, as when Kant made his famous confession of being impressed by two things, the starry vault above him and the moral law within him. The effect on us in the transition from Scene 1 to Scene 2 of

Rhinegold, as we rise first through water, then through cloud, to emerge at last on this celestial hill-top, is powerful; it carries us symbolically from the mother-world of unconscious nature to the father-world of light and bright intelligence. In contrast to the dwarfs, the Rhinemaidens or the giants, the race of gods is always more or less symbolical of consciousness.[1]

Wise though he is, Odin (Wotan) was not born so. He acquired wisdom by a persistent search for it, questioning all he met, and paying the price of an eye to the giant Mimir for a drink from the fountain of wisdom at the foot of the world ash tree Yggdrasil. The wisdom symbolized by such spring-water is introverted wisdom bought from the unconscious at the price of turning the sight half inwards, away from the outward world. The world ash tree is the tree of life itself, and is a symbol in close relation with the cross on which Christ hung crucified. Odin wounded himself with his own spear, and hung himself for nine days and nights on the world ash tree, suffering torment until he was able to read the runes written on it, which not only released him but filled him with new youth and new wisdom, as suffering willingly accepted can bring rejuvenation and insight. His voluntary suffering also accounts for the fact that whereas most sky-gods stand so high above the earth that they are experienced as remote (growing remoter as other more personal deities become added to the heirarchy), Odin kept in contact with the human race, taking a frequent and increasing part in the affairs of man. Odin himself first gave man the gift of spirit, which was the beginning of consciousness; he was the patron of poets and visionaries; by a dangerous adventure he stole, Prometheus-like, the divine mead or hydromel with which to bestow inspiration on favoured mortals.[2] He combines some of the attributes of the supreme deity and of the mediating (because suffering) saviour. But always his symbolism has to do somehow or other with consciousness.

WOTAN AS PSYCHIC CONSCIOUSNESS

Odin's many interventions in the affairs of men carry different meanings on different levels, but essentially they symbolize the impact of consciousness, not from the outside but from the inside. They stand for

[1] For the statements made in these paragraphs concerning the sky-gods, see the erudite and imaginative analysis in Mircea Eliade, *Patterns in Comparative Religion*, tr. Rosemary Sheed, London, 1958, Ch. II.

[2] Sources in the Eddas, but conveniently summarized in Larousse, *Encyclopedia of Mythology*, Engl. tr. London, 1959, pp. 258 ff.

insight derived not from ego but from the self. This is particularly true of the characteristic stories in which Odin exchanges question and answer, often with life staked as the guarantee of the knowledge exchanged. Whenever we meet Odin wandering disguised as an old man, we see him in an archetypal role, the role of the Wise Old Man, which has to do with our intuitive knowledge of the self, and with the actual intuitions which can often be gained through symbolic encounters of this kind in art, dreams and fantasies. Wotan's appearances as the Wanderer in *Siegfried,* after he has withdrawn from active interference at the end of the *Valkyrie,* show him mainly in this role. To a very considerable extent, the consciousness of which he has by then become a symbol may be described in Layard's term as psychic consciousness.

WOTAN AS EGO CONSCIOUSNESS

But it is not in such a role that Wagner first introduces us to Wotan. We first meet him here in *Rhinegold* as a figure in the prime of life; and the subsequent development of the human side of his character is one of the main issues through which the fundamental plot of the *Ring* is unfolded. Seen on this level, Wotan is a man approaching that crisis of the middle years of life in which we are called upon to pass, violently or gently as the case may be, wittingly or unwittingly, from the relative extroversion of our earlier years to the relative introversion of our later years. Most or all of us find this transition bewildering and disturbing in some degree; we resist it, put it off, try to escape it; but if we cannot go with it in the end, life itself will in effect have done with us.

In the first half of life, our libido pours itself readily into our conscious enterprises, and the self finds its natural outlet in furthering the plans of the ego. In the second half of life, this situation is in the ordinary course of events very largely reversed. It becomes increasingly important to be flexible and adaptable, not merely in relation to outer reality, but above all in relation to inner reality. It is time to relax the wilfulness of ego and the naïve assertiveness of youth, in favour of the maturer requirements of the self.

We shall soon find that Wotan has no present intention of relaxing his conscious authority; indeed, at the very moment at which we are now meeting him, he is at the climax of a formidable scheme for securing it against all possibility of outward attack. He does not appreciate yet that the real attack is going to come at him from within. It will be interesting to watch his reactions as this crucial point is borne in on him.

Meanwhile, a very prominent element in his symbolism is not directly concerned with the self or with psychic consciousness at all, but with ego and ego consciousness. On this level, Wotan's bid for the mastery of the world is ego's bid to retain that authority within the personality which in earlier life seems to belong to it by natural right. If ego's bid is finally successful, the personality itself will suffer the real defeat. If ego's bid is unsuccessful, and if ego can accept its own apparent defeat reluctantly but freely, the personality as a whole will win through to success in however unanticipated a form.

The visible symbol of Wotan's ego, and of his will to defend his ego against defeat, is the spear which even in his sleep he is now firmly grasping. In so far as he goes on dominating the situation more or less effectually by the power of his spear, with its powerful motive (73), Wotan is a symbol of ego consciousness.

WOTAN AS FATHER-IMAGE

A further point of contact between Wotan's divine and human sides can be seen in his character as a husband and father.

Like the priest whose private character may fall a long way short of the divine without detracting from the efficacy of his priestly function, Wotan, in what for want of a better term we may call his private life, has all the defects of his very great virtues. Through his function as sovereign god, Wotan carries the projection of our inner image of paternal authority. This image, being at the same time both positive and negative, may appear in mythology as the dual archetype of the Wise Old Man and the Wicked Magician: the good father and the bad father, who seem more distinct than they really are, since, as usual, they are really a single ambivalent symbol (*cf.* Jahveh). In this capacity as All-Father, Wotan calls up associations in us from the love and the hatred, the reliability and the incalculability, the friendliness and the irritability, the reasonableness and the irrationality we have all experienced in some measure from our physical fathers, or from substitute fathers. Behind these experiences there stands the archetype itself, whose image is latent in us by hereditary predisposition. Wotan, in short, like the other characters in the *Ring*, is no stranger to us. We know broadly what to expect of them even before they begin to act their parts.

If a child's father is too inhibited in his emotions to display this humanly ambivalent lovability and irascibility, the child lacks adequate material on which to continue developing his own inner father-image.

But if his father is ordinarily human and accessible, the child will love and hate him, admire and fear him, be desirous and jealous of him by turns, or still more disconcertingly, at the same time. He will try propitiation and he will try rebellion; he will try good behaviour and bad; in one way and another, he will assimilate and come to terms with father. In so far as he fails in this, his inner father-image will be tainted with unavowed bitterness and terror, and his dealings with the outer world will tend to be difficult and distressing, particularly in relation to authority. In so far as he succeeds, he will have the immense advantage of a father's strength and manliness at his inner command, and his outer relations will tend to be easy and assured.

Thus even as an archetypal symbol, we see how valuable it is that Wotan should be so warmly and fallibly human. If he were more perfect, he would be less recognizable as our own familiar father-image writ large. No child has or would want to have a perfect father, with all the immutability and inaccessibility which that impossible ideal would imply; he needs to be able to recognize his father as made of approachable human stuff like himself. A father who secretly though mistakenly thinks that he is perfect has his children in despair, because his unconscious hypocrisy keeps them out of touch with him as no mere bad temper can. An obviously bad father is better than a moralistic father who can never be got at.

Wotan is sometimes a bad father; Wotan can be got at; Wotan is reassuringly human. His strength, too, is as real as his weakness. He has our affection as a married man and father in the personal sense, and he stands all the better on that account for our collective father-image.

FRICKA AS PART OF WOTAN'S INNER FEMININITY

Fricka as Wagner presents her to us, sleeping peacefully for the moment by the side of Wotan, is not one of those great goddesses who carry our primary projections of the mother-image. She is presented as Wotan's consort. This means that she is seen, through man's eyes, as an aspect of man's (rather than woman's) experience of the eternal feminine. Like everything feminine she has, indeed, elements of mother, but these are not immediately obvious. What is immediately obvious, as soon as she wakes up, is that she is a nagging wife.

We shall never succeed in defining the eternal feminine, or the eternal masculine either. But one thing which has always been clear to poets and visionaries like Wagner, and which has been studied more prosaically now by modern psychologists, is that every man carries something of a woman's nature at the hidden centre of his masculinity. The counterpart to this is that every woman carries something of a man's nature at the hidden centre of her femininity. We have already given brief attention to this subject when considering some of the implications of Alberich's renunciation of love. We need to follow it up a little further here in connection with Wotan's loveless marriage. There is undoubtedly a level on which Fricka symbolizes some part of Wotan's inner femininity.

Jung calls a man's inner femininity his anima, using the Latin word for 'soul'; and a woman's inner masculinity her animus, using the masculine form of the same Latin word. Some of the best things men and women do, and some of the worst, are inspired by the anima or by the animus, whose influence wells up apparently uninvited, and sometimes so unconsciously that it takes possession of the will without our knowing it. But under more favourable circumstances there is a fertile exchange between the unconscious prompting and the conscious ego. A man's anima is his muse and his inspiration, the carrier of that inner creativity which he may often feel working through him as if it were another person; the carrier, too, for good and bad, of his irrational intuitions, impulses and emotions. A woman's animus is likewise her good daemon and her bad, carrying her rational, orderly capabilities and her legitimate ambitions, but also her potentialities for false logic and harsh assertiveness.

Wagner was immeasurably swayed by his anima, both at her best and at her worst. At her best, she helped him to produce some of the most warm, flexible and imaginative works of art our Western world possesses, besides endowing him with an insatiable aptitude for friendship. At her worst, she bedevilled these friendships and a great many other aspects of his life with touchiness, instability and megalomania. At her best, she bestowed on him the courage of an archangel; at her worst, the rigidity of a prig. Rigidity is more characteristic of the bad side of the animus than of the anima, and in this respect it has been suggested that the anima is actually imitating the animus: probably the mother's animus of the man in question introjected into him by unconscious imitation, and powerfully charged, as always, by the underlying archetype.

We shall find this kind of rigidity in Wagner's Fricka. She is impervious to argument. She has no lack of arguments herself; but much of her logic is borrowed masculine logic, not based on real feminine feeling. That is a typical manifestation of the animus when in the negative role, aping man at his falsely logical worst just as the anima when in the negative role will ape woman at her moody worst. This makes it fairly clear what this aspect

73

of Wagner's Fricka represents. It represents Wotan's (and by implication Wagner's) inner femininity (i.e. anima) in so far as it is under the influence of the worst masculine (i.e. animus) elements in his image of his mother. For Fricka is not moody at all; she is inflexible; and while her logic is in the main all too unassailable, it is also ever so slightly but exasperatingly off the mark. There is no answering it, and yet we get caught up in it without being altogether convinced in our hearts, as opposed to our heads. In Act II of the *Valkyrie* this becomes particularly conspicuous; but we shall already get the impression of it in the present scene.

This strangely borrowed element of counterfeit masculinity in a man is quite different from his real masculinity, though often confused with it both by himself and others. Since he may be thought to have absorbed part of it from his mother's animus and part of it from the archetype of the animus, it can, in the terminology I have just used, be described as introjected mother's animus. More simply, it is a part of a man tending to false morality, censoriousness and priggishness. When Wagner had behaved particularly meanly and deceitfully to Ludwig of Bavaria, and Ludwig, though knowing this, presently made humble and apologetic overtures, Wagner would answer with a verbose sermon all about his own—not Ludwig's—long-sufferingness and forgivingness and martyred endurance under adversity, until merely reading the letters at this distance of time we feel exceedingly uncomfortable. That was the Fricka in him: Fricka at her detestable and priggish worst.

False morality towards oneself or others is very much bound up with that important and often dominating formation in the psyche which Freud has so valuably investigated under the concept of the super-ego. We shall notice a prominent aspect of Fricka's attitude to Wotan in which she functions as if she were his super-ego personified.

A further and in some ways more obvious source of Fricka's character in the *Ring* may be found in the worst side of Wagner's relations with his first wife, Minna. Locked together through many years of intense mutual projection, unable either to part conclusively or to find a basis of compatibility, the pair of them probably gave each other more distress in the end than they had ever shared delight. The mutualness in such situations is like that of a pair of cogwheels; each sticks out where the other goes in, and they mesh together inseparably in projection and counter-projection until something is either undone or breaks. But because this is itself an archetypal situation, Fricka, as usual, is much more than a mere prejudiced portrait of Minna. Fricka with her nagging is indeed an aspect

74

of the eternal feminine, and one with which we all have to reckon in our inner life if not in our outward relationships: probably in both, though not necessarily in so extreme a form as Wagner's first marriage.

Moreover, even Fricka will prove to have a positive value, as we were bound to find if she is a truly archetypal image; and obviously she is. We shall see this too in Act II, Scene 1, of the *Valkyrie*, where Fricka tells Wotan something which he does not yet know and is not going to like when he does know it, but which he will have to know in his own long-term interests. For the present this must wait, and so must our consideration of Brynhilde as an enormously more sympathetically and elaborately developed representative of Wotan's inner femininity in particular and of the anima principle in general: of what Wagner and other German romantics were so fond of calling, after Goethe, the eternal feminine. Fricka shares with Brynhilde the beautiful (90A)!

OTHER REPRESENTATIVES
OF THE ETERNAL FEMININE

The *Ring* includes a number of other representatives of the eternal feminine, several of them considerably more important than Fricka. There are the Rhinemaidens; there is Freia; there is Erda the Earth-Mother; there are the Valkyries with Brynhilde at their head; there are the charmers called Wishmaidens, who if not identical with the Valkyries must at least be their very close relations, since when in the *Valkyrie* Act II, Scene 4, the Wishmaidens are mentioned as one of the attractions of Valhalla, the Valkyries' motive (47) is heard. Both act as cupbearers, in which role they carry positive mother-symbolism, but their favours do not stop at that. They merge with the fascinating tribe of Swanmaidens (mentioned in one source as in 'swan guise, for they were Valkyries') whose way it was to leave their plumage on a river's bank while they bathed; and he who took it from one of them might command her person or even (for a restricted period such as seven years) marry her. We find all these creatures, and others such as mermaids of the water, harpies of the air, and fates or Norns (three of these will confront us in *Götter-dämmerung*) so confused in the legends and so frequently changing roles that we can only regard them as varied personifications which stress this mood or that in turns, but which at bottom merge into one another with truly feminine inconsequence.[1]

[1] For examples see Jacob Grimm, *Teutonic Mythology*, tr. J. S. Stallybrass, London, Vol. I, 1882, pp. 417 ff.

All these images are to a greater or lesser extent coloured by our experience of the physical mother and by the quality of the love she or any substitute mother has been able to give us; but, as always, the underlying factor is our innate disposition to form an archetypal image. Because we experience mother's womb and breasts before we come directly to know father, the mother-image has a certain inalienable primacy even over the father-image. Both images are partly carried over into subsequent developments centring around brothers and sisters, friends, mates and other relationships. With their usual fluidity, the archetypal images are equal to all these complications. It is only we who may run into difficulties in our rational attempts to sort them out.

THE GODS' DILEMMA

Though the mists have cleared, we realize that it is still early dawn; and now the growing light catches a great fortress at some distance away on a cliff in the background. This effect should be dramatically brought out by strongly lighting up the stage and the fortress itself; when this is not properly done, the visual symbolism is not made clear.

Fricka starts up in agitation, and wakes Wotan to remind him that the fortress, of which we soon learn that it is Valhalla and that it has just been completed by a pair of giants, has now to be paid for. The price agreed was Freia (Freya), goddess of youth and youthful love; but Wotan has been relying on a vague promise by Loge, who recommended the bargain in the first instance, to find some way out of it.

Freia runs up in terror as the giants arrive. She has a beautiful theme in two halves, both of which are used as separate entities very frequently and in very important functions throughout the *Ring*. Both halves are more or less connected with what Loge presently describes as 'woman's delight and worth'. But the ways in which we value woman's delight and worth vary with the degree of naïveness in which we approach her. The naïver our approach, the more we take her for a radiant creature with whom to share the gay companionship and sensuous joys which should come so naturally in our younger years; and the less we see her in the round as a human individual complete with good moods and bad, so that when the bad moods appear and her shadow is in the ascendant, we are apt to feel surprised and aggrieved. This does not lessen the value of naïve love, which is among the best of human experiences. The first half of Freia's theme comprises a motive (6) of which the meaning has to do with the more or less naïve delight in love and love's sensuality.

There are, however, maturer experiences of love which do not preclude delight and sensuality, but which expand in ever-widening circles until they include all the warmth of compassion, understanding and sympathy which holds the world together. In using this expression 'maturer experiences', I have it in mind that maturity is very largely a matter of seeing both sides. But to see both sides is to be exposed to all manner of pain, distress and mental conflict. To experience the keenness of life's unavoidable opposites may be very disillusioning to our naïve expectations; it should not be so, however, to our real values. Many waters will not wash away love. But in so far as our naïveness is washed away, or burnt away by bitter suffering, we may grow more capable of holding both joy and pain at the same time, rather than swinging too blindly from one to the other and back again.

The second half of Freia's music comprises a motive (69) which most commentators have associated with the ideas of flight and of agitation. Freia here is both agitated and in flight, and these facts are reflected in the form taken by (69) at this point. Similar situations are found later on in which the motive is treated in much the same agitated fashion. But Deryck Cooke drew my attention to a very different aspect of the motive, and one which he rightly argues is much more fundamental to its meaning. In the first place, not only (69) but also (6) grow serener (being changed from the minor to the major mode) so soon as Freia is sufficiently relieved of her fears to appear in her proper colours (and also when the giant Fasolt, for example, or some other character is thinking pleasant thoughts about her or about some form of love). In the second place, (6) is the source of (37), the derivation being so intimate as to be essentially an identity. But (37) is a true love-motive, conveying only such elements of agitation as normally enter into our feelings of love, naïve or otherwise. We shall come to it later, especially in *Valkyrie*, Act I; but for the moment, it may not be too far-fetched to see in (69) a hint of all that side of love which is not unaware of pain and conflict, and which opens out into tenderness and compassion in their widest senses.

The giants come pounding after Freia with a motive (58) eloquent of their crude bulk, their vast strides and their heavy footsteps. Our earliest experience of such towering figures, with whose mere walk we can scarcely keep pace at the run, is of our parents. This is thought to be the main association underlying giants and gigantic ogres and ogresses in myth and fairy-tale. It almost certainly comes in here on some level. It is true that both Fafner and Fasolt are males; but gender is not always literal in mythology or dreams, where, for example, the darkest male element in a woman (the dark aspect of the animus) may often appear as a male ogre, dragon or other monster.[1]

Has Wotan been turning on to a problem of adult life the brutal aspect of parental authority as it may be experienced in childhood? That is a mistake for which we may pay by remaining ourselves to that extent under the domination of the parental image, experienced as guilty feelings and inhibitions such as Wotan, not without reason, has now towards these brutal giants, whose music resembles the important motive (70) known as Wotan's will frustrated (*see* 58, 59); these in turn are closely related to the descending stepwise motive (73) which represents Wotan's spear, the inhibiting bargains inscribed on the spear, and more generally, Wotan's personal wilfulness in his capacity as a symbol for the conscious ego.

It is our conscious ego which is liable to try to force an issue where only the slow processes of growth and persuasion can really avail. The giants command vast force; and Wotan has been using them to build up vast walls, behind which he hopes to secure his personal position, that is to say the position taken up by his conscious ego. The new danger to which he has thereby exposed himself is not, however, a danger from the outside; it is a danger from the inside. As we shall shortly see, he is in danger of losing the real source on which his strength depends; for that source is bound up with the symbolism of Freia, who is everything that the giants are not and who holds the real promise that Valhalla only seems illusorily to hold.

Valhalla seems illusorily to hold the promise of lasting security. But nothing in life can really be secure, except the security of knowing that nothing is secure, and of accepting that hard fact in all willingness as one of the conditions of being alive. What is not illusory about Valhalla is the value of genuine extrovert achievement. In the first half of life, extrovert achievement is our proper pursuit to an extent which becomes greatly modified as we reach the second half of life. Wotan is reaching the second half of life, and it is time for him to give extrovert achievement the second place. He can no longer afford to take it simply at its full face value, as he has quite properly been doing hitherto. He needs to grow more introverted; he needs to yield precedence to the inner promptings of his spirit; in Voltaire's unforgettable image at the end of *Candide*, he needs to cultivate his own garden. Or perhaps for the time being it will be sufficient if he does not make it impossible for Freia to cultivate hers, by yielding

[1] Erich Neumann, tr. R. F. C. Hull, *The Origins and History of Consciousness*, London, 1954, pp. 176 ff.

78

her over to the giants in accordance with the bargain to which he has so
dangerously assented.

The danger is precisely that in so far as we do contrive to cling to our
illusory security against the threatening aspects of life, we barricade out
the fruitful aspects. The more cleverly we evade the pain, the more
aridly we preclude the delight. If we cannot let life in whole as the bitter-
sweet thing it is, we cannot let it in at all. Both Wotan's guilty feelings
and his conventional inhibitions in relation to the giants, which prevent
him from fighting them outright, are connected with his attempt to find
security behind the barricade of Valhalla's impressive walls.

Wotan now pretends, clumsily enough, that the bargain had only been
intended as a joke, and invites the giants to name their own price. At
first incredulous, next patient, but finally indignant, the giants deserve
and get a large measure of our sympathy.

The giants are honest according to their lights, but stupid. They are
sometimes conceived as representing the reality-principle against which
Wotan has now run his head. So he has; but the stupidity in such cases
is our own stupidity, which only seems to be rising up against us like a
threat in the outside world because our projections are putting it there
for us to see, and perhaps actually calling it up into action against ourselves.

What particular kind of stupidity can we see in Wotan, or in Wagner,
which is presented to us here in projection on to these typical specimens
of the giant race? Perhaps it has to do with the unconscious stupidity of
projecting so many of our own inner difficulties on to the outer world.
Wagner's life, and the life's task with which he found himself confronted, were bound to be extremely difficult at the best. But he made
these difficulties very much worse by believing that every man's hand was
against him except for his own few loyal allies. Treating men in authority
almost consistently as his enemies, he did a great deal to make them so.
The miracle was that even his allies, on whom also he turned from time
to time, remained so loyal, and grew in number so rapidly and influ-
entially. His greatness must have glowed out unmistakably through his
covering of defensive aggressiveness; it must have become obvious quite
early on that he was the one man who mattered most at the time in
European music; his personal charm must have outweighed his unreliability; his fundamental integrity must have outshone his intermittent
trickiness.

Wagner evidently felt deep down that his own very genuine originality
could not have any value unless the whole contemporary art of his day

had none. His was to be the combined art-form of the future which was to superannuate such mere precursors as the existing arts of poetry, music, theatre, sculpture and architecture. He not only felt these things, but constantly repeated them in his published writings. It was very stupid of him; but he saw the stupidity in his environment, that is to say unconsciously projected. One of his favourite themes was the stupidity and indeed corruptness of most of the other people in the world.

It was not only stupid of him, however; in some strange roundabout way it was also magnificent. He fought against the giant enemies who were partly real, partly imaginary, and partly raised up by himself against himself, with a strength and heroism proportionate to the situation as he experienced it. The strength which he attributed to these giant enemies was in part a projection of the strength he developed to pit against them; the heroism was altogether his own. We are brought up, not for the first time in this book, against the mysterious connection between neurosis and genius, or more generally, between strength of delusion and strength of character. If Wagner had been free of persecutedness and free of inflatedness with regard to his prodigious life's work, it is by no means certain that he could have found in himself the sheer rebellious force of conviction to accomplish it. In one way or another, he certainly managed to overcome difficulties both real and imaginary which very few mortals could have survived at all.

In view of these experiences, it is to Wagner's credit that he was able to portray the giants in *Rhinegold* unmaliciously. He made them stupid, he made them large and he made them strong: the normal attributes of their kind throughout mythology. He is perfectly fair to them here, and he lets them make their case, which in terms of outer reality is a good one. As Freia's distracted cries bring Donner (Thor) and her twin brother Froh (Frey) running in, violence seems imminent. But Wotan, with difficulty, averts violence; his own sense of honour rejects that alternative, or is it mainly calculation? For if he merely repudiates his own pledged bargain, he believes, his authority as the upholder of law and order will be fatally undermined at the very moment when he is hoping to secure it by means of the castle of Valhalla finished by the honourable labours of the giants themselves. But he is willing enough to extricate himself by wile, if the giants can be persuaded to accept a wily alternative. And indeed it is just as true in the psyche as it is in the outside world that many a position which cannot be stormed by force can be turned by wile. In the inside world, here perhaps is a position which not only can be but should be turned by wile. We shall find presently that Wotan's bargains basically symbolize his inhibitions. We cannot overcome our inhibitions by mere force of will-power; they are too strongly and, above all, too unconsciously entrenched for that. A kind of inner wile in getting round them is the normal means used by the psyche to get the flow of life moving on again; and it may be this which is now being so eagerly awaited by Wotan and the others.

The eagerly awaited representative of wile is Loge, at whose advice Wotan first struck his bargain with the giants. We all have a Loge in us, and Wagner's inner Loge was a very highly developed example of this perfectly normal ingredient in our human composition. Even to the conventional eye, however, Loge does not look so consistently reprehensible as Black Alberich; and as he arrives now in the nick of time, and is immediately pressed with threats and insults to redeem his promise by propounding a mutually acceptable remedy, we may take an unprejudiced look at his antecedents and standing in mythology. We shall find many things against him, but others which tell surprisingly in his favour.

LOGE THE TRICKSTER AND HIS TRICKY REMEDY

Loge is a fire god, the patron of smiths and all who make good use of fire as the servant of man. Fire, however, is a good servant but a bad master. Firelight flickers and is never still, like Loge's restlessly chromatic music. Loge is the god of lies as well as the god of fire; the patron of thieves as well as of smiths. 'The first father of falsehood', says the Prose Edda,[1] he had 'artifices for all occasions; he would ever bring the Aesir into great hardships, and then get them out with crafty counsel'. Loge is the arch-trickster of Norse mythology, and ambivalence is his second name. This too his music (20, 20A, 20B, 21) conveys.

Such trickster gods are to outward appearance cunning but not wise.[2] They all have this habit of getting themselves and others into scrapes and out of them again, generally with a whole skin if not with dignity. Their tricks range from mischievous to spiteful, but they have always an excuse ready and are more often threatened than punished. We have more sympathy for them in their misdeeds than we may admit to ourselves, and are none of us quite above making use of the qualities they symbolize. They may at times come to the rescue of their own accord with unexpected thoughtfulness and goodwill, having uncanny powers at their

[1] *The Prose Edda*, tr. A. G. Brodeur, London, 1929, p. 41.
[2] See Paul Radin, *The Trickster: a Study in American Indian Mythology*, with commentary by C. G. Jung, London, 1956; Maya Deren, *Divine Horsemen: Living Gods of Haiti*, London, 1953, pp. 102 ff.

disposal when they are in this helpful mood. Even their seeming follies have a way of producing good results which could never have been planned deliberately.

Loge is mythologically closer to Hermes (Mercury) than he is to Hephaestus (Vulcan), whose nearer counterpart is Wieland (Wayland) the lame smith. In medieval and renaissance alchemical literature, Mercury, the volatile, sometimes appears as fire. He can be the fire of the Holy Ghost; he can, in this alchemical imagery, be the heavenly dew or rain of grace; he can be the transforming water in the *vas hermeticum* or alchemical bath. He can be the hermaphrodite produced there by the union of male and female opposites in the symbolical 'sacred marriage'; or he can be the 'divine child' of it, symbolizing, like the alchemical gold itself, renewal and rejuvenation. Like all alchemical imagery, that attaching to Mercury stands for states of the psyche rather than of the chemical substances employed as matter on which to project them. Mercury, in his extreme ambivalence, sometimes almost seems to stand for the vast play of contrary forces in the psyche itself; and even the little-loved Loge presents us with a suggestion of the same impressive paradox. Loge himself was hermaphroditic enough not only to beget children but also to bear them, 'which', as Odin justifiably remarked, 'I weened was a woman's lot'.[1]

So great was Loge's ambivalence that he was sometimes split into two characters, one tending to be spelt Loge and the other Loki, of which the former had more favourable attributes and the latter less favourable; but the distinction was not maintained.[2] Even the Christian devil (with whom, especially as Lucifer, Loge has obvious affinities) displays ultimately the same ambivalence. The limp commonly thought to be shared by Loge, the devil, Vulcan, Wieland the Smith and others suggests, as we saw when considering Alberich's dwarfish deformity, the flaw or trauma found so typically in creative characters; the wound in the psyche which in its positive aspect drives them into creativeness by depriving them to some extent of ordinary contentments. Wagner was himself a driven man in both respects.

One consequence of a trickster-god's mischief may be the uncovering of new self-knowledge which would not otherwise have come to light. Loge (like Mercury in his role as messenger) is a conveyor of knowledge from one part of the psyche to another, and a revealer of valuable if

---

[1] *The Elder or Poetic Edda*, trans. Olive Bray, London, 1908, p. 255; cf. p. 221.
[2] Jacob Grimm, *Teutonic Mythology*, tr. J. S. Stallybrass, London, Vol. I, 1882, pp. 241 ff.

unwelcome truths. An attempt was once made to sew up Loge's mouth; but it was unsuccessful.[1] There is an entire and very entertaining book of the Poetic Edda called *Loge's Mocking*,[2] in which he pierces the complacency of each of the gods in turn by reminding him of the one episode in his legend which he least wants to remember. Loge is punished for this by being bound to a rock with a serpent dropping venom on to his face, though his wife caught the venom in a bowl except when it became full and she had to move away and empty it.

In a commoner rendering Loge was punished in this way for causing the death of Baldr the Beautiful—a being so perfect that he plainly represents something to do with our ideals. But even our ideals have a positive and a negative side to them. No doubt they are positive in so far as they are genuine; but ideals taken over consciously or unconsciously from the community do not all ring true for the individual; and even the individual saddles himself with ego-ideals, conscious or unconscious, which are not all true to his own inner nature.

Ideals can make a man very rigid and very priggish without his knowing it. They can make him very hard on himself as well as on other people. They can make him unrealistic, so that he continually lets the best be the enemy of the good. Conscience in the shape of what Freud defined as the super-ego can be a cruel and unyielding master. No man is as good as his ego-ideals tend to make him think; and if, on the negative side, Baldr symbolizes the Norse gods' idealistic illusions about themselves (i.e. a projection of our own idealistic illusions) it may well have been necessary for Loge to trick them into killing him, just as it may well have been necessary for Loge to remind the gods of the more discreditable sides of their own symbolism.

On the positive side, Baldr's symbolism is connected with creative sacrifice and resurrection, of which for us in the West the supreme example is Christ. Judas, whose part in Christ's passion was necessary, hung himself out of remorse. Loge was punished by the gods with venom, a fit symbol of hatred whether from outside or from inside. His punishment, bound to the rock as he was, again reminds us of Prometheus, another defier of the gods whose crime was certainly in the interests of the human psyche in its quest for consciousness and civilization. The close relationship of Loge and Prometheus has long been recognized.[3]

[1] Snorri Sturluson, *The Prose Edda*, tr. A. G. Brodeur, London, 1929, p. 147.

[2] *The Elder or Poetic Edda*, tr. Olive Bray, London, 1908, pp. 244 ff.

[3] Cf. Jacob Grimm, *Teutonic Mythology*, tr. J. S. Stallybrass, London, Vol. I, 1882, p. 247. For Loge's punishment, see Snorri Sturluson, *The Prose Edda*, trans. A. G. Brodeur, London ,1929, pp. 75–77.

Loge and Prometheus are both, in their different ways, late and sophisticated examples of a very primitive line of trickster gods. The more primitive the trickster, the more clearly he stands for some autonomous part of the personality so cut off from the conscious ego that it can play tricks which ego would never knowingly risk or tolerate. There are some American-Indian animal tricksters, rather like our Reynard the Fox, who repeatedly learn by their own uncomfortable experiences to get into a more realistic contact both with the world outside and with their own natures inside.[1] It is the great advantage of the trickster in us that he can get behind both our ego-ideals and our ego-fears. He can be of enormous value to us on that account.

At his worst, the trickster may tempt us into twisty conduct from the complications of which even he may be unable to extricate us. At his best, he may prompt us with some inspired stratagem which is both ingenious and legitimate. This is as true inwardly as it is outwardly. The trickster may at one time appear to encourage our inner evasions, but at another time he may expose them by one of his most mischievous-seeming ruses, greatly to our benefit. On one level, as Deryck Cooke pointed out to me, Loge meant for Wagner the sceptical rationalism of the Age of Reason, above all of Voltaire, for which like other romantics Wagner felt a partly justified mistrust. On another level, Loge represents a certain most curious but creative kind of inward trickery, which works somewhat as follows.

Both the forces and the resistances which operate in the psyche unconsciously are enormously stronger than anything in the conscious will which we can oppose to them. Our only hope of modifying them is by somehow turning their own power round against themselves. This cannot be done by force of will. It can be done if the trickster in us comes to our assistance in his own wily fashion. In legend after legend and myth after myth, we find the hero successful only when he adopts some ruse or trick suggested to him by a magic figure, often an animal figure, from the deep unconscious. Not only are such tricks the commonplaces of myths and fairy-tales; they appear just as typically in our dreams and fantasies, and with just as valuable results if we can accept them either intuitively or with the help of psychological analysis. It was already an age-old principle when Plato drew attention to it: set a thief to catch a thief.

This is exactly what Wotan decides to do, after listening to a long and famous narrative in which Loge recounts how he has searched the world in vain for any treasure which men will take in exchange for woman's

[1] Paul Radin, *The Trickster*, with commentary by C. G. Jung, London, 1956.

delight and worth. We hear a motive (79) which begins with a fragment of the 'renunciation' motive (76) and ends with a variant of that falling semitone (68)—often from minor subdominant to dominant seventh— used already in passing, and very much used subsequently, for grief or for the tragedy or evil lying behind the grief. The new motive (79) con- veys a mood not unlike that of the 'renunciation' motive: it speaks of grief and destiny; it also speaks, not in all but in some of its harmonic and dramatic contexts, of acceptance and resignation. It is followed here by the first part of Freia's music, i.e. motive (6), since she holds for the giants as for everyone else the promise of woman's delight and worth.

But now Loge tells the whole story, which the gods and the giants had not yet clearly known, of Alberich's theft of the gold. Slyly Loge hints at the power offered by a ring forged from the gold; and not only the giants, but the gods too, are caught up in the temptation of that power, and also in the gnawing fear that if left with Alberich it may be turned against themselves. For next they learn that the unwelcome con- dition of forswearing love has already been fulfilled by Alberich. The ring has been duly forged, and a golden treasure piled up by the dwarfs who are now subjected by Alberich to the ring's power.

The giants succumb to the lure thus cunningly displayed to them. They agree to accept the gold in place of the goddess. It only remains to steal the treasure from Alberich with the tricky help of Loge, who in providing all this valuable information about the underworld situation has already shown himself in his Mercurial capacity as messenger between one part of the psyche and another.

At once the giants retreat, taking Freia with them as hostage. The light grows strangely dim; the faces of the gods themselves grow grey. Loge tells them why. Each morning the gods are given magic golden apples to eat by Freia; now she has been taken from them, and there are no apples with which to start the new day. It is these apples which keep the gods perennially young and radiant; but Loge claims not to miss them, never having been given his fair share.

Gold again! What are these golden apples of youth? We have seen two primary mythological meanings attaching to gold: as a symbolical equivalent to fire, it stands for libido; as a symbolical equivalent to light, it stands for consciousness. In the *Ring*, the Rhinemaidens' gold itself seems to represent value submerged in the unconscious, and brought into use only after being not merely lit up, but, at a cost, taken away and forged. But the golden apples have been grown in the full light of day. In the Bible, eating an apple brought knowledge of good and evil: in a

85

word, consciousness. In Norse mythology, the main emphasis seems to be on life and the abundant energy of life, as when a barren woman becomes pregnant through being given a magic apple to eat. It seems possible that Freia's golden apples symbolize the supply of libido which at any given time is available to the ego for its own conscious purposes.

People who wake to each new day with an abundance of natural energy are apt to take that precious boon for granted. But it is only while we and our conscious purposes are sufficiently in harmony with the self and its underlying purposes for us that this abundance is continued. Most of us, perhaps all of us at times, know what it is to feel deprived of natural energy. If that condition becomes at all permanent, the complexion may in actual outward fact become visibly grey. Though manic moods remain possible, paid for by corresponding depressions, there will be no waking to each new day wide open to the keen joys and pains of simply being alive. Freia will not give an abundance of her golden apples.

If this explanation is approximately correct, we can see why Loge in his capacity as fire does not need Freia's golden apples; for fire itself is a still more general symbol for libido. The gods need Freia's apples not so much to keep them literally young in years as young in spirit. Freia is not a goddess of love in quite the direct sense of Venus or Frau Minne. One of Freia's gifts is to set mortals in love with love; but that is only one consequence of a still better gift, which is to set mortals in love with life.

The music bears all this out after its own unargumentative fashion. Freia's golden apples have a motive (7) closely related not only to the part of Freia's motive (6) which suggests the naïver delights of love, but also to the group of nature motives centring on (2). We can take small delight in life if we get too far out of touch with nature. Happy love, which most emphatically includes naïve love, is one of the great channels along which our natural delight in life can flow. But it is quite possible, if things turn out that way, to live a full life without any of the naïver delights of love. It is not possible to live a full life without love in its wider meaning of delight in life itself.

That is the ultimate deprivation now threatening the gods under the symbolism of losing Freia and her golden apples. The crisis thus coming to a head could hardly be more serious. But Loge the trickster is ready with his tricky remedy, and we can only hope that it will prove more satisfactory than his own unsatisfactory reputation makes in any way certain. At all events, he still acts in a manner reminiscent of Mercury, this time in the latter's capacity as leader of souls through the under-world. 'Down through the Rhine?' asks Loge of Wotan. 'Not through the Rhine!' exclaims the god, in a violent spasm of guilt at his own secret determination never to let the Rhinemaidens see their gold again. 'Then through the sulphur cleft', concludes Loge, and down into the under-world he leads Wotan to steal from Alberich his stolen treasure.

CHAPTER V

Rhinegold, Scene 3

--------- ❄ ---------

THE PARADOX OF THE SITUATION
BROUGHT OUT IN THE MUSIC

Black vapour has filled the stage, and condensed into impenetrable cloud (it is usual to bring a curtain down at this point, but the effect can be very well produced by projecting a film on to it). The cloud rises continually upwards, so that we have the sensation of sinking. Soon the cloud changes into rock, which still rises. We are or should be left in no doubt as to our journey down into the bowels of the earth.

Not only this journey, but the entire situation is made still more explicit to us in the music. This begins with a whirl of chromatic passage-work (20) indicative of Loge and his tricky scheming, and further suggesting a general sense of transition and of dissolving boundaries. Everything seems in flux; but there is certainly no lack of vital energy. Now (20) is interrupted by the diatonic strength of (79), the new motive of grief, with its paradoxical hint of nobility and acceptance. It is a stepwise descent from the saddest of minor intervals, the third of the scale. The hint of nobility partly comes from the mere directness of the harmony; but at its third entry here, this changes to a dominant major ninth, than which no one chord conveys a warmer or more poetic feeling. As to the melody of (79) its notes are all of them identical with the main notes of the second part (69) of Freia's motive. But Freia's (69) hints at the compassion and understanding of love in its widest meaning as the delight in life; these after all are the very notes of which the wonderful love-motive (37) is also formed. Grief, destiny, compassion, understanding, love, delight in life: it takes a subtle image to bring such contrary emotions into conjunction. But music is the most elusive of the arts, and for that very reason its potentialities for subtlety are unsurpassed.

This is not all. The chromatic flickering is finally ousted by a rapid

88

version of the original falling semitone of woe (68). To add to our sense of ambiguity, the metre becomes nine-eight superimposed on three-four; and the falling semitone expands into—the second half (69) of Freia's motive again! Not, this time, in its slow, romantic form, but in its rapid, agitated form, which is nevertheless comprised melodically of just the same notes.

A harshly minor version of the gold's motive (44) breaks through, followed by a particularly sinister version of the ring's motive (8), with its harmonic basis at its most uneasily chromatic. Thereupon the sharply dotted nine-eight rhythm here given to (69), with the slightest of modifications, leads on to a motive (50) which presently thins to the sound of many anvils, while other anvils persist simultaneously in three-four. As the orchestra falls silent, we see nothing except a vague red glow of hidden fires in various directions; but our ears give us an uncanny sense of passing through or near some vast echoing cavern where the dwarf smiths are at work, so that ever afterwards we associate this motive (50), or even the mere rhythm of it, with dwarfs and with smithying in general. As the orchestra takes up again, the anvils soon fade away, and we are back in the oppressive rock passages until the curtain rises and we are out into another great cavern, just visible in the murky gloom.

If so many contrary emotions can be brought so intimately into relationship by the music, the implication is that the grievousness and the resignation, the harshness and the compassion, belong to one another. Evil is not a foreign body which some clever surgeon of morals can neatly excise; it is a part of ourselves which we have to learn to live with. Grief is not a poison we can vomit out of the system; it is an ingredient in human experience which we have to assimilate. We can accept all this, and still be in love with life, which we cannot really be if we merely repudiate the darker side of it. The bitterness and the sweetness of life are quite inseparable. But we can delight in our bitter-sweet cup provided we do not expect it to be only sweet, which is simply the fantasy of blissful irresponsibility and the infantile longing for the mother-paradise all over again.

Wagner could hardly have summed up the poignant paradox of life more pointedly than when he wrote to Roeckel (25 Jan. 1854): 'Without death as a necessary concomitant, there is no life; that alone has no end which has no beginning.' Wagner must have known more than most people about the bitter-sweet cup; and this knowledge glows through his music. A passage of the present quality moves us just because it is so true to that most fully human of our moods, when we accept ourselves for the mixed, vulnerable and indeed mortal creatures that we are. Music is at its greatest when it puts us in mind at once of our own mortality and of life's worth and beauty, and reconciles us to the paradox.

Indeed I cannot help feeling that fundamentally this is what all great music, perhaps all great art, is about. Music is equal to all our moods. Music can range from tragedy to comedy and touch on anything which lies between. Music can make us want to laugh or want to cry; but it is never more typical than when it makes us want to laugh and cry at the same time. Under all our moods there lies this master mood which in some degree is always present. The best comedy is that which holds a hint of tragedy, and the best tragedy is that which is relieved by comedy: Shakespeare is a supreme example of this familiar principle. Nothing moves us so much as being confronted with our own hidden awareness that our mortal existence is a fitful compound of light and shadow, coming from the dark and ending in the dark, bounded by death yet radiant with life, a finite thing yet somehow infinitely worth while. Sentimental music only reminds us of what it is easy to remember, that there can be sweetness. Great music further reminds us that there can be bitterness, but that the bitterness does not cancel out the sweetness. This is not so easy to remember, and we have always needed the resources of art and religion to help keep us in mind of it.

Freud, the extrovert, coined the term 'oceanic feeling' for an emotion which he confessed he neither understood nor greatly shared in, but which has to do with this spacious sense of being in touch with the extremes of our nature and of our natural conditions, without resenting them. Jung, the introvert, understood it very well, and came to the conclusion that the fundamental problem common to his patients in their approach towards the second half of life was a problem of religion: that is to say, the search for a meaning. Not that we all find the same meaning; we may have to make our individual search; but we all need a meaning. In this age of weakened religious understanding, the arts have more responsibility than ever for quickening our intuitive awareness that life does hold a meaning to be discovered by each in his own individual way. If the pain cancelled out the delight of living, life could not hold a meaning. But pain and delight do not have to cancel out; they can add up to an immense aliveness of which the value is indestructible even if mortal life itself is not. And something very like this is as plain in Beethoven as it is in Shakespeare, or in Rembrandt: as plain as I believe it is in Wagner's music dramas. Great art reconciles elements which are harsh, and in themselves even ugly, with other elements which are warm and beautiful.

Great art reconciles the opposites, and in so doing helps us to reconcile them and to become reconciled with life.

THE UNDERWORLD OF NIBELHEIM

The cave now barely visible gives us little more than the impression of receding buttresses and vaulting. But the underside of our imagination, already stirred by the music, gets to work on it at once.

Our fairy-tale memories are full of such places, and they will almost certainly have come into our dreams.[1] We know of the underworld of the Greeks and Romans, where Pluto keeps Persephone for one-third of the year, and Orpheus recovered his Euridice and lost her again. We know the Christian hell of condemned sinners, into which nevertheless Christ had to descend: many of us will have classical images from Virgil and medieval images from Dante and late Renaissance images from Milton. Below these perhaps lie intimations of the underworld as the womb of the Great Mother and the unseen, unknown centre of life from which vital impulses well up for good or bad. The underworld is a primary archetypal symbol of the unconscious.

Deep water stands for all that is most fluid and elusive in the unconscious, all that is most fecund after the indiscriminately prolific fashion of acquatic life. The underworld is womb-like; but only mammal life is actually moulded in the womb and thereafter nourished by breasts; mammal life in these and other ways is more highly differentiated than acquatic life. On the other hand, the underworld also corruscates with lifeless but precious stones and metals, symbols of value waiting inertly to be mined and forged for human use. In mythology, the great miners and metalworkers are the dwarfs; and here we are now in Nibelheim, the home of the Nibelung dwarfs, with Alberich now their unchallenged master.

Here is Alberich in the very act of bullying his weaker brother Mime. Wagner has often and with good reason made their music harsh, but it is intended to be sung with as much natural expressiveness and vocal beauty as it allows, and not barked out unmusically. We must be able to feel the positive elements in these harsher characters after their own fashion. Alberich's have already been discussed. Mime's are not so clear-cut; nothing about him is; he is a shambling, loose-limbed and loose-spirited little creature, hardly strong enough to be a villain, certainly not

---

[1] There is a valuable discussion of the archetype of the underworld in Maud Bodkin, *Archetypal Patterns in Poetry*, London, 1934, pp. 127 ff.

amiable enough to be anything much else. Yet he will have the enterprise to bring up the infant Siegfried to manhood. Admittedly that is in further-ance of his own tortuous ambitions; but it takes considerable qualities to bring up a child, even as oddly as Siegfried was brought up. Another quality we must not overlook in our estimate of Mime is the fact that he is a smith of unusual skill. At this very moment he has just finished forging for Alberich the magic helmet Tarnhelm.

But though Mime has the skill to make magic objects, he has not the wit to use them, and now Alberich, snatching Tarnhelm from Mime, offers a practical demonstration by becoming invisible and giving poor Mime the beating of his life. There is no resisting an invisible assailant, particularly when that assailant has all the power of the magic ring at his command.

THE RING AS A SYMBOL FOR THE SELF

A ring is a circle, a continuous flow with neither beginning nor end. In mythology, theology, alchemy, dreams and even musical notation, the circle stands for perfection. Since no human being is perfect, the perfec-tion refers not to ego or any other component, but to the totality which at the same time includes all aspects of the psyche and is its guiding principle: i.e. to the archetype of the self, of which various symbols make a most insistent appearance in dream imagery and elsewhere at any stage in a man's life when he is developing in the direction of wholeness. Symbols for the self, whatever their form, point towards an integration of our opposing tendencies, and in particular of our conscious with our unconscious tendencies. They are uniting symbols.

A ring is one such uniting symbol (that is why we wear engagement and wedding rings). An extension of this is the famous *Uroboros* or tail-eater, a mythical serpent who creates, feeds on and transforms himself all in one magnificently continuous gesture, by swallowing his own tail. He stands both for the undifferentiated union of all the opposites in an unconscious state of nature, and for the highly differentiated union of opposites towards which it is the underlying purpose of the self to lead us through the increase of consciousness. Thus in alchemy he plays the same ambivalent role as Mercury, with whom he is often equated. He may wear the golden crown of royalty, again symbolic of the self, like the golden ball held by royalty in the opposite hand to the sceptre.

The significance of the ring which gives Wagner's *Ring* its name is greatly complicated by the fact that it so obviously means different things at different times and to different characters in the drama. For Alberich, the ring means the power for forcing slaves to enrich him and women to yield to him, with the eventual aim of supplanting the gods as rulers of the world, which would seem, as things now stand, to include in its meaning the usurpation of ego's authority by the shadow: no slight catastrophe. For Wotan, it is not yet decided whether the ring means the power to entrench the authority of ego or the power to ransom Freia in token of recovering love in its widest sense as the delight in life itself: that crucial choice has still to be made, and whatever Wotan may so far suppose, it is not one in which he can have it both ways. For Fricka, the ring means the power to curb Wotan's infidelities, in token of preventing him from following new ideals as well as new desires. For the giants, the ring will seem to indulge a passive acquisitiveness not directed to any active use or purpose at all. For Siegfried and Brynhilde, the ring will become a love token, though a love token with very singular properties. To Gunther, it will be a corrupting temptation, to Hagen a life-long obsession.

The common factor in this wide range of uses and abuses is power itself. A man's power turns in the direction in which his effective values lie; and he has very little direct control as to where that may be. Power is ultimately an expression of libido, and libido has its source not in the ego but somewhere deeper in the self.

The primary symbolism of a ring is, traditionally, the self. This particular ring has been made out of a lump of gold standing for individual value, in short for libido lying unused, though it was revealed each day, at a deep level of psychic consciousness, by the penetrating rays of the sun. The opportunity thus daily offered was eventually taken by Alberich at the fearful cost of which we know. For good or ill, the gold was forged and the libido represented by it was made available. But since the ego had no knowledge of this at the time, and no part in it at all, the power thus released still rests in the hands of the shadow by whose initiative it was released. It is not available to the ego. Yet it seems that the ego now needs it very badly indeed. Whatever the eventual rights and wrongs of the matter, it will be a bad day for the gods if Wotan returns empty-handed.

It will be a bad day for them because the gold, in its new shape as the ring, somehow stands for our individual experience of the self. So long as the self only impinges on us as a deep but nebulous mystery, our own individual worth remains undiscovered and inoperative. But when the self begins to become present to us in sharply focused images, we get an individual experience of it by which our personality develops and our own worth comes better into our possession.

The ring is a self-symbol so sharply focused that it certainly stands for an individual and not merely a nebulous experience of the self. Getting possession of the ring includes, as part of its meaning, getting possession of this experience. Unless the gods can do this, bringing the power now wielded by the shadow further up into the light of day, they will never extricate themselves from their immediate peril. What they will do with this power if they do get their hands on it is another question, only to be settled when the time comes. But meanwhile we feel instinctively on the side of Loge and Wotan in their present adventure. We may be a little uneasy about its further implications, but there can be no doubt at all that we want it to succeed.

TARNHELM AS A SYMBOL
OF UNCONSCIOUS FANTASY

Tarnhelm resembles the ring in being a magical object. Magic is a name for the operation of powerful forces which are not understood, including unconscious forces in the psyche. But whether we understand them or not, such unconscious forces are not arbitrary. We shall find that the power of the ring itself is neither arbitrary nor unlimited. The power of Tarnhelm appears to be both arbitrary and unlimited, which may lead us to wonder whether it is real at all in the sense in which the power of the ring, where it is applicable, is unquestionably real.

Tarnhelm reminds us of various cloaks or helmets of invisibility, seven-league boots and so on, the common property of which is that the wearer can wish himself into a choice of conditions or situations which would otherwise be attainable only by great and difficult effort, if at all. This is suspiciously suggestive of wishful thinking. Now we all of us in some degree have fantasies of omnipotence in which it really seems that we have only to wish for something harmful to our enemies or beneficial to ourselves, and it will happen. Though these fantasies are essentially infantile, they persist into adult life, and in certain states of mind can swamp both our judgement and our personality.

As to invisibility, it is one of the symptoms of a schizoid inclination that we assume our most blatant actions to be unobserved, although this is usually very far from being the case. Another such symptom is the well-known invisibility to the right hand of what the left hand is doing. The degree of our wishful thinking can vary enormously, and so can the severity of our schizoid inclinations, but we are all liable to a certain amount of them, and we all indulge in unconscious fantasies up to a certain point. These fantasies are often very convincing for a time not only to ourselves but to the people around us (chiefly by acting in turn on their unconscious). Our fantasies weave spells which to primitive thinking are plainly magical spells. They are a source of endless complications and no little trouble and danger. These effects are very real; but the illusions producing them are not. It seems possible that the persuasive but ultimately unsubstantial workings of Tarnhelm have to do with the treacherous potentialities of unconscious fantasy.

THE TRICKING OF ALBERICH

Fortunately for us, our unconscious workings may as easily be helpful (when they may pass for white magic) as harmful (when they may pass for black magic). But nothing at all helpful is happening for the moment to little Mime. His lamentations fill the stage as Alberich at last leaves him alone. Wotan and Loge emerge just in time to hear his sorry tale before Alberich returns, driving a crowd of dwarfs in front of him. They heap up gold at his command. As he brandishes the ring at them, they clearly suffer agonizing pain; and their screams are taken up by the orchestra into a symphony of harsh compulsion met by impotent dismay and panic. Alberich next sees his visitors, and hurries Mime and the other dwarfs off-stage before confronting the two gods, which he does with all possible suspicion. He is nevertheless soon trapped, by one of Loge's most cunning wiles.

I can scarcely believe, says Loge, that you can really transform yourself as you claim. In the twinkling of an eye Alberich has turned himself by means of Tarnhelm into a vast writhing snake (worm or dragon: they are all one in the German). The music (18) for Tarnhelm is haunting and beautiful, but oddly hollow (indeed it comes to a bare fifth, and the scoring with muted horns emphasizes the hollowness). We hear at once the potent spell and the ultimate emptiness of unconscious fantasy. Then comes the growling, clumsy motive (57) in the bass which we shall later associate with Fafner, in his form as the dragon Siegfried has to fight. His symbolism can best wait until we come to him, but there can be no mistaking the boundless menace of the beast. He is a devourer and destroyer of men, if ever there was one in myth or fairy-tale.

Alberich's vanity is now vastly tickled. He is delighted to be showing the two gods what a formidable fellow he has become. So he falls without a thought into the trap next laid for him. Ah, says Loge, seeing is believing; but that you can make yourself as small as before you were large, small enough to hide from your enemies like a toad in a rocky cranny, that is more than I can credit. Next moment, Tarnhelm has done its work again. Alberich is a little creeping toad; which is interesting in itself, because symbolically the toad carries suggestions of transformation (he is said to be the first transformation of the dragon as *prima materia* in alchemy) and on a long view transformation of character is the main subject of the *Ring*.

Now in a flash Loge has his foot on toad-Alberich; the two pull Tarnhelm off him so that he is in his own dwarf-form again; they bind him with ropes; and he has lost his liberty to guile, where force could have been of no avail. He makes no attempt to turn the tables by brandishing the ring at his captors; it seems he is enough of a realist to know that it can have no power against destiny, in other words against the underlying purposes of the self, for which the ring is primarily a symbol.

So far Loge's remedy is prospering. Set a thief to catch a thief; call on the trickster in us to counter the tricks our unconscious is playing on us. It is the time-honoured remedy of myth and fairy-tale.

CHAPTER VI

Rhinegold, Scene 4

———— ❀ ————

WOTAN ACTS THE RUFFIAN

We return to the abode of the gods by means of music as graphic as that which brought us down. Alberich is harshly told to purchase his freedom with his golden hoard. He summons his dwarfs to bring it up, objecting more to the indignity of being thus mastered in their presence than to the actual loss, which he tells himself that he can soon more than replace by the continued use of the ring's power. The reality of this power, where it can be used at all, is again made plain by the agonizing quality of the music to which he forces the terrified little creatures to his will. It is one of the great climaxes of *Rhinegold*, and makes an overwhelming impact when properly conducted. The material of the music is the insistently rhythmic little motive (50) of the dwarf smiths; the falling semitone (68) of woe and evil superimposed on it—but with a peculiar remorselessness of harmony adumbrated when Alberich drove the dwarfs to work in Scene 3, and often to be heard again, particularly in the more violent scenes of *Götter-dämmerung*; and a version of the dragon motive (57), used here and subsequently to indicate the treasure-hoard soon to be in Fafner's sole possession, as the dragon guarding it. Gold when hoarded is useless; life-energy is only of value when it can flow freely and continually replenish itself. Hence the aptitude of this massive motive to represent the hoard, as well as the dragon guarding it.

Having rendered up the treasure, Alberich asks for Tarnhelm back. It is refused—but no great matter, he again says to himself, since Mime can be made by the ring to forge another. Now Wotan sees the ring itself still glinting on Alberich's finger, and claims this too. From that the dwarf recoils in immeasurable horror: My life, but not the ring! Wotan disingenuously accuses him of having stolen the gold it is made from, and Alberich cries back that the god too wished though he would

97   G

never have dared to commit this crime, the price of which was to curse love. Without the slightest scruple, Wotan pulls the ring off, and Alberich is bereft indeed.

What are we to make of this high-handed act? The music gives us part of the answer. We have been hearing that stepwise descending motive (73) which stands for Wotan's spear, the symbol of his worldly authority and also of that wilful authority which in his role of ego he still wants to exert over the psyche. He still hopes that stone walls and ruthless action will afford him a security which nothing in life can really guarantee; he has undertaken to give away the free source of life and delight in life itself as the price of it; he hopes to evade the undertaking by the wiliness of the unconscious trickster in him, while shutting his eyes to the inherent impossibility of having the advantages of both courses.

We now hear a rising inversion of (73) as a suitably distorted accompaniment to this stubborn blindness—or does the very fact that it is rising suggest that the outcome will be other than Wotan expects, and better? Again, the motive (44) of the gold, usually diatonic even when in the minor, is chromatically distorted into a diminished seventh as if to stress the violence now being done to it. So it was when Alberich first wrenched the gold away from the Rhinemaidens' rock; the music thus underlines the parallel between these two thefts. As his ring is wrenched away, Alberich utters a terrible cry of despair, alone and unaccompanied on his top F sharp. That becomes enharmonically G flat for an eerie fragment of the ring motive. This enharmonic transition is the slightest yet subtlest of hints that transformation of character is still the fundamental issue. It is not merely that the ring is changing hands; the ring is itself at work to bring this change about, as we may infer from the very fact that it does not avail Alberich to prevent the theft. This does not alter the further fact that there is a level on which Wotan is committing a crime against Alberich, thus bringing inevitable consequences on to his own head throughout the remainder of the *Ring*.

On a deeper level this crime serves a purpose not unlike Alberich's own original theft of the gold from the Rhinemaidens. The first of these thefts enabled the latent power of the gold to be made actual by the forging of the ring; the second brought the ring up from the dark realm of the shadow. But not in order that it should remain on Wotan's finger; not in order that ego should try to misappropriate the authority of the self in the attempt to bolster up its own wilfulness. That is the deeper crime which Wotan commits, not so much on Alberich as on himself, and as a result on the psyche as a whole.

We feel extraordinarily shocked. It was distressing enough to watch Alberich wresting the Rhinemaidens' gold away from them; but at least that seemed quite in character from all that we had previously seen of his appearance and conduct. But Wotan's appearance is not dwarfish but palpably godlike, and his conduct so far has not flatly contradicted his appearance. Now he acts the ruffian, and not merely through his agent Loge, but in his own godly person.

The incongruity is appalling. It is perhaps the first time in the *Ring* that we feel utterly confused and dismayed. It is obvious that Wotan is just as confused, though he does not know it. He is the very picture of a man blinded by his own unconscious.

Yet even this alarming spectacle has its value if it makes us realize that the noblest or wisest of personalities is not noble or wise all through. It is not the bad men who do all the evil and the good men who do all the good. We are all mixed and vulnerable and mortal creatures. Everything hangs now on whether Wotan is going to be able to realize as much about himself, not necessarily all at once, but in the slow course of his own development. However, he will need to learn the start of this lesson with uncommon speed if the immediate situation is not to take a catastrophic turn.

ALBERICH CURSES FOR THE SECOND TIME

'Defeated, destroyed,' sings Alberich: 'of sad wretches the saddest.' We are at least half on his side in this lowest state of his fortunes, and at least half antagonistic to Wotan in so tyrannical a triumph. These despairing words of Alberich's are set, strikingly enough, to the crucial motive (79). In so far as (79) conveys the bitterness of grief and the inexorability of that which is (we call it destiny), this is not surprising. But neither here nor anywhere else where this motive enters can I escape the impression that something more than grief and inexorability is being conveyed. There is something in the motive itself which sounds noble. It is a healing nobility: we are made aware of grief, and in the very same music we are reconciled to grief.

There is nothing out of the ordinary in this mixture of emotions. It is very typical of our human feelings, which get their poignancy just from being so mixed. But that Alberich in the downfall of what was after all in any obvious sense a highly nefarious ambition should be allowed in the music this hint of a healing nobility is certainly surprising, and calls for explanation.

Perhaps the first point to be made in Alberich's favour is that he does at least accept the situation as a fact. So many of us try to soften a reverse of fortune by not quite admitting to ourselves that it has really happened or that it is really so very bad, still less that it might have been in any way our own fault. Alberich blames himself squarely for a fool, tells us in so many words that he means to learn his lesson, and then, when the fatal blow falls, takes the full impact of it on the instant, yet never for one moment loses either his courage or his independence. It is in every way an impressive performance.

It may next be as well to remind ourselves of a certain difference between crimes in outer reality and crimes in fiction. In outer reality, if a man commits robbery with violence, we probably ought to credit him with the desperate courage of his illusion, such as, for example, that he can somehow force from the world an equivalent to the mother's love of which he has almost certainly been starved as an infant; yet at the same time we have to deal with him in a practical way as a pestilential grown-up menace to life and property. In the *Ring*, Alberich robs, Wotan robs with violence, Siegmund and Sieglinde are guilty of incest, Siegfried of infidelity and treacherous violence to a woman, Hagen of murder, Brynhilde of being an accessory to murder, and so on. There is no factual loss to life or property; all the singers get up again and live to sing another night. There are, indeed, morals to be drawn, but they are not altogether these on which practical considerations usually compel us to concentrate in outer reality. The symbolic aspects of the crimes in question may claim our effectual attention.

This does not imply that our horrified reaction in the opera-house is out of place. Shocking deeds on the stage are meant to shock, and if we failed to react to them in the natural and obvious way we should be failing to respond to the drama as a whole. But it is here that the autonomous action of symbolic images comes in. On any obvious level, we are shocked because crimes of violence are rightly shocking in outer reality. In the opera-house, our sense of shock simultaneously reaches down to a level on which we are intuitively aware that all important changes in the psyche are experienced as shock and violence.

Even in outer reality, the same symbolic strata are touched by crimes of violence; but practical considerations peremptorily intervene. In the opera-house, we have not got to do anything practical about the matter; we have simply to sit in our seats and take it all in. We take in the obvious levels consciously enough, but there is nothing to prevent our taking in the less obvious levels intuitively yet just as vividly; and I am sure we do so. The positive value in these symbolic crimes of violence does not fail to impinge on us, however surprising it may seem to our rational faculties when we first begin to notice what we have been responding to intuitively all along.

Surprising or not, it is a very well established fact that changes in the deeper levels of our own personality feel like terrifying violence at the time of experiencing them. There is no limit to the power with which the autonomous psyche may assail us from within. If it did not do so, we should never develop, and life would lose its real point and meaning. Yet our experience of this power in its formidable aspect is a terrifying experience, as we can often see explicitly in our dreams and elsewhere. It is evidently part of our nature to be extremely frightened of a new stage of growth and to resist it with a desperation not far short of panic.

If we actually panic to the extent of not yielding at all, we may pay for our rigidity by psycho-somatic or mental illness. In such a condition, a breakdown may occur, holding at least the possibility of our development being resumed, since what has primarily been broken is the stalemate. More ordinarily, we go with the power of the autonomous psyche before breaking-point is reached; but we still suffer unavoidable fear and distress in course of doing so. This fear and this distress are very closely allied to the fear and distress we experience in a dramatic scene such as the present.

It may be helpful to ask what such a scene would imply if it were occurring not in a drama but in an ordinary dream. Our dreams are populated by figures many of whom are more or less drawn from outer life. We can often learn something about our outer situations from watching what these dream figures do or say, just as we can learn something about the outer world and how to behave in it and towards it from watching Wagner's characters. But any inferences of this outer kind to be made from a dream are secondary and incidental compared with the inferences we can make about our inner situation. A dream only uses outside personages in so far as we have already projected our own inner material on to those personages in waking life. The dream is about the projected material rather than about the personages. Everything that happens in a dream is part of the dreamer: it is his dream. The fundamental insight which we can gain from a dream is insight about ourselves (including our relation not only to the outer world but to the archetypes of the collective unconscious in so far as these are active in us at the time).

A work of art differs from a dream in that its inner material is organized not only by the unconscious but also by the conscious faculties of the artist. But the inner material itself is still only secondarily and incidentally drawn from outer life; it consists primarily of projections made on to more or less lifelike characters and other symbols.

Wagner had not only the artist's intuitive understanding of this important fact. He was able to put a good part of it into words, as he did in one of his best known letters (to Roeckel, 23 Aug. 1856) where he wrote: 'While, as an artist, my intuitions had such compelling certainty that all my creations were moulded thereby, as a philosopher I was attempting to construct an entirely contrary explanation of the universe, an explanation which, though stoutly upheld, was always being dismissed out of hand by my instinctive, objective artistic perceptions, much to my own astonishment.' At the time of writing this, Wagner believed that he had found, in Schopenhauer, a philosophy to fit his intuitions. Schopenhauer's 'explanation of the universe' is summed up by Wagner in this letter as depending on 'the high tragedy of renunciation, the deliberate, reasoned, ultimately necessary negation of the will, in which alone is salvation'. Wagner felt that he had always intuitively 'discerned the nature of the universe itself in all its conceivable phases and had recognized its nothingness'. But whatever either Schopenhauer or Wagner may have supposed, these are explanations not of the outer but of the inner universe.

The 'necessary negation of the will' is indeed the main intuitive theme of the *Ring*. In the language I am using here, we may paraphrase it as the necessary yielding by the ego to the underlying purposes of the self. That is an issue of paramount importance in any life-story; but it is an inner issue projected by Wagner the artist on to Wotan and the rest. It is also an archetypal issue, so that Wagner's projections are far more than merely personal, and Wotan and the rest carry perennial truths. These are certainly truths about the universe, but with regard to the psyche, not with regard to physics. The 'high tragedy of renunciation' works itself out very thoroughly in course of the *Ring*, and we shall be considering it in greater detail in connection with the end of *Götterdämmerung*.

It has long been known that the hold which fiction takes on us results from our identifying ourselves with its characters and their fortunes. By far the most obvious of our identifications is naturally with the hero, for a man, or the heroine, for a woman. The ego is only too pleased to see itself mirrored in so favourable a light. Besides, we all have a genuinely heroic streak in us somewhere. But there is much more to it than this.

A man further sees in the heroine an image of his own anima, and the woman sees in the hero an image of her own animus. But not a total image: there are other and less acceptable aspects of the anima and the animus, and fiction includes plenty of characters to carry the projections of these darker aspects too, and others again to carry the projection of the shadow itself.

These are all parts of us, and intuitively we know that. Intuitively we identify ourselves not only with the hero or heroine but with all the characters. This does not prevent us from taking sides, and wanting the hero and heroine to win. It does prevent us from rejecting even the villains completely. If they were merely alien to us, we should not have enough interest in them to arouse our hatred; and hatred is notoriously close to love. They are both expressions of our deep concern. We are concerned with the characters of fiction just so far as they resemble something in ourselves.

The darkest and most hidden part of ourselves is the part which Jung refers to as the shadow. It is in this part of ourselves that we in the audience are identified with Alberich. Certainly we hate him and certainly we think of him as evil. We have real grounds for doing so. Yet the only ultimate way of dealing with the shadow in ourselves is by getting to know him better. In so far as we can bring him up out of his invisibility to us (he is by no means so invisible to other people) and put him into the picture, we may be able to accept him and become reconciled with him.

A classic case somewhat of this kind comes at the end of Aeschylus trilogy on the story of Orestes, who is represented as having killed his mother for very good reasons both ostensible and symbolical, but as being hounded by furies of guilt and remorse presumably from his own deep unconscious, in the shape of the Erinyes (euphemistically known as the Eumenides, the kindly ones). At last a reconciliation was effected by the anima in her manifestation as the wise and chaste goddess Athena, who recommended the Athenians to pay due recognition to those dark forces of the underworld by setting up a shrine to them: advice which was very sensibly followed, as students of early Greek history will be well aware. The degree in which Wotan manages to become reconciled with Alberich in course of the *Ring* is much less complete and therefore much less healing than this; but he makes unmistakable progress in that direction, as we shall discover in the Second Act of *Siegfried*.

Meanwhile, here is Alberich meeting defeat to music, i.e. motive (79), which though it in no way softens that defeat nevertheless gives it the dignity, and even the inherent nobility, of all suffering which is fully acknowledged and not evaded. If only for his suffering, we have at least some fellow-feeling for him; and that is just as well, in view of the fact that he really is our fellow in the sense of symbolizing something which is in ourselves. We also accord him, however grudgingly, a measure of respect for his courage and his indomitable independence. He goes on being himself. He goes on acting the villain; but since that is his allotted role in the drama, we should have a much poorer opinion of him if he failed to do so.

Rising now to the full stature of his villainy, and to the accompaniment of an obsessively and sinisterly syncopated harmony known as the motive (15) of the Nibelungs' hate, Alberich gathers himself together for his revenge. On the notes of the most powerful and baleful of all the Ring's many powerful motives, the curse motive (13), Alberich curses for the second time. 'As by curse it came to me, so be this ring accursed!'

ALBERICH'S CURSE: SHEER DISASTER
OR BLESSING IN DISGUISE?

Alberich's curse is that neither triumph nor contentment shall reward all future holders of his ring, but envy, care and death. What has the music to add to this straightforward statement?

The music has something very interesting to add. The curse motive (13) rises by striding leaps on the harmony of a minor seventh complicated by a pedal bass which is usually F sharp against an emerging C major tonality (or the same relationship in different keys): i.e. at the unquiet interval of the diminished fifth (augmented fourth), concerning which the old musicians wrote *tritonus est diabolus in musica*, the tritone is the devil in music. Yet the same disturbing relationship to a pedal bass is often given to a motive which might easily be expected to contrast with the curse motive (13): i.e. the motive (8) of the ring. The more these two motives are compared, the more alike they are found to be.

The word which best expresses the common element in these two superficially dissimilar motives is the word so often used already in this book: ambivalence. They are tonally ambivalent; and this tonal ambivalence is uncommonly disquieting. We have only to compare them with another close relative, indeed an offshoot of the ring motive (8) in order to show up just how disquieting they are. We have only to compare them with the imposing Valhalla motive (63), which is tonally quite unambivalent. The symbolism of the Valhalla motive (63) suggests the very opposite of ambiguity. It suggests the plain man's view of outward wordly success as something solid and reliable.

Worldly success has its own solidity on its own level, but it is in no way reliable, and there are other levels on which even its solidity is illusory. The plain man has no need to know this, and even when his intuitions are in fruitful contact with the inner world, as they very often are, he may still have apparently not the slightest inkling that such a world exists. In so far as Wotan is determined to rely on Valhalla's solid walls and shut his eyes to his very considerable inklings of another plane of reality on which all their solidity is of no avail, he is clinging to the plain man's view, the common-sense view, against his own growing realization that the inner world of dreams and visions cannot simply be pushed aside as of no account. But dreams and visions are ambiguous through and through, being perfectly true to the nature of inner reality in this and other ways.

There is nothing idly fanciful about dreams and visions provided they are not misconstrued in too outward and literal a sense. It is the un-ambiguous view, with its illusory confidence in security and solidity, which really might be called a little fanciful. Such confidence has im-mense value for extroverted characters, and even for introverted char-acters during the earlier and more extroverted decades of their lives. But Wotan has reached a stage of his development at which he very badly needs to lose some of his undue confidence in stone castles and worldly achievement generally. He is losing it surely enough. But will he just react in a negative way, clinging to the remnants of his illusions and his old, outworn attitudes until they finally destroy him? Or will he react positively, moving of his own free will into the new phase he cannot in any case avoid, thus reaping the immeasurable gains of it as well as the inevitable losses?

As he stands there now with Alberich's ring glinting on his finger, and throws stubborn glances on everyone around him, we realize with great dismay that already the curse just placed on the ring has claimed its first victim. Nobody could look less contented or genuinely triumphant. Care sits on his every feature. Envy was also prophesied, and death as the end.

It is not easy to see the ambiguity in all this. But unless there is an underlying ambiguity, Wotan's story is the story of a failure, and the best that can be said for him (it is already a great deal) is that he accepts his failure eventually with a noble resignation. As Wagner explained it to Roeckel (letter of 25 Jan. 1854): 'Wotan rises to the tragic dignity of willing his own destruction.' So he does, in his capacity as the representative of a naïve ego; but the fascinating question is whether he can turn this failure or seeming failure of ego's authority to advantage by winning through to success in his own deeper role as a representative, however imperfect, of the self.

Wotan is entitled to this deeper role in virtue of his undoubted godhead. Whether he can win through to it, however, is not at all a foregone conclusion. On this level, we can only think of him as an example of godhead incomplete and in the making. That, of course, is what renders him dramatically so interesting. It puts him so much in the same position as ourselves. We all have, in our measure, an element of godhead in us of which the development or otherwise is not a foregone conclusion.

When St. Paul (I Cor. 15, 31) cried in painfully difficult and anguished acceptance, 'I die daily', he meant not physical death but the necessary death of cherished illusions and outworn attitudes without which we can expect no growth of character, yet which however often repeated and manfully accepted never ceases to feel like shocking violence and distress of spirit; and he also meant the creative anguish which a man who is driven on by his own inner tensions, as Wagner was driven, must unavoidably undergo. Because they tend to feel so like a dissolution, such inward deaths are habitually depicted in myths, rituals, dreams and fantasies as outward deaths: all too literally so in the case of human sacrifice. In the tragic confusion of madness, too, the very impulse which may be healing if experienced inwardly as a symbol may be a psychotic crime if misplaced outwardly as arson, rape or murder.

All these three crimes occur in the *Ring* at least once: Brynhilde herself burns the house down in *Götterdämmerung*, having previously been carried away by the bewitched Siegfried and having contrived his murder in return. But we know very well that these events have an inwardness which precludes our taking them merely at their face value. In short, they are ambivalent, like any other archetypal symbols, and have to be taken on more levels than one. Since they are all consequences flowing from the curse here placed so dramatically on the ring by Alberich, we must certainly look to find a corresponding ambivalence in this curse itself.

The curse commits its victims to unavoidable discontent, with death as the end. Its ambivalence lies in the fact that both these results can be taken positively as well as negatively. Discontent can be creative. Death can be a symbol for transformation. Since we need both the discontent and the transformation if our life's growth is to open out in the way it is potentially capable of doing, any occurrence which compels that potentiality to become actual has a positive as well as a negative side. It may very well seem hateful to us and be not at all to our liking. The point is that we need it.

A further question is where Alberich got the power to make his curse effective. It seems extremely unlikely that he could have done anything of the kind if it had not been for this underlying necessity within the psyche. On this level, the curse appears to be a symbol for something we know intuitively is inherent in our human situation and has got to happen to us, but which we nevertheless cannot help mistakenly thinking of as directed against us in a hostile spirit. We project our resentment but also our sense of inevitability on to Alberich. That is why Wagner presents him and we accept him as so blackly malevolent; but it is also why we credit him with the power to enforce his will.

It is absolutely essential to the tension of the drama that we should experience Alberich both as malevolent and as powerful. We are not all-seeing beings who can dispense with illusion and look at everything just as it is in its inmost essence. We are human beings in the thick of the conflict. If we were perfect beings we should have no need of drama, and no capacity for creating it, since we should see nothing but the ambivalence, and there would be neither tension nor suspense. In the opera-house we feel all the tension and all the suspense; our sense of the ambivalence is the merest hint of an unrevealed mystery beneath the surface. Yet it is this mystery which, without our thinking much if anything about it, keeps our attention riveted on an apparently nursery-tale cast of gods and dwarfs, giants and mermaids, legendary heroes and heroines.

We may keep Alberich's ambivalence, then, in the background of our minds. In the opera-house we have only to let the full horror of him and the terror of his curse take possession of our hearts.

ERDA PROPHESIES TO WOTAN
AND FREIA IS RANSOMED

Off slinks Alberich and back stump the giants. Since they bring Freia with them, the air clears, the light glows brightly and the gods regain their youthful freshness. Only the distance where the fortress stands is still hidden in a lingering remnant of the recent mist.

At this point, the giants themselves show in their measure the signs of differentiation already foreshadowed. Fasolt is reluctant to lose Freia for gold; Fafner has not a moment's hesitation. It is agreed that enough gold must be piled up in front of Freia to hide her completely from the giants' sight. Fafner finds a cranny; Tarnhelm has to be thrown in to fill it up. Fasolt still catches a last glimpse of Freia's radiant glance, and the presence of both parts of her melting motive (6) and (69) in the orchestra tells us the effect of it on his susceptible heart. The gold seems surely all spent now—till Fafner points to the ring itself, which has so significantly found its way, not to the pile of treasure, but on to Wotan's finger, where it gleams out with its now literally accursed faculty for attracting covetous and ambitious eyes. And Wotan refuses outright to give it up. He acts, for the time being, as a man possessed; and so he is possessed, by blind fantasies of world dominion and ego authority which are ultimately as unreal as they are compulsive.

In this possessed state, Wotan behaves as if he could use the power newly activated by his own dark shadow, Alberich, not through the slow, healing process of coming to know and accept that shadow, and not by letting the underlying purpose of the self work freely through him, but by the ruthless exercise of his conscious will. Other forceful men have made the same mistake: it may seem to succeed for a time; in the long run it is calamitous. We are witnessing a turning-point in Wotan's development. If he makes the wrong decision here, he may find it difficult or even impossible to get back on to the forward path again.

On the very verge of a perhaps irreparable blunder, and at the height of his obdurate deludedness, with his own personal feminine intuition either silenced or actively aiding and abetting him, Wotan has an archetypal vision. We hear a majestic motive (3) in C sharp minor; majestic, yet quiet and without pomp. We recognize it as a minor version of the first melodic motive (2) of the *Ring*, the partly arpeggiate, partly stepwise motive which stood (but in the major mode) for the unconscious state of nature; we shall last hear motive (3) inverted as the motive (4) of the god's decline at the end of the *Ring* when what began in nature returns full cycle back to nature, though with a vast difference.

To this quietly impressive music, the light of day fades strangely, and out of the earth, lit by an uncanny green-blue light of its own, a woman's figure emerges to half its height, the lower half remaining buried in the solid rock. It is Erda, the Earth Mother, in Wagner's own words here 'the eternal woman possessed of all the world's wisdom'. She is, then, an image of the *anima mundi*, the world's anima, and not merely of the anima as developed in any one individual's psyche. As her title of Earth Mother states and her music confirms, she can be seen as an aspect of mother nature, but with the emphasis less on nature's blind maternity than on nature's instinctive wisdom.

The growth of consciousness has largely cut us off from nature's instinctive wisdom, but not altogether, or we could certainly not survive. Erda only appears in the *Ring* at moments of profound uncertainty and desperate need. When she does appear, she shows a knowledge of the underlying situation which none of the more conscious protagonists possesses. She reveals this knowledge, however, only in dark riddles which it tests the hearer's entire character to understand.

In this she resembles other genuine oracular images, whether imposing or apparently trivial, and ranging all the way from the Sphinx or the Delphic Oracle down to the Three Witches in *Macbeth*. When every rational recourse has failed, or alternatively when every appearance is favourable but a fatal step is about to be taken unrecognized, we may find ourselves acting on some dark hint from the deep unconscious without knowing why. The hint is bound to be dark, because if we could see daylight we should not be in so serious a crisis. Dark as it is, Wotan now takes his hint. Macbeth failed to take his: that is where the test of character comes in.

Erda's warning to Wotan is typically cryptic, but at least she tells him plainly what he must do to save the immediate situation. He must give up the ring. Wagner informs us (letter to Roeckel, 25 Jan. 1854) of a most interesting change of mind which he had with regard to the libretto here. He originally intended Erda to sing: 'A dark day dawns for the gods; your glorious race shall yet end in shame, unless you give up the ring!' This implied that if Wotan does give up the ring, he can still save his own ruling authority. The passage as Wagner revised it reads: 'All that is, ends! A dark day dawns for the gods; I counsel you, give up the ring!' We hear Erda's (3) inverted as the 'downfall' motive (4).

Giving up the ring is no longer presented as an alternative to the end of the gods, but as the equivalent of accepting the end of the gods. Giving up the ring is the first step towards giving up the wilful authority of the ego in favour of the increasing claims of the self, and that is the positive meaning of the end of the gods. But this is a transformation of character such as always feels like defeat and even death. It is certainly in one sense a dark day which dawns for the ego when such developments are in train, but it is nevertheless a day very much to be desired, and Wotan is already beginning to get some distant premonition that this may really be the case.

Naturally enough, Wotan, filled as he is with foreboding at so elusive a prophecy, would like to hear about it in a great deal more detail. But that cannot yet be. He makes a half-crazed attempt at detaining Erda; but she sinks quietly into the earth again, taking her mysterious green-blue light with her. He gazes at the rock as it closes over her. Then all of a sudden he lets his obstinacy fall from him like a garment. He gives up the ring to be added to the ransom-pile. It closes the last chink. Fasolt can no longer see Freia's eye. He lets her go. So far as the immediate situation is concerned, the gods are saved.

THE CURSE GETS TO WORK:
FAFNER MURDERS FASOLT

Not so the giants. In a furious quarrel which at once breaks out over the division of the booty and the possession of the ring, Fafner fells Fasolt lifeless with his staff. The curse has not been long in getting to work again.

We have previously felt a certain tolerant affection for this clumsy pair of stalwarts, and more particularly for Fasolt in his tender yearnings towards Freia's youth and beauty. It is yet another hideous jolt to our feelings when, having made what seems a foolish choice in taking the golden treasure in place of her, the pair fall out among themselves, and the harsher of them commits this brutal murder of the gentler.

But was it such a foolish choice? Even on a purely personal view of the matter, we cannot help noticing that Freia was desperately reluctant to be carried off. The giants are just as repugnant to her as Alberich was to the Rhinemaidens, and though they could have forced her person they could not have forced her love. The second situation is a fairly close repetition of the first. Alberich turned from the love he could not have to the gold and the power he could; so, in effect, do the giants, although they do not admit to themselves that the love of Freia was not really within their reach either.

When we take a mythological view, their optimism seems much better justified. Beautiful goddesses frequently mate with giants in Norse mythology; Freia herself spent a night with each of three dwarfs in turn, none of them any handsomer than Alberich, for the sake of a necklace of which this was the price agreed. But there we are moving on a level of symbolism which is not quite that of human love, either in its sensuous or in its romantic aspects.

The element in the giants' symbolism which is perhaps most important here has to do with their massive stupidity. Giants are always conservative forces, on the side of the past rather than of the future. They have to do with the weight of parental authority in its obstructive rather than its constructive manifestations, not so much in the actual parents as introjected into our inner parental imagery, the super-ego included. The giants further have to do with the stupidity we find ourselves up against in the outside world very largely because we have ourselves projected it there, the really relevant stupidity being our own. To let them carry Freia off would suggest letting our own fresh delight in life be overborne by our regressive tendencies. To buy them off by the gold and the ring itself suggests having to pour a priceless supply of libido into the mere feat of keeping our regressive tendencies in check; it further suggests putting our most creative underlying purposes into the sterile keeping of those same regressive tendencies.

From this point of view, our sympathy for the giants is not perhaps wasted, but it is certainly misleading. Sentiment towards our actual parents is proper enough; but sentiment towards our inner parental imagery can be a dangerous weakness, because it can prevent us from fighting as ruthlessly as we need inwardly to do for our own independence. Fortunately for the psyche which is the ultimate hero of the *Ring*, Siegfried is not going to show any such sentimental weakness towards Fafner when the great battle with him in his dragon shape comes off; but that battle is a long way distant still, and meanwhile we seem to have reached a temporary stalemate. Freia has been rescued, and that is undoubtedly the most important thing. But the ring has passed into Fafner's keeping, the implication being that the price paid is a certain blockage in the onward flow of the underlying purposes of the self for which the ring is primarily a symbol. It will be some time before we see how that blockage can be released, as it will undoubtedly have to be before the onward flow in the psyche can be fully resumed again.

No sympathy is altogether wasted, however, which helps us to make contact with an inner figure. Gentleness and tenderness are components of our parental imagery as much as oppressiveness or conservatism. On the assumption that death in a myth is primarily a symbol for transformation, we may ask where Fasolt's gentler spirit went when Fafner killed him. The answer, according to mythological precedent, must almost certainly be: into Fafner who killed him.

The sequel is as follows. Fafner, as we later learn, goes off and turns himself into a monstrous dragon, the better to guard his own perfectly useless treasure. It is perfectly useless because he is too conservative to do anything with it except put it into a cave and prevent anyone else from making any use of it either. He becomes, in consequence, his own jailer. By the time death and transformation come round to him in his turn, he has grown too tired of life to put up any formidable resistance. Not only this; he also shows a quite unexpected gentleness and concern towards his youthful slayer. The gentleness can be accounted for by regarding it as the assimilated spirit of his murdered brother. This would not make sense in outer reality, except to a primitive mentality, by which it would be taken very much for granted. But it makes excellent sense in the world of inner images, of which the essence can commonly be integrated into the personality as a whole only by wrestling with them, overcoming them or killing them in one symbolic manner or another.

None of this lessens or should lessen in the slightest degree our present sense of horror, nor that of the assembled gods themselves, as Fafner marches off before our eyes with his ill-won and ill-fated booty.

VALHALLA THE IMPREGNABLE FORTRESS AT LAST

At last the way is clear to the fortress. It is outwardly impregnable; but like so many of the defences we interpose against the full impact of life, it will prove illusory in the long run. Such defences are not without value; even assumed confidence may be better than none for a time; and indeed Valhalla does not only stand for illusory defences but for genuine worldly achievement, as is confirmed by the impressive grandeur of its music (63).

Donner, the forthright, unreflecting thunder-god of extrovert activity, swings his great hammer, which always returns to his hand of its own accord (64). A storm soon gathers, most excitingly represented in the orchestra; the lightning flashes to a splendidly jagged motive (46) of its own; the thunder crashes. These are very powerful symbols, and represent equally powerful inner realities.

Lightning has always symbolized the descent of the spirit in its most potent aspect: it terrifies; it electrifies; if it does not destroy outright, it implants new life. Rain stands for a gentler aspect of the spirit, descending as healing grace after the manner of a baptism, but likewise impregnating with new life. There is no reason to doubt that these traditional associations are operative beneath the surface here. Whatever the weaknesses of the present situation, a tremendous amount has been achieved since first we saw the Rhinemaidens' gold glinting innocently but uncreatively beneath the waters. There has been a mighty release of libido, a surging uprush of life. Wotan will spend the middle years of his prime strongly ensconced with his attendant gods and goddesses in Valhalla; and he has every right to enjoy these middle years while the changes in his character which we have seen instigated slowly mature. The self does not grudge a man the outward achievements of his prime provided that he is getting ready underneath to turn inwards as the time comes round.

In Norse mythology, Donner (Thor) wields the thunderbolt which is elsewhere reserved for sovereign gods such as Zeus (Jupiter). This is in general a symbol of male virility, including male assertiveness, aggressiveness and anger. From one angle, Donner stands here for Wotan's aggression. If looks could kill, Wotan would have killed the importunate giants outright in Scene 2. He must have badly wanted to kill them; but he knew the impossibility of that on account of the bargains inscribed on his spear, in token of the limits he has inwardly imposed on himself as a means of persuading himself (mistakenly) that he is secure. So Donner had to threaten them for him; and Wotan had, though with difficulty, to hold Donner back (a point of which Deryck Cooke suggested this meaning to me). Some part of Wagner must have wanted to kill Hanslick and the other hostile critics. We all of us have more or less of a problem with our repressed aggression; but in so far as we can turn it into creative channels, it is invaluable to us.

Donner's thunderstorm here is apparently what generates the energy to create a link between the present condition of the gods and the condition in which they are to pass the next phase of their development. As the clouds disperse no less quickly than they gathered, Freia's twin brother Froh (Frey) spins out of the rain and the evening light his rainbow bridge. Neither Donner nor Froh are at all fully presented in the *Ring*; their few remarks are not such as to do them much credit, as when Froh says in Scene 2 that it should be quite easy to steal Alberich's ring, and Loge rounds on him with justifiable irony. But the archetypes behind them are of no small significance.

The rainbow itself has its own beautiful symbolism as a pledge of hope. Faith and imagination have more to do with hope than the outward facts have, and Froh is a more poetic and introverted figure than solid Donner, who in Norse mythology was not allowed to cross the rainbow bridge for fear his weight would break it. This does not prevent hope from being one of our most rewarding attributes. The gods are now full of hope, and it will carry them a long way before the inherent vulnerability of Valhalla becomes evident.

Loge is not full of hope, and foresees quite clearly and sceptically that for all their confidence the gods are moving towards their end. He tells us as much and the gods too if they cared to listen; but they show no signs of doing so. He makes up his mind to return to his old shape as fire, ready to burn up the gods themselves at the far-off climax. As fire he is pure libido again, not subject to hope or disappointment: a sheer flux of inexhaustible energy.

Wotan is full of hope, but by no means blindly. He has been standing in a fit of brooding, obviously a prey to misgivings. He throws this off with the impressive gesture of a man who has just had a far-reaching thought, and got great comfort from it. He does not put this thought into words until he is much older and wiser, in Act II, Scene 1, of the *Valkyrie*; it is brought to our attention here only by the music. We hear a motive (45) which we shall later associate with the magic sword left by Wotan for Siegmund, after which it passes to Siegfried. The motive also suggests the heroic character fitted to the use of the sword. It leaps arpeggio-wise on the notes of a major triad, covering a total interval of a tenth.

This gives us the mood of Wotan's thought, though it is only in the light of after-knowledge that it could possibly convey the thought itself; nor does the traditional (but best forgotten) piece of stage-business help which Wagner is said to have suggested in rehearsal, and by which Wotan is made to pick up a sword left over from the treasure and wave it in the air. The thought is the astonishing one, for a sovereign god still in his prime, of begetting a hero to supplant himself and exert a freer authority than his own compromising bargains any longer permit. This is the first appearance in Wotan's imagination of an archetype of the utmost subsequent importance to the drama, namely the hero archetype, and it is one of the few significant moments in the *Ring* which are almost bound to be missed unless the musical symbolism has been examined beforehand.

As the gods line up for their ceremonial entry into Valhalla, there breaks into the confident Valhalla music, of all poignant inspirations, the song of the Rhinemaidens, out of sight down there in the river below. Up float their voices in three-part harmony, creamy as ever, piercing our hearts with sudden longing, melting our bones with nostalgic desire, unreal, sweeter-seeming than any reality, making the grandeur of the gods momentarily of no consequence and the perilous bliss of their own siren seduction the one attraction. 'Rhinegold, Rhinegold, give us back our Rhinegold!' Only Loge, who knows too much about unreality from the inside, remains unshaken; but no one has any intention of giving

them back their gold, even if it were now possible. Their cry goes un-
heeded—but not unheard. We are none of us too mature to be enchanted
by the sirens' song.

Besides, what if the sirens' song is not unreal? What if the grandeur
of the gods is the hollow semblance, and the call of nature the true
reality? There is a renegade in every one of us to whisper this doctrine
into our willing ears. It has enough truth in it to make us waver, and
indeed we would be glad enough to believe it. So much of our vaunted
civilization is artificial, not to say hypocritical. Reason can run so shallow,
and learning so dry. Consciousness can bring heavy cares, and instinct
promises a blessed relief from choice and responsibility. Nature is blind,
but nature is warm. What can man's laborious achievements set against
the call of nature?

Nothing at all, if we get out of touch with nature. Whatever is human
has an element of compromise. If we reject the part of the compromise
which keeps us in touch with nature, we are completely lost. But we are
just as lost if we try to evade our commitment to conscious civilization.
Just because the Rhinemaidens' cry makes Valhalla look shabby, we
cannot give up all that Valhalla stands for and go back to the state of
nature with which *Rhinegold* began. Shabby Valhalla may partly be, but
it stands here for our average human condition, and we need its uncertain
shelter and its overrated justice, culture and amenity. It is a stage to be
passed through, and there is no avoiding it. On the other hand, it is not
the end of the journey. Wotan's intuition on both these aspects seems
sound enough.

The confident Valhalla music takes over again. The gods pull themselves together; and as at last the procession gets into motion, the curtain
falls.

CHAPTER VII

The Valkyrie, Act I

———————— ❀ ————————

INCEST PHYSICAL AND MYTHOLOGICAL

The subject of the *Valkyrie* is on the face of it a surprising one. Incest is an unusual situation in a comparatively modern work of art, or if it comes to that in modern life. However, any sufficiently experienced social worker will know that it still remains a problem of the most literal kind. It has always been a problem, and the more primitive the civilization, the closer the problem.

In addition to the problem of literal incest, physically enacted, we find in more primitive cultures a widespread and important mythology of incest. The meaning attached to this was not at all the meaning attached to literal incest; in certain ways it was the very opposite. Incest between men and women has been prohibited since the earliest human cultures; incest between mythological beings was at the least condoned, and at the most endowed with the highest sanctity possible.

We have thus two apparently contradictory lines of tradition, both of them already of incalculable antiquity in the mid-medieval period during which the myths drawn on by Wagner in the *Ring* were taking literary shape. In reality, these traditions are intimately connected, and the mythological aspect is at once a compensation for and a complementary opposite to the literal aspect. The emotional intensity of the literal incest-longings which the earliest human cultures found it so necessary to sacrifice was transformed over into the sanctity attaching to so many instances of mythological incest. There is a subtle interplay of these two aspects going on in the background of the *Valkyrie*, and this helps to shape the course taken by the very moving events in the foreground.

INCEST A DANGER IN THE FLESH
AND IN FANTASY

It is generally felt that incest is unnatural. That is, however, precisely

116

what it is not. Nature has no more objection to incest than a cattle-breeder or a cat-fancier. Why should she object? Incest is closest of all with the mother (i.e. where the son fertilizes the very womb which bore him) and has in any case the psychological effect of turning libido inwards into the matriarchal situation, which is nature's own situation. There are other closely incestuous relationships, but they are all inward-turning, including both father-daughter incest and brother-sister incest, of which the last-mentioned is the variety with which the *Valkyrie* is concerned. All incest implies a failure to break the tie with the mother-principle. Why should nature object? What we call nature is the very embodiment of the mother-principle.

But what we call culture does not depend on the mother-principle; it depends on the father-principle. Matriarchy goes on perpetuating itself from generation to generation with a minimum of change. Every change from nature towards culture is a step, however small, in the direction of patriarchy. In so far as men's libido is effectively drawn back into the mother-world of nature, culture is held back too.

This does not affect the question of whether women are as capable of culture as men. No doubt they are; but the beginnings of culture had to be painfully built up by the struggles of men to free themselves from the natural dominion of perennially parturient women. That could only be done by enduring the frustration of not returning to the mother's embraces, either directly or under the near (and physically more attractive) equivalent of daughter or sister. The bitterness of that frustration and the difficulty of maintaining it are amply witnessed by the universality and severity of the incest taboo in every known primitive community. Only a natural desire of the greatest strength needs such extreme precautions to prevent it from breaking out and swamping the community.

The reason for these precautions is that very primitive communities live so close to the state of nature that they are in continual danger of being drawn down again. Their achievements in human culture are so precious, yet still so small and precarious, that only a constant vigilance can protect them. This vigilance is intuitive, not rational, but it is on such intuitions that primitive institutions develop, and develop with a tenacity of conservatism which we can hardly understand. Primitive institutions may not seem to us to represent a very advanced degree of consciousness, but on their own level of civilization they are the very frontier-posts of consciousness; indeed their value is likewise something which we have great difficulty in understanding, and which previous generations of

missionaries and others did much to destroy for lack of that understanding. However, the incest taboo is an institution which we still
maintain, and if we do not need to enforce it with such severe penalties,
that is only because the taboo itself has become like second nature to us.
A taboo which has to withstand a natural instinct needs to acquire the
force and appearance of an instinct if it is to become adequate to its
purpose.

The purpose of the incest taboo is to prevent our slipping back from
our measure of human consciousness and responsibility into an animal
state of unconsciousness and irresponsibility: i.e. into that very state of
nature which we saw so enticingly depicted at the opening of *Rhinegold*.
It begins to appear that incest is a topic by no means so irrelevant to the
underlying subject of the *Ring* as might superficially be thought. In so
far as the Rhinemaidens included in their symbolism a projection of our
own unconscious mother-longings, when in our weaker moments we
indulge in unrecognized but insidious fantasies of blissful irresponsibility,
Rhinegold has already brought up the topic of incest.

If it were only a question of incest in the flesh, we might not find it
particularly interesting, since this is so rare an occurrence under average
modern conditions. But unconscious fantasies of incestuous reunion with
the mother are not rare occurrences. On the contrary, we are all liable to
them, whether or not they are ever brought into the open, as by psychological analysis. They are among the factors which pull us back from
living as courageously, as freely and as consciously as we otherwise
might. In this sense, incest is still a danger to us, and for the same
reason that it has always been a danger to the human state. It is a danger
because it has still its old power of pulling us backwards from whatever
measure of consciousness and responsibility we may have achieved.

While incest remained very much of a danger in the flesh as well as
in fantasy, one very primitive compromise by which the situation could
be dealt with was sister-exchange. Of two men, each marries the other's
sister; hence each gets a certain indirect satisfaction of his unconscious
incest-longings, by proxy, and at only one remove. But marriage so very
endogamous severely confines the spread of the tribe by wider alliances,
and presently new forms of cousin-marriage replaced sister-exchanges.
Still freer and more exogamous marriages next became the rule, though
to begin with always at the cost of terrifying conflict between the conservative and the innovating tendencies.[1]

[1] See John Layard, 'The Incest Taboo and the Virgin Archetype', *Eranos-
Jahrbuch*, Vol. XII, Zürich, 1945.

As the scope for marriage widened, the scope for the physical satisfaction even by proxy of unconscious incest-longings dwindled. The
energy thus increasingly diverted from nature by the incest barrier
turned towards culture, where it poured into the vast effort of building
civilization.[2]

On the no longer very primitive level of civilization at which we first
meet the original mythological material here incorporated by Wagner,
literal incest has long since ceased to be a general danger. Unconscious
incest-fantasies are the danger obliquely referred to as a part of the
symbolism of the Rhinemaiden's seductiveness, and now to be brought
up more openly in connection with the fate of the brother-sister lovers,
Siegmund and Sieglinde.

TRANSGRESSION OR HEROIC ACCOMPLISHMENT?

The mythological significance of incest, though inseparably connected with the literal significance, and with the unconscious fantasies
ultimately derived from the literal significance, represents emotionally
an opposite pole. The current of emotion is the same; but in one case the
sign is in general negative, and in the other case positive.

Some confusion does, indeed, exist between these two extremes, and
we are not sure in every mythological situation whether we are supposed
to be condoning a transgression or witnessing a ritual. That may largely
be due to the fact that the ritual itself gains in sanctity from representing
what under ordinary mortal circumstances is an undoubted transgression.

This is a factor worth remarking on. There are numerous myths and
fairy-tales of which the whole point is that some particular action is
forbidden, yet is the one action necessary in order that the story shall
unfold. The forbidden door in Bluebeard's castle is one famous example;
Pandora's box is another, and so is the box Psyche could not resist
opening on her way back from the underworld. Psyche had already
broken Cupid's ban on seeing him: in this part of the tale, he came to
her each night in the dark, but forbade her to bring a light to him. Nor
did she, until her reputedly wicked but in reality ambivalent sisters put
into her mind the doubt whether he was not perhaps a hideous serpent.
She lit a lamp and saw all his winged beauty; a drop of hot oil woke
him; he left her; and the terrible adventures began for her by which

[2] John Layard, 'Identification with the Sacrificial Animal', *Eranos-Jahrbuch*,
Vol. XXIV, Zürich, 1956.

against all expectation she became reunited with him on a far more realistic basis than before.

Yet another example is the plot of *Lohengrin*, where asking the forbidden question as to what his name is deprives Elsa of her magic lover, but restores to her (a point commonly underestimated) her actual brother. Symbolically, both are images for her animus, but the actual brother represents a higher degree of reality than the magic lover. In *Parsifal*, it is the hero's failure to ask the right questions at the right time which involves him in such wanderings and sufferings before he is mature enough to redeem the situation; in that case the questions were not forbidden outwardly, but they were prevented inwardly by the fact that he was not yet ready to ask them.

The common element in these and other similar situations is that there is something hidden to be brought into the open. For a time, there is no need to do this. Naïve living, with all the real problems still hidden from sight, may be successful for a time. But a stage comes when so unconscious a state must be outgrown. To take this necessary step forward feels exceedingly dangerous, as steps into the unknown are apt to do. It also feels guilty, for the reasons already discussed in Chapter II. In short, it wells up in our symbolic imagery as a forbidden act.

The hero or heroine of this class of tale always ignores the prohibition sooner or later, and is always right to do so; an intuition deeper and stronger than the unavoidable fear and guilt takes command, and the essential gain in consciousness is duly achieved. Commonly the way forward is strewn with the corpses or the enchanted forms of other aspirants who have come to grief among its very real dangers; often these are automatically restored so soon as the youngest son or the slighted daughter or some such usually humbler aspirant succeeds where the others have failed. These others may stand for earlier attempts within the same psyche. The story naturally concentrates its chief attention on the more or less successful attempt which follows.

The difference between the unsuccessful and the successful aspirants is to be found in nothing so much as the spirit in which the task is approached. It is not the wisest nor the cleverest nor the strongest who is successful; it is more likely to be the one with the kindest heart and the simplest wits, who helps animals and follows their good advice, or the apparently bad advice of envious people, or mere human curiosity. From this angle, Siegmund and Sieglinde are like courageous but ill-starred aspirants, and Siegfried is the successful simpleton; but there is much more to it than that.

Underneath all the unsophisticated detail of the fairy-tale, and showing up still more clearly in the underlying layers of myth (which are seldom unsophisticated) we find a conviction that the one deed which is most prohibited to mortals is most sacred in those more than mortal beings who serve us as images for the archetypes. This is nowhere more obvious than in the case of incest.

MYTHOLOGICAL INCEST AS A RITUAL MARRIAGE

In mythology there is no possible doubt as to which variety of incest is primary, namely mother-son incest. We find under every variety of manifestation a Great Mother who having created herself out of herself gives birth to a son who is also her lover. As the young fertility god, he dies and is reborn in the recurring cycle of death and rejuvenation. One meaning of this widespread myth is that consciousness is born out of the matriarchal womb only to be repeatedly swallowed up again. But this has a patriarchal sequel when the son ceases to be a helpless victim, no sooner mated to her than lost in her. Instead, he begins to fight her for his independence. He gets a firmer hold on consciousness.

The unconsciousness of nature is often presented symbolically as a hermaphrodite whose male and female principles are undifferentiated. This is a primordial incest of opposites which are not yet distinguished, still less reconciled; it has in our fantasy-life a retrogressive fascination. But when consciousness has developed far enough for life's opposites to be seen apart, the possibility arises of reconciling them in a hermaphroditic union which on the contrary is differentiated and regenerative. This may be shown through a return to incest symbolism in the form of the sacred marriage, such as that of Osiris with his twin sister Isis (and its ritual externalization in the brother-sister marriages of the Pharaohs) or of King Sol with Queen Luna in alchemy; we may compare the mystical union of Christ with his bride the Church. All gradations are possible between these two extremes of retrogressive and regenerative incest.[1]

The most classic and certainly one of the richest of all incest myths is that of Oedipus, a hero exposed at birth in token of the more than human (because archetypal) role in store for him. He was also lame,

[1] See esp. Erich Neumann, *The Great Mother*, tr. R. Manheim, London, 1955; also C. G. Jung and C. Kerenyi, *Essays on a Science of Mythology*, tr. R. F. C. Hull, New York, 1949; and C. G. Jung, *Psychology of the Transference* (1946), Coll. Ed., Vol. 16, tr. R. F. C. Hull, London, 1954; *Psychology and Alchemy*, tr. R. F. C. Hull, London, 1953.

in token of the creative flaw in his character which drove him on. He killed his father and married his mother, but in ignorance, which suggests the level of unconscious fantasy rather than of outward reality; and on this part of the myth, Freud based one of his most valuable and irrefutable contributions to our knowledge of depth psychology. In between these two achievements, however, Oedipus overcame the Sphinx, a female monster and a symbol for the devouring aspect of the mother-image. This in turn suggests that his incest was not simply retrogressive, but had regenerative possibilities. It is, indeed, an essential stage in the development of individual character in either sex to pass more or less effectively through the Oedipus complex; people who for one reason or another (such as the absence of a strong enough parent of the opposite sex) largely escape it often seem to grow up only half at grips with life.

The turning-point in Oedipus' story arrived when he became conscious of his actual or fantasied situation as the supplanter of his father in his mother's embraces. He tore his own eyes out, ostensibly as a self-inflicted punishment for his own unwitting guilt. But this guilt was only a case, though an extreme one, of the usual heroic accomplishment of the most forbidden act. We may compare this episode with Wotan's self-inflicted loss of an eye in token not of guilt but of new insight. Samson, again, had not much inner wisdom until his eyes were put out. Blind Oedipus became a seer, and ended his days by walking gladly off into the unknown, beyond the reach of mortal eyes, not because he knew too little but because he knew too much for us any longer to follow him (I am indebted to John Layard for this interpretation.) The symbolical implication of blinding or partial blinding is turning the sight inwards.

Nevertheless, it is certainly significant that the typical variety of incest used to carry regenerative symbolism as a ritual marriage is not mother-son incest but brother-sister incest. To transfer our main unconscious incest fantasies from the mother to the sister is a normal stage of growth, and prepares us for the later stage of separating our sexual desires from our incest-longings still farther in ordinary mating. It is worth recalling that Wagner went through a stage of very close emotional attachment to his sisters. From this point of view, as from certain others, the incestuous mating of Siegmund and Sieglinde may be regarded as a preparatory rehearsal for the much more independent (though not entirely unincestuous[1]) mating of Siegfried and Brynhilde.

A particular significance attaches to the fact of brother-sister incest

[1] See Genealogical Table on p. 13.

122

being between twins. This is very often the case with mythological incest, as it is with Siegmund and Sieglinde. One implication is that the incest is as close as it is possible for the brother-sister variety to be, we might almost say as close as the primary mother-son incest itself. Isis and Osiris were lovers even in their mother's womb. But all such legendary improvements on the merely biological possibilities have an ulterior purpose: to stress the symbolic interpretation at the expense of the literal interpretation. Sometimes one twin is mortal and the other immortal, in order to represent the duality inherent in human nature as part animal and part spirit; sometimes, as here, there is one mortal and one divine parent, with the same implication. Any such detail of the imagery which tends to give the symbolic aspect prominence over the literal aspect adds to the probability that a mating of siblings is primarily an image for the sacred marriage. Brother and sister are classic symbols for animus and anima.

It is probably this mythological rightness underlying the symbolism of Siegmund's incest with Sieglinde which does most to account for one remarkable fact. Whatever our ingrained resistance to the idea of incest in the ordinary outside world, we are completely on the side of the lovers as we sit watching them in the opera-house. We share in Wagner's own feeling that the world has blossomed into warmth and fruitfulness after the strained, inhibited congestion of Wotan's plotting and Alberich's hatred in *Rhinegold*. There love herself, in the person of Freia, was held to ransom until Wotan was at last brought by his vision of Erda to let go his reliance on wilful power in the place of compassionate tenderness and understanding. Here, compassion, tenderness and understanding flow freely again, and love brooks no obstacles.

The conflict of compassionate love with wilful power is not yet finished with, but it is held in abeyance by such an upsurge of warm and immediate feeling that we too are warmed and moved. The very darkness of the setting makes the story of Siegmund and Sieglinde more deeply affecting. We are not only on their side; we are absorbed in them with a completeness of sympathy not very often achieved by any work of art. Without haste and without delay, without irrelevance and without faltering, the mystery and the enchantment unfold. There is no operatic act quite to compare for balanced perfection of form and content with the first Act of the *Valkyrie*. In the background of it all, there is a wealth of mythological significance; and in the foreground, the most lyrical of Wagner's love-stories.

SIEGMUND AND SIEGLINDE IN THEIR HOUR
OF DESTINY

As prelude to the *Valkyrie*, we hear some wild weather in the orchestra, to music (74) somewhat reminiscent of Wotan's bargain-bonds (73). Donner's thunder and lightning motive (46) breaks through as at the end of *Rhinegold*: one of the same group of leaping energy-motives which also includes the gold, the sword, the Valkyries and others. It is the climax of the storm, which dies down rapidly before the curtain rises to reveal the interior of a rough but impressive forest chieftain's hut, its roof-tree, a mighty ash, rising in the middle.

A small door at the back opens and an unarmed man, Siegmund, clearly exhausted and in flight, breaks in, to a motive so heroic and yet at the same time so resigned that we know him immediately for one who is undaunted although he has had much to daunt him. This motive (35), which has harmonically an inclination towards the diminished seventh, grows melodically out of the storm-music, and like it has its derivation in the descending stepwise motive (73) of Wotan's spear, which in turn suggests him in his role as ego. Siegmund's motive (35) has, indeed, a warmer and less angry tone, and turns expressively upwards at the end; we sense, nevertheless, that in some crucial respect Siegmund is an extension of Wotan's personality and has not wholly grown up as an independent adult. Events will confirm this interpretation relentlessly enough.

Siegmund sinks down in front of an open hearth on our right, where Sieglinde, entering, left, from an inner chamber, finds him. Within a few bars' space her main motive (36) is heard in such companionable counterpoint with Siegmund's that we are left in no doubt of the imminent mingling of their destinies. Like his, her motive is of the rarest beauty and expressiveness; and the same is true of the further motives given to this wonderful couple, so unfortunate in everything except the crowning good fortune of their shared experience. Wagner must have found more of his own inner nature in their vulnerable heroism than in all the assertive brilliance of Siegfried and Brynhilde, with whom he was superficially more identified. We find in the love-music here a passion of tenderness and a depth of yearning nowhere again quite equalled until the still maturer understanding and stronger loveliness of *Götterdämmerung*.

It is most important to the symbolism that this Act should be produced with scenery representing the hut tangibly enough to look capable, in the first place, of withstanding the frightful storm outside, so that we share Siegmund's relief at shelter; in the second place, of turning into a prison when its owner, Hunding, proves to be an enemy; in the third place, of ceasing to be a prison with the most dramatic of contrasts at the climax. For if Siegmund finds shelter there, that shelter partly symbolizes his own need for reassurance; if the shelter becomes imprisonment, that partly symbolizes the problems of his own driven nature rising like walls around him wherever he tries to settle; if these very walls open for him in his hour of destiny, that partly symbolizes his courage opening to it without fear or reservation. The roof-tree carries suggestions of the world-ash Yggdrasil on which Odin (Wotan) voluntarily crucified himself for nine days in search of deeper wisdom;[1] and indirectly of that other Tree of Life, the cross on which Christ hung in fulfilment of his own redeeming destiny. Siegmund, too, has a tragic destiny to fulfil which in its lesser way is necessary to a purpose greater than himself.

Sieglinde, mistress of this house but like it the property of Hunding, feels the first stirrings of compassion for the unknown fugitive; and the hour of their shared destiny has struck. He cries out for a drink; and as she fetches him a hornful of water, the music (39) pours over into such a flow of concentrated beauty as tells us how deep his thirst lies, and how much more than drinking-water is being offered him in this simple act of hospitality. There is no lovelier moment in the *Ring* than the seven bars here compounded of an inspired expansion of both their motives, which only once recurs, when she fetches him a second drink a little later in the same scene. Water so yearned for as this may well symbolize the water of life, for which she is becoming a channel for him.

He looks next into her face, and out of nine unharmonized bars of his own questing motive (35) there grows the first statement of their love-motive (37). It is on the same melodic sequence of notes as the second part (69) of Freia's motive, but drawn out into a lingering tension which carries all the compassionate tenderness of love mature enough to include an awareness of pain and suffering. The almost unbelievable poignancy and lyrical perfection of the first Act of the *Valkyrie* are due as much as anything to the mastery with which the bitterness of pain and the sweetness of love are blended, after the manner usual with the greatest music.

As the tonic B flat of Siegmund's motive (35) becomes the suspended 4 of a dominant 7–5–4 for the return of the harmony and the entry of the love motive (37), a new world is born. But the new world of love is also

[1] *The Elder or Poetic Edda*, tr. Olive Bray, London, 1908, p. 103.

a very old world. Falling in love is falling into one of the most archetypal of situations. New lovers often feel as if they had always known each other, always been fated for one another. What they are recognizing is not literally each other, but the archetypes of the anima and the animus which they carry and reveal for one another. The music itself may seem to us in some strange manner familiar, not simply because it grows out of material previously heard in *Rhinegold*, i.e. motive (69), but because it is in itself a closely fitting image of the archetype behind our human loves. I heard this first Act of the *Valkyrie* as a child before I heard *Rhinegold*; and yet everything seemed natural, everything seemed familiar in a way which I took for granted at the time, as a child will. It was my first experience of Wagner; yet I felt not that I was entering a wonderful new world, but that I was recognizing with wonderful new delight a world I somehow knew inside me very well already. Looking back on it, I can only regard this as one more confirmation that the archetypes are innate within us, so that any fresh encounter with their images gives this sense of recognition.

All our love and indeed all our experience is at bottom bitter-sweet; but this poignant quality is somehow more than usually prominent in the love of Siegmund and Sieglinde. They are such a particularly vulnerable pair. We hear this very quickly in the music, which at the fifth bar of the new motive (37) is twisted (37A), not harshly but with gentle inexorability, into enharmonic modulation (E flat taken as 7 of the dominant F of B flat major is left as if it were D sharp as the leading note of E major, then through A minor to a major dominant ninth on C, etc.).

On learning that her guest is wounded (though he makes little of it), Sieglinde fetches him a second drink, this time of mead. This symbol hints at the heavenly mead or hydromel which Odin stole with great difficulty and peril from the giants; who had tricked it away from the dwarfs; who first brewed it from honey and the blood of the murdered sage engendered by the Aesir gods from their own spittle and that of their reconciled enemies the Vanir gods; and this mead achieved through so much conflict and transformation is the source of poetic inspiration.[1] There is also mead given to the gods daily by a divine she-goat from her udders,[2] which seems to combine the satisfaction and nourishment of mother's milk with the intoxication and inspiration of a manly brew. All this Sieglinde gives Siegmund in symbol, as the music overflows for the second time in the same ecstatic fashion as before (39); but now he

---

[1] *The Prose Edda*, tr. A. G. Brodeur, London, 1929, pp. 92–96.
[2] ibid., p. 51.

insists on her drinking from the horn before he drains it himself. It is as if, without yet knowing it, they pledge each other to the fateful ecstasy they are about to share. The love music glows out again in all its searching intensity as they meet each other's eyes.

He makes to go on his way, but she asks who is in pursuit of him, and is told that he is and always has been a man pursued by misfortune, which he does not want to bring on to her head (81). She answers that he cannot make her any more unfortunate than she is already; and he stays to wait for Hunding's arrival.

SIEGLINDE AND HUNDING HEAR
SIEGMUND BEGIN HIS STORY

Hunding arrives with a promptness which is an obvious dramatic necessity, but which on another level might also be taken as hinting that as Siegmund's shadow and hidden source of misfortunes he has in a sense been here all along and is conjured into visibility by their thoughts of him. Hunding symbolizes Siegmund's shadow in the sense of presenting us with the underside which must somewhere exist to his heroism. Hunding is sluggish and conventional and cold at heart. He is, as we should expect, a man dark in appearance and character, since these two things go together in the simplest archetypal imagery, as any frequenter of Wild Western films will readily confirm. His music grows in its harmony out of the music which has been accompanying the latest mingled emotions of the other two, just as his arrival grows out of their thoughts of him. He has a motive (60) baleful in tonality and powerful in rhythm, to match his personality. His greeting is cold but correct (12).

As the three settle to a rough meal, Hunding notices a great resemblance in feature between the other two, including a strange marking of their eyes, like a snake or dragon. In the Sagas, such a marking might indicate kinship to Siegfried as the dragon-slayer. Here it is treated as a hereditary characteristic of the Volsung race, Wotan's children. When Hunding notices it, the orchestra sounds Wotan's spear motive (73), which suggests that we were right in regarding Siegmund as in part an extension of the wilful aspect of Wotan's personality. We shall see presently how this partial dependence affects Siegmund's fate, though not his actions.

In answer to Hunding's dour questioning and Sieglinde's shy eagerness, Siegmund tells his story, under the self-styled name of Woefull. This story itself, or rather the story of all the Volsung race, has a motive (77), a nobly arching melody the first notes of which recall the last notes of Siegmund's own motive (35). They share a certain inclination to include intervals of the diminished seventh (though an upwards major sixth is also prominent). Since Siegmund's story will from now onwards embrace Sieglinde's story too, we shall find many future references to their joint experience conveyed by this present motive, which is strongly emphasized here by being heard unaccompanied.

It seems that Siegmund's father has planned that he should grow strong under adversity, as hardy characters, although not soft ones, can. Returning from a hunt, father and son had found their homestead burnt, the boy's mother killed and his twin sister vanished. Thereafter they lived the turbulent life of outlaws, until presently the father vanished too, leaving as token an empty wolfskin; for Wolflings was the name by which they passed, though the music by sounding the Valhalla motive (63) tells us that the father's true identity is Wotan, and another motive (66) in the same general group as the Valhalla motive soon appears to characterize the heroic Volsung race itself as Wotan's offspring.

An interesting light is thrown on this part of the story by the corresponding episodes in the Volsunga Saga.[1] In this Saga, the generations are much more numerous than the shortened genealogy given by Wagner, though in both cases the line is directly descended from Odin (Wotan). Sigmund (Siegmund) has taken refuge in the forest where his twin-sister Signy (Sieglinde) seeks him out, but in a disguise assumed by witchcraft, so that although she knows who he is, he does not know who she is. He gives her shelter, and they spend three nights at each other's side. They have a son, and though he is not Siegfried he becomes a great hero. His training, which is extremely hard, resembles that which in Wagner's version Wotan gives to Siegmund.

We are told that Signy sewed a glove on to her son's hand and pulled it off skin and all as a test of his courage; when he did not flinch, she sent him out into the forest to live as an outlaw with his father. This is reminiscent of male initiation rites by circumcision or subincision such as still occur in the few surviving stone-age societies,[2] since the hand is commonly a token for the phallus. The pattern of these rites is first to shock the young initiates out of their childhood bondage to the mother-world of women, and then to reassure and comfort them in their new allegiance to the father-world of men.

In the forest, father and son repeatedly assume the form of werewolves. One day the father bites his son's throat in this form, and nearly

[1] Tr. E. Magnusson and Wm. Morris, London, n.d., pp. 20 ff.
[2] John Layard, *Stone Men of Malekula*, London, 1942.

kills him, but heals him by a herb whose use has been learnt from an animal. This, too, is reminiscent of male initiation rites, which by first hurting and frightening the boy, but then cherishing and reassuring him, help to wean him from the mother-image in his psyche as he has previously been weaned from his mother in the body. The two themes of incest and of weaning are clearly connected in this story; by making the boy the actual offspring of incest, the problem of psychic weaning is all the more clearly underlined. The problem is to wean him away from incest-fantasies and into the incest-renouncing company of men.

Sigmund next tests his son by leaving him to bake bread from meal in which a live snake has been hidden. Two of Signy's sons (not by Sigmund) have already failed this test and been ruthlessly killed off as cowards; this son kneads the meal and bakes the bread, snake and all, thus symbolizing his unfearing acceptance of the dangerous but creative mystery of phallic power. But the father, who can himself eat snake's venom unharmed, will not let his son eat it, as it would kill him (and in the end it is a poisoned drink offered by an animus-ridden woman which does kill him); he can only endure snake's venom externally, we are told. Meanwhile, both father and son are buried alive by the boy's grandfather, Signy's father, whom they subsequently kill; for Signy has smuggled their magic sword into the barrow, and they cut their way out with this token of their manhood, in a fashion reminiscent of ritual rebirth. With such a start in life, the boy was already well launched on his heroic career.

It is interesting to notice what parts of this Saga have been taken over by Wagner, and what have not. In the Saga, both parents act as good parents intuitively do. The symbolism for this is so forceful that it gives us quite a shock; but necessary actions within the psyche are apt to feel like shocking violence on account of our unavoidable resistance to them, which it takes a great deal of inner pressure to overcome. The necessary action here shown symbolically is for the mother herself to push her son out into the world of men, and for the father to receive him there with a calculated mixture of hardship by which to temper him, and loving care by which to reassure him. It is a process which our physical parents can greatly help or greatly hinder by their own conscious and unconscious attitudes, but which is essentially the work of our own inner parent-images. It is essentially an inner process. Initiation rites are designed to help it, but there are few remnants of these valuable rites in modern society beyond a little schoolboy bullying.

Wagner, as part of his telescoping of the Volsung generations for

I

dramatic purposes, made Wotan apply to Siegmund (his own son in Wagner though not in the Saga) treatment comparable to that applied (in the Saga) by Sigmund to his incestuously begotten son (not, in the Saga, Siegfried). Wagner has left out the torture, with its hidden reference to initiation rites, but retained the hardship. That is understandable, since even in the Saga the reference to initiation is an indirect and highly unconscious one. But it is remarkable how much Wagner seems to stress one aspect of Siegmund's story which from the Saga we might not expect. As Siegmund goes on with his melancholy narrative, to which the falling semitone of woe (68) adds its grievous though by no means self-pitying comment, we realize more and more plainly that he has brought one misfortune after another on to his own head. Half his troubles, including the one from which he is now in flight, are of his own making.

SIEGMUND TELLS US OF
HIS UNQUIET AND LONELY LIFE

On Siegmund's own showing, as often as he tried to make friends he only stirred up new enemies. As often as he intervened in a good cause and with the best of intentions, he only found that no one, not even the victim he had rushed in to save, took the same view as he did of the rights and wrongs of the quarrel. As often as he tried to take any part in the ordinary affairs of men and women, he seemed to get out of step. He could find no settled place for himself in human society anywhere.

The indications which this history gives us with regard to Siegmund's character correspond strikingly enough with what we know of Wagner's. There is a letter from Wagner to Pusinelli on which Ernest Newman made illuminating comment.[1] In it Wagner described himself as quite incapable of finding his bearings anywhere in the outer world which so puzzled and eluded him. It was the inner world which was real for him. The outer world, he confessed, was for him a shadow world through which his legs carried him, but which he simply could not understand either in principle or in practice. Yet he was always ready to rush in with some grand scheme of artistic, social or political reform, and was always hurt and surprised when it met with opposition, some of it reasonable, from vested interests or disinterested dissentients. Even in success he was liable to feel cut off, as when he had his first triumph with *Rienzi*, and stood there unable to feel that the thunderous applause

[1] Ernest Newman, *Richard Wagner*, Vol. I, 1933, p. 398.

was really for himself: indeed, unable to feel anything at all, a not uncommon sort of attack with him.

At Weber's reinterment in Dresden, Wagner listened to himself
speaking with such disassociated pleasure, as if to another person, that
he waited for that other person to go on during a quite embarrassing
space of time before he realized again that the other person was himself.
The least contradiction or disagreement was enough to make him very
angry, and he would fall into fits of uncontrollable, ranting abuse of
which a number of very circumstantial accounts have come down to us.
His mere verbosity was interminable, and his invective was vitriolic.
He would weep and he would shout. Suddenly it would all stop, and he
would drift away into some serene haven of his own, leaving his victim
dumbfounded and at a loss to know what to make of the whole nightmare
scene.

These are not merely neurotic but near-psychotic symptoms, and
unfortunately they grew worse rather than better with advancing years
and fame. But as Newman pointed out, here was the very same driving
force which created Bayreuth—a project which no merely sane and
balanced reformer could have thought for one moment of attempting,
and still less have carried through. Wagner's notorious ingratitude to
his friends, his intolerance and his possessiveness, his obstinacy and
his touchiness, his obsessive domination of everyone who could be
brought into his personal or professional orbit would have been beyond
all endurance but for the equally extreme genius, integrity, charm and
sheer lovability which were inseparably bound up with them. Newman's
first conclusion was that we ought to distinguish Wagner the artist from
Wagner the man, and judge them separately, on the not ungenerous
assumption that an artist can be great in spite of being dreadful as a
man. In his later writings, Newman began to recognize that Wagner
was Wagner whether as man or as artist, and that he was shot through
and through with contradictory qualities. Newman never quite saw that
the contradictions themselves add up, and that Wagner was not great
in spite of them, or because of them, but simply in being them.

It seems possible that Wagner developed his genius instead of developing a psychosis. Without his genius, he might have come to a bad end
(perhaps in the role of political adventurer, as he nearly did in the
Dresden revolution); but then he was not without his genius. That
does not tell us what genius is, but it gives us a line of approach to the
familiar problem that genius is akin to madness. No one who is able to
live a balanced and contented life wants to get across the world as

genius is so often compelled to do. The least driven genius that I can think of is J. S. Bach; and even Bach's relations with his colleagues, though amiability itself compared to Wagner's, were chronically quarrelsome enough to suggest a certain amount of paranoid obstinacy and intemperance. Wagner, like Beethoven, was more characteristic of his kind in this respect. The kind to which such creative people (though not only creative people) belong is the same kind as that of which Siegmund seems to be a representative.

Siegmund's story reminds us at several points of the familiar experiences of a 'bad mixer' who through no conscious fault of his own always finds himself too 'different' from other people to settle down with them on ordinary terms of give and take. 'I am differently organized', said Wagner to Eliza Wille: 'the world ought to give me what I need.'[1] It is the typical conviction of a man who is mother-bound in the sense of not having outgrown his infantile dependence sufficiently to expect to have to provide for his own welfare. 'The world owes me a living' is the tacit assumption. The world does not always see it in that light, even when the claimant is a genius, which, of course, more often he is not.

From this point of view, Siegmund's early loss of his mother and sister takes on a rather more complicated aspect than it presented when we were thinking of him as being deliberately schooled in misfortune to harden his character. It is true that he was old enough to have been out hunting with his father on the day of the catastrophe, so that the deprivation did not occur during his infancy, when it would have been much more damaging still, nor even very early in his childhood. But it was nevertheless an appalling experience, which must have left its mark.

We have no direct evidence as to the quality of the mothering Siegmund and his sister received before the catastrophe, but it may not have been so good as we are inclined on romantic grounds to assume. The father's contribution to the twins' upbringing must always have been irregular and uncertain, coming from so habitual a wanderer. Wagner himself is thought to have suspected and perhaps to have believed that he was fathered out of wedlock by the same Geyer who subsequently became his stepfather; and such a suspicion or belief is one more unsettling element to be taken into account over the development of his own character. Presumably the illegitimate children even of a god have also

---

[1] Cited by Ernest Newman, *Wagner as Man and Artist*, London, 1914, p. 83, from *Richard Wagner and Eliza Wille*, pp. 74–75.

something to contend with in this respect; and their mother, too, cannot have had an easy time of it, which must again have reflected unfavourably on her influence conscious and unconscious over her children.

It is not the children given an ample allowance of mother's and father's love during infancy and childhood who tend to grow up unduly dependent, in the sense which depth psychologists mean by the terms mother-bound and father-bound. It is the children deprived of an ample allowance, so that in later life they are haunted by a strange, restless ache which sends them perpetually in unconscious search for it.

This search is tragically self-defeating in so far as it is directed outwards towards other people, who are almost bound to end by resenting a demand for reassurance not really to be satisfied by any outside person. There is no satisfying the insatiable, as Wagner's friends and helpers found to their cost; there is no real possibility in the outside world of catching up with authentic mothering and fathering if we did not get enough of them at the proper time. But in so far as we can direct our search inwards, we may learn to do our own mothering and fathering for ourselves, with incalculably creative consequences for the indirect benefit of the world as well as the direct benefit of ourselves.

When a mother is so impoverished in her own life that she tries to live it through her children, she may destroy their independence by an excess of smother-love. Severely but not disastrously deprived children will at least escape that fate. They cannot hope to find life easy, but they may find it uncommonly interesting. They are perhaps more likely than better-loved children to grow up as artists, visionaries, creators, or in the language of mythology, heroes. They are heroic in so far as they are driven into exacting tasks, inward rather than outward, which more equable people are spared. Their creativeness is their reward, though they may pay a high price for it in loneliness. Wagner often felt a 'terrible emptiness' in his life (letter to Liszt, 17 Dec. 1853), as 'an artist and nothing but an artist—that is my blessing and my curse' (letter to Roeckel, 23 Aug. 1856). 'The subject of *The Valkyrie* affects me too painfully', he confessed to Princess Caroline (letter of Nov. 1854); 'truly there is not a sorrow in the world which does not find its most agonizing expression here.' Like his own Siegmund, Wagner was too 'different' to get on easy terms with ordinary people. He knew just what it is like to be driven into a heroic destiny.

SIEGMUND'S STORY SHOWS HUNDING
TO BE HIS ENEMY

So soon as Hunding has noticed the snake-markings in his wife's eyes and his guest's, his demeanour suggests that he has made the obvious inference. He knows in effect who Siegmund is before Siegmund knows that he knows, and long before Siegmund and Sieglinde mutually recognize each other. Siegmund himself is now too absorbed in his own story, and in Sieglinde's compassionate response, to sense the deterioration in an already unfriendly atmosphere. But to us in the audience the explosiveness of the situation has been growing plainer all the time.

The snake-markings are an interesting detail. The snake is traditionally a phallic symbol in the widest sense, with all the usual ambivalence between positive and negative suggestiveness. There are snakes of healing associated with Aesculapius; there are snakes of transformation into new life associated with Mercury. There are soul-snakes and ancestor-snakes. There are deadly snakes growing in place of hair on the Gorgon's head, as was also sometimes the case with the Furies (Erinyes) of the underworld, who alternatively had torches instead of snakes in their hair or their hands: a conjunction which interestingly enough links the phallic symbolism of the snake with the libido symbolism of fire (indeed they lie very close). Snakes are also linked in many other ways with the underworld, and particularly with pursuing or avenging spirits, which reminds us of the snake's venom dripping as a punishment on Loge's face. A snake tempted Eve so that she and Adam did eat of the forbidden fruit, and as a result got knowledge of good and evil. The Python was a snake-dragon killed by Apollo, the stench from whose decaying body, entering his priestess the Pythoness from below, inspired her to prophecy, rather as the blood of the snake-dragon Fafner is going to teach Siegfried the speech of the birds.

Dragons are traditional symbols for the devouring aspect of the mother-image. The heroes who have to fight them are those on whom the mother-image exerts an exceptional fascination, so that they must overcome this fascination by a direct encounter, or perish in the attempt. Siegmund and Sieglinde carry the sign of the snake in their eyes partly in token of their own heroic destiny, and partly in token of the dragon-slayer Siegfried whose parents they are to become in pursuance of that destiny.

Now the smouldering hostility at the supper-table comes out into the open. As Siegmund describes the conflict from which he has just escaped, we hear Hunding's motive (60), and we quickly realize that Hunding is a blood-relative of Siegmund's latest foes, who have already broken his weapons though not his strength or his courage. As my guest you are safe for tonight, Hunding tells him; tomorrow, guard yourself well. The irony of these words is not lost on us, nor on the weaponless Siegmund. Sieglinde's agitation appears in an excited extension to her motive, very much as the second part (69) of Freia's motive takes an agitated shape where the dramatic situation requires it.

Bidden to prepare Hunding's evening drink and await him in the inner chamber, Sieglinde fills a horn and drops some spices into it; she glances first at Siegmund, and then long and meaningfully at the roof-tree, while the sword motive (45) rings softly out for a reason we shall shortly see; then at a curt gesture from Hunding, she goes. He follows, and does not reappear in this Act. It is as if the symbolic representative of Siegmund's shadow, having been to some extent confronted, has no more power to interfere with him during the one night which is going to make sense of his whole life-story.

WHY WOTAN IS ENTANGLED IN HIS BARGAINS

Left alone and almost in darkness, Siegmund falls to brooding, as well he may. His father has promised him a sword against the time of his greatest need; and surely that need has come upon him now. He ponders, too, on the unhappy wife for whom he has felt not only desire but a strange emotion he cannot yet understand. The firelight stirs a little; and the light of it catches the hilt of a sword plunged deep into the roof-tree. We in the audience see it quite plainly; but he thinks dreamily that it must be the woman's bright glance lingering behind her. The fire falls in again, and the gleam of the sword-hilt fades.

We realize, even if Siegmund does not yet, that here is his father's sword waiting for him to claim. This is the sword of which we heard the motive (45) at the end of *Rhinegold*, when Wotan had his great thought of begetting a hero to cut through the entangling bargains of which there seemed no other way of getting rid. Siegmund is the hero, and this is the task to which he has been trained up with such severity.

The bargains, on the face of it, are quite literally the bargains or treaties with which Wotan has buttressed his power and established his worldly authority. He made one such bargain with the giants in order to get his castle Valhalla built; and we are to suppose that this is typical of a number of others recorded among the runes on the shaft of his spear.

On this level, Wotan's problem is that each such bargain, though safe-guarding some aspect of his authority, does so at the cost of concessions which limit that authority in another aspect, until eventually he has lost all real liberty of action. He cannot break his bargains without destroying respect for authority in general, including his own authority. In the case of the giants, he cannot afford to honour his bargain either, and is driven back on actual dishonesty in order to buy them off.

It is a vicious spiral of which the coils are growing narrower; and the only hope he can see is that his hero son, not being under any obligation to respect father Wotan's bargains, will cut his way out without bringing down any more penalties as a consequence. Provided the son is really not under any obligation to the father's bargains, this seems to offer a solution which though it will not leave much effective authority to Wotan, will at least keep it in the family, i.e. in the hands of the gods. But what about this crucial proviso?

As a specimen of either political or commercial morality and realism, we may as well admit at once that the project is no more rationally convincing than some of the more dubious of Wagner's own business propositions. Can obligations be disregarded merely by getting another member of the family to do the disregarding? Not if they are genuine obligations; and if they are ungenuine, why is it necessary to employ a proxy? Wotan's dilemma and his proposed solution for it, which are perfectly convincing in the opera-house, would not be so if they did not correspond to an inner situation which carries conviction not so much to our reason as to our intuition. This situation has to do not with outside bargains but with the unconscious inner bargains which from earliest infancy we begin to strike with ourselves and with our environment as we experience it.

We each make our own world, in the sense of coming to our own unconscious conclusions about what the world is like. So far as our reactions to it are concerned, that really is our world. Our conclusions have an archetypal foundation which ensures that they have a great deal in common, quite apart from the influence exerted by the reality-principle. But even the same realities are not experienced as the same by people whose reactions are different, nor by the same people when in different moods.

Since birth, indeed already in the womb, we have been adapting ourselves to what have seemed to us to be the possibilities offered by life. For all its archetypal foundation, our view of these possibilities has been heavily conditioned by mother's attitude, and later by that of father and others. Did mother feed us lovingly or grudgingly, and handle us reposefully or anxiously? It will make a difference to our later confidence in the world and in its willingness to accept and nourish us. Did she convey in a thousand unpremeditated ways that life in joy or pain is of wonderful value, or on the contrary that it is disappointing, or shameful, or terrifying? We are bound to pick it up, and it will affect our own unconscious choice of attitude. Did she take pleasure in our first sturdy efforts at independence and make us feel respected as the true little personalities we were already striving to be, or did she invade us and swamp us with the intentional or unintentional determination that we should grow up the way she wanted us to go? In so far as it was the first, we are helped to relate easily and undefensively to other people, but in so far as it was the second, we may go in constant fear of losing our own individuality so soon as we come into contact with anyone else's.

It is in response to such early experiences that we build up, on an archetypal foundation, the world we are going to live in.[1] It seems to us the only world there is, and it is hard to believe how different it may be from the next man's. This is the case in sanity, and still more so in madness. Sane or mad, we strike bargains with ourselves. If we inhibit our libido from this dangerous direction, perhaps it can more safely flow in that? If we avert our awareness from this quarter, supposedly guilty, perhaps we shall be allowed a freer enjoyment of the other? A network of tacit compromises and unspoken assumptions grows up, which, however hampering it may be in many ways, at least makes possible some sort of a working adjustment to the facts of life. The danger might really be all the better for being confronted; the guilt is in all probability misplaced; the bargains constitute an obligation which is ultimately not genuine. Yet we need our bargains, since we could not face life at all except from the varying degrees of apparent security they offer us. In this sense, Wotan's bargains are his inhibitions; but even our inhibitions have their positive as well as their negative function. Nevertheless, we need to outgrow them as far as we can.

As, therefore, we grow in character, we modify our compromises; but with the best will in the world it is a difficult and gradual process to change a tacit assumption or to leave an entrenched position of whose very existence we may on the rational level be unconscious. It can only happen through experiencing a developing series of symbolic images to

---

[1] The experiences of infancy as the start of our outlook on the world are magnificently studied by D. W. Winncott, *Collected Papers*, London, 1958.

which we respond intuitively. What with our blindness and what with our fears, we cannot help resisting our own progress as well as desiring it. Thus it is seldom smooth; and it not infrequently gets blocked. Such a crisis of re-adaptation often accompanies the transition from one main stage of life to another, and particularly the transition from earlier to later manhood on which Wotan is now engaged. The sword which he has left in the tree suggests his own predominant desire to make a clean cut, and Siegmund suggests the heroic strength of character by which to make it.

When an image of the hero archetype takes shape in us, the implication is that our inmost need is calling up hidden reserves of heroic strength. We have such a dread of the unknown, such reluctance to sacrifice the apparent security of our existing compromise with life, and such tenacious illusions as to ego being in full command of the situation, that we can seldom free the hero in us to act as an autonomous archetype at the first attempt. But even an unsuccessful attempt, throwing us into bitter discouragement and distress, may open up the way more than we can realize at the time.

The heroine is as necessary as the hero, since she is an image for the archetypal compassion and inspiration of the anima. Both Siegmund as hero and Sieglinde as heroine have the tempered courage of misfortune long endured, in the true tradition of myth and legend. The only sign so far of their father's helping hand is the sword itself.

THE SWORD IN THE TREE

The sword in the tree is not the first object we have seen waiting to be pulled away subject to a necessary condition being fulfilled, nor the last that we shall see. What is the common element in this recurring theme?

The gold on the Rhinemaidens' rock was a symbol for libido lying unused in the unconscious until lit up by an access of psychic consciousness and stolen by the fulfilment of an abhorrent condition: the forswearing of love. But the accompanying symbols were those of the creation, i.e. of the birth of consciousness, and of that renewed creation in the individual's life which can have the effect on him commonly described as rebirth.

We noticed at the time the strange mirror-correspondence between the abhorred forswearing of love by Alberich and the admired forswearing of love by the knights of the Holy Grail. Libido denied a sexual outlet often pours into creative outlets of some other kind. Libido recovered from unconscious mother-longings can go straight into the building of character. Since sexuality is not debilitating in itself, the power which often accrues to celibates probably comes from their enhanced resistance to the unconscious mother-longings which can never be entirely excluded from any sexual relationship. It is not the sexuality itself but the compulsive dependence on sexuality which they gain strength from overcoming, because that dependence is a form of mother-dependence. The legends of Parsifal and the Holy Grail have largely to do with the overcoming of unconscious mother-ties under the very appropriate symbolism of sexual seduction; so, we saw reason to believe, has *Rhinegold*; and here in the *Valkyrie*, this basic theme of incest, as an image for retrogression in the psyche, comes directly into prominence.

The retrogression symbolized by incest can lead to a regressive entanglement in escapist infantile fantasies; or it can lead on to a regenerative reliving of infantile situations, in such a way as to give them a more progressive outcome than occurred in actual infancy. The first is a step back into illusion, but the second is one step back to take two forward. We may therefore regard it as a favourable sign that this further object waiting to be pulled away, namely the sword in the tree, also carries associations with the saving image of rebirth. One of these associations is the rebirth of Osiris from a mother-tree as Egyptian mythology moved away from its matriarchal beginnings towards its subsequent patriarchal development.[1] That is connected with the weaning of the spirit away from the mother-world of nature towards the father-world of culture, which in turn depends on the sufficient overcoming of unconscious mother-longings. It may well be counted a prefiguration of rebirth for Siegmund if he can win his manhood under the symbolism of pulling his father's sword out of a tree related, as this tree undoubtedly is, related, to the mother-world of nature. The condition here is simply to be the right hero: i.e. to accept his own heroic destiny for weal or for woe or for some of each.

We feel sure that Siegmund is going to pull the sword out when first we catch sight of the gleaming hilt, and it will do no harm to anticipate here by mentioning that when he does pull it out, we shall hear, in its original dark key of C minor, a full statement of the 'renunciation' motive (76) first heard when the Rhinemaidens were describing to Alberich the condition on which their gold could be pulled away. The

[1] Erich Neumann, tr. R. F. C. Hull, *The Origins and History of Consciousness*, London, 1954, p. 237.

words sung by the Rhinemaidens to this wonderful motive, which is at once so deeply sad and so nobly resigned, are: 'Only he that renounces the power of desire, only he that forgoes the delights of love, only he gains the magic to enforce the gold into a ring.' The words sung by Siegmund to the same motive are: 'Holiest desires, highest need, yearning love's compelling need, burns bright in my breast, urges to deed and death.' In this Siegmund shows the intuitive foreknowledge often attributed by the Sagas to heroic characters (including Siegmund himself in his last battle as the Volsunga Saga relates it): the deed will be the begetting of Siegfried on Sieglinde; the death will be Siegmund's own. This is not renouncing love; it is accepting a destiny shaped by love even at the price of death. But it is renouncing escapist fantasies. Renouncing escapist fantasies and accepting the full impact of one's destiny are two descriptions for the same act of courage. Motive (76) might just as well be called the 'acceptance' motive as the 'renunciation' motive.

The words used by Wolfram von Eschenbach to symbolize this combined renunciation of escapist fantasies and acceptance of destiny are: 'He who would to the Grail do service, he shall women's love forswear.'[1] He who would find the creative aspect of the eternal feminine (here symbolized by the Grail) must stand out against the seductive aspect: that is what this symbolism means, even for the majority of us who do not have literally to forswear women's love.

We all of us have to wrest our inner strength away from the mother-image, since that is where it lies as in a matrix. We have to fight and defy her for it. Whatever the symbolism may be under which this fight and defiance appear, it is liable to be affected by a sense of guilt. Any defiance of the mother-image is apt to feel wicked. Alberich's theft of the gold felt wicked at the time. Siegmund's union with Sieglinde is going to feel wicked to her in her subsequent frenzy of remorse, as well as being judged wicked by Fricka and by Wotan on the strength of Fricka's arguments. Part of Siegmund's heroic courage lies in his ability to pull out the sword, as a preliminary to carrying off Sieglinde, without pausing to consider that at least the second portion of this combined operation must certainly come under the heading of a forbidden act. In myth and fairy-tale, the forbidden act is the needed act: the heroic act.

---

[1] *Parzival*, tr. Jessie L. Weston, London, 1894, Vol. I, p. 284.

THE SWORD ITSELF

The fact that both the gold and the sword have an access of power to offer him who has the force of character, dark or bright, to win them is underlined by the similarity of their motives in the music. The motive (44) of the gold and the motive (45) of the sword have a leaping potency shared to some extent by other more or less triadic motives such as Donner's lightning (46) or Siegfried's gay and virile horn-call (48). They are all related to the group of motives directly based on the upsurging arpeggiation of (1) at the start of *Rhinegold*.

We have just seen the firelight catching the metal hilt of the sword and causing it to glow like fire, as the sunlight caught the gold under the Rhine and caused it to glow like fire. The closeness of the relationship between these three symbols, i.e. gold, sword and fire, can be further confirmed from Nordic mythology, and has evidently an archetypal foundation.

We have already noted that one of the poetic synonyms for gold in Skaldic convention was 'Fire of Waters or of Rivers'. In the same way, a poetic synonym for a sword was 'Odin's fire' (Wotan's).[1] A part of the Nibelungenleid not drawn on by Wagner makes Gudrun (Gutrune) tell her second husband Atle (who had dreamt, prophetically as it turned out, of being pierced by her with a sword) that 'to dream of iron is to dream of fire'.[2] In the Volsunga version, this very sword which we are seeing here in the *Valkyrie*, after being reforged for (not in this version by) Sigurd (Siegfried) from its broken pieces, gave off light 'as though fire burned along the edges thereof'.[3] We hear of another sword which when hardened in dragon's blood resembled fire.[4] There is also the blazing sword of fire wielded victoriously by the giant Surtr at the twilight of the gods.[5] That may put us a little in mind of the angel with the fiery sword who prevented Adam and Eve from slipping back into the supposedly blissful unconsciousness and irresponsibility of Eden.

The common factor in the symbolism of gold, sword and fire is their underlying suggestion of the burning force of life itself: i.e. libido. If the sword which bars the primrose path back to Eden and the sword which helps and rewards the heroic encounter with unconscious fantasies of

[1] *The Prose Edda*, by Snorri Sturluson, tr. A. G. Brodeur, New York, 1916, p. 186.
[2] Quoted by D. A. Mackenzie, *Teutonic Myth and Legend*, London, n.d., p. 345.
[3] *The Volsunga Saga*, tr. E. Magnusson and Wm. Morris, London, n.d., p. 51.
[4] V. Rydberg, *Teutonic Mythology*, tr. R. B. Anderson, London, 1889, p. 565.
[5] *The Elder or Poetic Edda*, tr. O. Bray, London, 1908, p. 293.

Eden are both fiery, that is because the same force of life inspires both
the ban and the encounter. With similar ambivalence, the same image
which appears in some contexts as the sword of justice appears in others
as the sword of violence by which he who takes it up shall die. The
sword, again, is another phallic symbol: but, as usual, its penetrating
point suggests general male adventurousness as well as specific male
sexuality; its cutting edge suggests the keen inquisitive edge of male
reason, tending to divide this category from that and establish order and
logic, where the female tendency is to join and contain and incubate.
The hardness of the steel suggests the obduracy of the will but also
the integrity of the spirit; its malleability when heated suggests the
feminine fluidity and susceptibility to feeling on which the male spirit
depends to keep it warm and approachable. Libido itself is neither male
nor female, but takes its quality from its living vehicles. Libido is a
primary manifestation of life, and its symbols are as diversified as its
channels of activity. No wonder Siegmund needs his father's sword.

THE LONG WINTER ENDS
WITH THE COMING OF LOVE

There is a wonderful hush as of great events preparing in this quiet
interlude in the drama and the music, with Siegmund thinking over his
position more resignedly than hopefully down there by the sinking fire,
and the darkness of the hut relieved only by the intermittent glow on the
hearth and the answering gleam of the sword-hilt in the tree.

Then against all his expectation Sieglinde slips in from the inner
chamber door; tells him that she has put a sleeping potion in Hunding's
drink; and relates a strange story of a mysterious stranger with a great
hat drawn down over one eye. The Valhalla motive (63) in the music
further identifies this stranger for us as Wotan. In among the guests he
strode at her forced marriage to Hunding; thrust the sword into the tree
with a mighty thrust; and departed with no word but with a smile for
her alone, whereupon she knew him for her father, and knew, moreover,
for what hero the sword was meant, though many for whom it was not
meant have since tried to pull it out in vain. The story is a compressed
version of some more scattered incidents in the Sagas, and it bears the
stamp of authentic mythological mystery and truth. If you are that hero,
ends Sieglinde, and were in my arms, all my ill-fortune would be
retrieved.

Siegmund has her in his arms at once; for she, too, is everything that he has been waiting for without knowing what it was. And of its own accord not just the little wicket door by which Siegmund and Hunding entered, but the great door swings wide open at the back. There is a blaze of moonlight. The whole forest outside is aglow with it, the hut within is brilliantly illuminated, and for the first time the two see one another clearly.

Ha, who went there? she cries. No one went, but one has come, he answers quietly: the Spring has come. Beautifully he describes it. You are the Spring, she replies; and so the radiant love scene unfolds (38, 86). They speak more and more plainly of their uncanny likeness to one another, and as their stories fit like the pieces of a jigsaw, their mutual recognition approaches certainty. He will no longer answer to his pretended name of Woefull: Joyfull is better; but she shall name him afresh. She does so, with his own name of Siegmund. As he gladly assents, he draws the sword out of the tree, naming it Nothung (Needfull); she names herself Sieglinde; and in the full and delighted knowledge that they are indeed twin brother and sister they rush out into the forest, as the curtain falls, to consummate their union.

CHAPTER VIII

The Valkyrie, Act II

———————— ❀ ————————

BRYNHILDE AS VALKYRIE
AND MORE THAN VALKYRIE

Act II opens with a ferocious overture of which the material is the second part (69) of Freia's motive, in its agitated form. In the previous Act I, this material has mainly been heard in its more lingering form as the love motive (37) of Siegmund and Sieglinde. At the end of Act I, the material became agitated, but in delight, not distress. Now, however, the sense of distress conveyed by the music's agitation is acute and unmistakable (69A). We are instantly aware that something has gone wrong since the ecstatic ending of Act I.

Another marked feature of this overture is a plunging dotted rhythm which has already been prominent in the 9–8 section of the music which carried us down into the underworld of Nibelheim between Scenes 2 and 3 of *Rhinegold*. It is as if the love of Siegmund and Sieglinde blazing out in the light above has stirred up some deep agitation down below in the unconscious; and when the lovers next appear, which is not until Scene 3 of the present Act, this supposition is confirmed. We shall find there not only that they are literally in flight, but that Sieglinde has become almost unhinged by exhaustion, guilt and remorse. We can already imagine her pressing on through the forest with Siegmund trying not very successfully to restrain her. The music gives an all too clear representation of their state of mind.

But soon the plunging dotted rhythm takes on quite a different mood. The harmony becomes full of the challenging, restless intervals of the augmented triad, while the rhythm continues almost as before. The result is one main motive (22) of the Valkyrie sisters in general, and of the Valkyrie aspect of Brynhilde in particular. The connection is not difficult to understand. Freia, Sieglinde and the Valkyries with Brynhilde at their head are temperamentally contrasted in many ways, but

144

they have it in common that they are manifestations of the eternal feminine.

The Valkyries are among the innumerable lesser representatives of that basic femininity, whose primary image is the Great Mother. But the Great Mother is both the Good Mother and the Terrible Mother. She is a creator and a destroyer; she is a force equally capable of transforming men so that they are symbolically born again, and of seducing them so that they are symbolically devoured. Only by running the gauntlet in some symbolic encounter with the Great Mother can men get free of her downward pull.

The Valkyries show both sides of this ambivalent character. The negative side of their legend is seen in their provoking men to war and slaughter, so that they can batten like vampires on the blood of corpses. In this they seem to symbolize the devouring propensities of the unconscious, which may swallow men's independence as a vampire swallowed blood. But it is also possible to be swallowed by the unconscious as Jonah was swallowed by the whale, not for destruction but for rebirth. The positive side of the Valkyrie's legend is seen in their choosing heroes slain bravely in battle for a joyful after-life in Valhalla. In that they seem to symbolize the transformation of character which may reward a sufficiently brave encounter with the mother principle.

In virtue of their characteristic energy, the Valkyries have another motive (22A–22B) which is demonically chromatic like the fire motive (20–20C) given to Loge in his elemental capacity as fire, that is to say as a symbol for libido, the burning energy of life. The Valkyries display an abundance of sheer energy both negative and positive. Anglo-Saxon glossaries equate them with the Greek Furies and other carriers of vengeance, conflict and madness. They are active as witches; but equally active as protectors of men caught in storms at sea. They habitually ride through the thunder-clouds, but they also serve rapturously as cup-bearers and wish-maidens. We have already had occasion to note that Wagner's Rhinemaidens, his Valkyries and his Norns are all members of the same family with different characteristics uppermost.[1]

For a man directly, and for a woman through him, the archetype of the anima is inextricably associated with that of the Great Mother. For a man, the magical maidens encountered by the heroes of legend

---

[1] See Jacob Grimm, *Teutonic Mythology*, tr. J. S. Stallybrass, London, Vol. I, 1882, pp. 417 ff; Erich Neumann, *The Great Mother*, tr. R. Manheim, London, 1955, p. 164, p. 232; Brian Branston, *Gods of the North*, London, 1955, p. 184, pp. 186–194.

carry mainly our projections of the anima, just as for a woman the heroes carry mainly our projections of the animus. The older characters carry more of our projections of the mother and father images. Since, however, we are all of us inwardly bisexual, we all to some extent see the characters from the point of view of the other sex as well. Thus the relationship of the images to one another and to ourselves is often very complicated. On the hero's ability gradually to sort out the other symbolical figures he meets, and to deal with them in appropriate ways, his progress depends, just as our understanding of his progress depends on our ability to sort them out in the same intuitive fashion. Wotan's relation to Brynhilde is an excellent example of this kind of development as the legend unfolds.

Wagner first shows us Brynhilde as the undeveloped Valkyrie she starts by being. Wotan briefly instructs her, in her traditional role as chooser of the slain (which can mean either choosing who is to be slain or choosing who of the slain shall join the select heroes), to give victory to Siegmund in the conflict now imminent, but on no account to admit Hunding to Valhalla. She assents in a high-spirited yodel, but points to Fricka angrily approaching, and light-heartedly leaves Wotan to engage in *this* conflict unaided, merely warning him to take good care to give himself the victory.

WOTAN AND FRICKA

Wotan views the approaching Fricka morosely enough. He has had plenty of experience of her censorious attitude to himself, and knows that her obvious agitation foreshadows trouble. Yet the music tells us of something deeper than their habitual and mutual resentment. At the very moment of her approach we hear a strangely troubled and uneasy but unmistakable version of Erda's motive (3). It is highly unexpected, but the implication can only be that we are to take Fricka, in spite of appearances, for one more aspect of that mysterious feminine wisdom deep within the psyche of which Erda herself is the most primordial image in the cast of the *Ring*.

This does not mean that Fricka's negative aspect is in any way unreal. It does mean that we must expect to find a positive aspect in addition; and so it will prove. The singer who takes her part has a nice problem here in the portrayal of character. Fricka's harshness and her intemperance must certainly be in evidence; we must be aware of the inexorably jealous woman in her; but we must also be aware of her archetypal dignity, and even of some considerable warmth of feeling. She must not merely scream and rail; she must sound fully convinced of being in the right. Little though we like her attitude, she must be able to enlist enough of our sympathy to reveal her positive side and thus to preserve the necessary dramatic balance. Fricka is a queen; Fricka is a goddess; Fricka is the image of an archetype, facing two ways like all other archetypal images.

She immediately makes any sympathy for her difficult, however, by demanding that Siegmund shall die, at Hunding's hand, in requital for two transgressions in one: the adultery and the incest. She demands this in her capacity as Wotan's consort, which Wagner interprets as making her the guardian of lawful marriage.

This is dramatically effective and mythologically acceptable even though the Sagas present her as much more of a nature goddess, not at all clearly differentiated from Freia herself, and like Freia, more interested in love and fertility than in social propriety and expediency. Even in the Sagas, Fricka displays the jealousy if not exactly the morality of a lawful consort, and Wagner has done her no violence in developing this side of her at the expense of the nature goddess in her. It is, however, important to remember that in the *Ring*, fond as Fricka is of invoking nature and natural law to reinforce her arguments, she is not strictly a representative of nature at all. She is, on her negative side, a representative of the kind of conventionality which takes itself so much for granted that it calls everything opposed to it unnatural.

Both Fricka's charges are admitted, and the argument is merely concerned with the question whether they deserve punishment, condonement or outright approval. To the charge of adultery, Wotan replies that forced oaths are unholy oaths and that love is stronger than law. He argues, thus far, on the side of nature. Fricka then turns to the incest, which shocks her, in effect, because she thinks it so unnatural. 'When was it heard of for siblings to fall in love?' she asks. Wotan so far shares in her tacit assumption that he replies: 'It has been heard of now: learn to accept what has happened of its own accord, even though it has never been seen before.' And he asks her to put her divine blessing on this unprecedented pair. But they are not an unprecedented pair; it has been seen before; and so far from being unnatural, the real social objection to incest is precisely that it could pull society back to the state of nature.

Fricka, at that, breaks out into a fury of righteous indignation. If she were really the natural matriarch she seems to want us to take her for, she would be putting love before law; but her argument suggests much more the very type of womanhood so long reconciled to patriarchy as to mistake it for the natural order of things. Our civilized rejection of incest is not an instinct, though it has had to acquire the force and appearance of one in order to overcome our aboriginal desire for incest, which does derive from instinct however resolutely repressed. Fricka is therefore voicing the basic patriarchal argument when she goes on to warn Wotan that to condone the incest is to undermine the entire civilized structure of law and order which he himself in his strength and wisdom has built up. On the social level, that is all true enough. Unfortunately she now rather spoils the dignity of her case by bringing up all Wotan's personal infidelities to herself. She gives vent to an accumulation of jealousy which unlike her basic argument strikes us immediately as nature in the raw.

Wotan takes both argument and jealousy with quiet patience. He is used to the jealousy and has never yet let it incommode him; he has, or thinks he has, an answer to the argument. He replies that she cannot see beyond the existing law and precedent, but that he has to take into account the possibility of change. This is true not only on the social level but on the deepest levels which symbolism can touch, as Wagner himself was partially aware.

In his celebrated letter to Roeckel of 25 January 1854, Wagner wrote: 'Alberich and his ring could do no harm to the gods if they were not already ripe for evil. Where, then, is the root of this evil? Look at the first scene between Wotan and Fricka which leads on into Act II of the *Valkyrie*. The strong chain which binds these two, forged from love's instinctive error in wanting to prolong itself when change has become inevitable, in seeking mutual guarantees against the law of eternal transformation and renewal in the world of phenomena, compels both of them to a reciprocal torment of lovelessness. Thus the whole unfolding of the drama illustrates the need to recognize and accept the diversity, the perpetual changing, the eternal renewals of reality and of life.'

There are echoes here of Wagner's own bondage to his first wife Minna, long after their love had largely succumbed to reciprocal misunderstanding and hurtfulness. But what bound them was not that she deliberately clung to him; she made several abortive efforts herself to effect a parting. What bound them was that their mutual projections meshed together in the usual manner of more or less neurotic relationships. If one of them clung more than the other, it was quite possibly Wagner. Hidden deep beneath the marital bond on his side lay a more elemental and formidable bond: the unconscious mother-bond (on her side the father-bond). Wagner's intuitions waged a perennial combat against his mother-boundness, and against the entire network of unconscious assumptions and inner compromises which defined his life's problem but also his life's opportunity. It is just such assumptions and compromises as these which are symbolized by Wotan's entangling bargains.

In speaking of 'the law of eternal transformation and renewal' Wagner was not only describing the outer 'world of phenomena' to which he consciously attributed it, but the inner world of which he had an intuitive rather than a rational awareness. It was his own inmost need to obey that law. But it is not within the direct power of the ego to bring about transformation and renewal; the most that the ego can do is to open itself to the process. We all find that hard enough, and Wotan is no exception. But in so far as we can do it, we open the way to the next stage. That is the extent of ego's contribution; but it is a crucial contribution, and may make all the difference between a developing life and a life that has somehow got stuck half-way through.

Wotan in his role as ego has learnt by now that he can do nothing of his own accord to cut through his entangling bargains. The climax of his answer to Fricka is that the gods need the help of a hero who has neither wish nor instructions to help them and does not even know that he is helping them, but who will nevertheless do what they need simply in pursuit of his own heroic destiny.

No wonder Wotan thinks this argument is conclusive. He has been quietly working it out ever since that moment of premonition at the end of *Rhinegold* when the music told us of his great thought, but he was not yet ready to put it into words. Now at last he has done so, for Fricka's benefit and ours. In the next scene, he is going to amplify this same information in confiding the depth of his troubles to Brynhilde; and when, in that scene, he sings the key-phrase 'only one is able', the motive to which he does so is motive (5). This motive is, note for note, a combination of Erda's quietly impressive motive (3) and the restlessly urgent motive (70) known as Wotan's Will Frustrated.

The 'one who is able' to help the gods out of their present impossible position is the free hero of Wotan's thought, and it is Wotan's belief that this free hero has now come into action in the person of Siegmund. Motive (5) makes two profound comments on this belief. The first is to the effect that the thought itself comes from the part of the psyche symbolized by Erda's wisdom, and is therefore right. The second is to the effect that Wotan's conscious will to power is still very much caught up in the thought, and may well bring it to frustration; for the motive (70) of Wotan's frustration is in its turn a contorted version of his powerful spear motive (73), and is thus intimately connected with his obsessive assertion of ego's wilful authority.

Fricka goes straight to this one grave flaw in Wotan's argument. She simply points out that so far from being a free hero, Siegmund is no more than Wotan acting vicariously. Wotan protests than he has not helped or sheltered Siegmund. Fricka replies: 'Then do not help him now; take back the sword.'

Wotan's reaction to this deadly thrust is immediate and conclusive. He is shaken to the core. His answer to Fricka has proved to be no answer; for she has made him see in that one terrible instant that Siegmund is no more a free agent than he is himself. Because Wotan created Siegmund for the purpose of setting Wotan free, Siegmund can do nothing to set Wotan free. Siegmund's courage is the courage that Wotan breathed into him. Siegmund's sword is the sword that Wotan left ready for him. Siegmund is Wotan himself at one remove.

But in bringing this to Wotan's knowledge, Fricka stands for something more than a mere nagging wife. She stands for something more even than the super-ego with its rigid conscientiousness and its cruel moralism and its guilt-ridden resistance to change and freedom in themselves. She stands for a part of Wotan's inner femininity which knows better than he does himself what, after all, he needs to know, since it is profoundly true and important to him. We can see now why when first she arrived on the scene we heard that wry but recognizable version of Erda's motive (3). Like Erda herself, Fricka has her roots in the eternal feminine.

In the long run, Wotan and the ego stand to gain from being thus painfully forced out of their entrenched positions. Here and now, we acutely sympathize with his distress, brought out in the music by ceaseless convolutions of the motive (70) of Wotan's Will Frustrated. He agrees dejectedly to let Siegmund die, and confirms it with an oath. Fricka departs to the grim sound of the motive (13) of Alberich's curse, now palpably working itself out on Wotan. The gloom is deepened by the singularly depressed tonality of E flat minor.

THE SACRIFICIAL SIGNIFICANCE
OF SIEGMUND'S DEATH

Yet why does Siegmund have to die? Why should it not be sufficient for Wotan to admit the failure of his plan to push his responsibilities off on to Siegmund, while still leaving him with the sword intact to fend for himself? Indeed, since Fricka has convinced Wotan that the real responsibility remains his own, why should he not accept it in full and protect his agent Siegmund?

Part of the answer is that ultimately Siegmund does not exist except as an aspect of Wotan. This aspect consists in his attempt, as yet over-conscious, to call up in himself the autonomous archetype of the free hero. The attempt dies when this fatal weakness is exposed; and Siegmund, as its symbol, dies with it. Hunding, representing here not so much Siegmund's shadow as the shadow principle within the psyche of which the *Ring* is a composite portrait, has to be allowed to kill Siegmund in order to symbolize his re-absorption into the unconscious from which he was first evoked by Wotan's intuitive longing to abdicate some at least of his ego authority.

A further part of the answer is that, being symbolic, this is pre-eminently a death of transformation. The aspect of the psyche for which Siegmund stands is to be reborn in the person of Siegfried. The first attempt by the ego to submit itself to the hero archetype is to go down in apparent defeat only to reappear more effectively at the second attempt.

We pick up subliminal associations here from the great mythological theme of the saviour god who has to be sacrificed in order to be reborn. Hunding's roof-tree has already brought up a hint of Yggdrasil, the world ash-tree or tree of life, on which Wotan once hung himself in search of wisdom and renewal. To hang on a tree or a cross has symbolically the significance of returning to the Great Mother in search of rebirth. It implies sacrificing the masculine assertiveness of the conscious ego; it implies enduring the torment of transformation; it implies going down into the feminine submissiveness which lets the autonomous psyche do its work of transformation; it implies yielding to the unconscious not in order to be swallowed up in the illusion of blissful irresponsibility, but in order to emerge more conscious and responsible and masculine than before.

Wotan wounding himself with his own spear and hanging himself for nine days and nights on the Tree of Life is an image related to the Christian crucifixion. Wotan descending into the dark underworld of Nibelheim is an image related to Christ's descent into Hell. But it is one of the great doctrinal revelations of Christianity that God the Father gave not himself but his son to be crucified and to descend into hell. This implies a discrimination between the principle of the patriarchal spirit of consciousness itself and its incarnation in a human being. It is the human incarnating that spirit who has to suffer torment as the sacrificial saviour.

Pagan though Wagner's rational attitude was at the time of the *Valkyrie*, he was like the rest of us irrationally influenced to his own immeasurable advantage by the Christian tradition. It may have been this underlying Christian influence which led him to shape his plot in such a way that Wotan in the role of father has to sacrifice Siegmund in the role of son. We have already seen how closely Wagner identified one part of himself with Siegmund, and how close the connection was between Siegmund's sufferings as a driven man, kept apart from his fellows by his own heroic turbulence, and Wagner's sufferings of the same kind and from the same cause. There is a very real and important sense in which a man such as Wagner, driven to the verge of distraction by a temperament indissolubly compounded of turbulence and creativeness, is actually in the position of a saviour god destined to be sacrificed for the benefit of mankind.

Throughout the poignant opening, the radiant climax and the tragic continuation of Siegmund's and Sieglinde's story, we are on their side, not only because of the tender truth and beauty with which Wagner has clothed this story, but also because its mythological implications are true. The human union is deeply moving; the symbolism of the sacred marriage, with its theme of reconciliation within the psyche, is deeply convincing. Wagner's own longing for such a reconciliation of himself with himself was so intense that it sometimes broke into open realization, as when he wrote to Mathilde Wesendonk (18 Sept. 1858): 'I had been distressingly but more or less decidedly disengaging myself from the world; everything in me had turned to negation and rejection. Even my artistic creativeness was distressing to me; for it was longing with an insatiable longing to replace that negation, that rejection, by something affirmative and positive, the marriage of myself to myself' (Sich-mir-vermählende). Seeing himself as Siegmund and Mathilde as Sieglinde while he was composing the *Valkyrie*[1] did not lessen Wagner's intuition that Sieglinde (and Mathilde) also symbolized something of his own inner femininity, i.e. of his anima, and indeed of the archetypal anima. The sacred marriage is a union of opposites seen as the masculine and feminine principles: just such a union as Wagner longed for inwardly.

But the death of the partners as a preliminary to rebirth is a traditional element in the imagery of the sacred marriage, as we shall see still more

[1] Cf. Ernest Newman, *Life of Richard Wagner*, London, Vol. II, 1937, p. 485.

clearly later on in connection with Siegfried and Brynhilde. Thus the death of Siegmund, and of Sieglinde after the birth of Siegfried, also carries conviction to our intuitive sense of what is right and fitting. It is mythologically, which is to say symbolically, intelligible.

That this image of the sacrificial god superimposed by Wagner on the incest symbolism, and not the incest itself, is the fundamental explanation of Siegmund's death may perhaps be confirmed by a comparison with Wagner's chief source for the events of the *Valkyrie*, which is the Volsunga Saga.[1] Sigmund was not there a son, though he was a descendant, of Wotan. Sigmund's incest with his sister Signy was not punished. Only after a long lifetime of heroic accomplishment was Sigmund's sword, which he had pulled as a young man from the roof-tree where Odin had thrust it for him, broken in battle by Odin. Sigmund then accepted the omen, refused to have his wounds dressed, and died that night on the battlefield in the arms of his lawful wife, who was pregnant at the time with their future son Siegfried.

The Nordic bards and their audiences, though well enough disposed towards sexual escapades which did not involve breaches of the kinship system, were hostile to those that did, when human beings were in question. The Poetic Edda even treats the mating of human first-cousins as incestuous enough to be self-evidently wrongful. But with regard to mythological beings we find in the Sagas the same robust and somewhat humorous attitude towards incest which is usual in other mythological traditions. It is in this tolerant and half-admiring spirit that the Poetic Edda describes the god Frey (Froh) as the son of an own brother and sister, and none the worse for that; while Frey in his turn had intercourse with his sister Freya (Freia), who is herself in some versions both wife and sister of Odin (Wotan).[2] Since Wagner has incorporated in his version of Wotan's consort Fricka some of the characteristics of the Greek goddess of wedlock Hera, with her somewhat puritanical fidelity (which the original Norse Fricka partly shared), it may also be worth recalling that Hera, for all her fine airs, was herself the sister as well as the wife of Zeus (their father was Cronos).

Thus the gods are never in a very strong position to take exception

---

[1] *The Volsunga Saga*, tr. E. Magnusson and Wm. Morris, London, n.d., esp. pp. 17–18.

[2] *The Elder or Poetic Edda*, tr. Olive Bray, London, 1908, p. 291, p. 259, p. 257; Brian Branston, *Gods of the North*, London, 1955, p. 291. E. Tonnelat, in Larousse *Encyclopaedia of Mythology*, tr. R. Aldington and D. Ames, London, 1959, p. 275, interestingly conjectures that Froh may originally have had a single hermaphrodite parent.

to incest. Indeed, even allowing for the modifications of character introduced by Wagner, we can hardly imagine his Wotan, who is still a wandering adventurer of a god, allowing himself to be nagged into restoring the matrimonial honour of a consort not much less matrimonially disreputable than himself, at least in the originals, by condemning Siegmund to death on grounds either of adultery, socially unsettling as this may be on the human plane, or of incest, potentially dangerous as that may be on the human plane. Nor can we believe, in view of Wotan's habitual behaviour even as presented by Wagner, that such respect as the world may have for his authority can really depend on his own respect for law and order as exemplified at all literally by the enforcing of matrimonial conventionality. Yet symbolically it is true enough that ego's comforting illusion of being in full command depends on suppressing any disturbing tendency to yield the autonomous psyche a greater freedom of action.

We can view the incest of Siegmund with Sieglinde, followed as it is by the death of both of them but also by the birth of Siegfried, as a regenerative descent to the Great Mother, as a sacred marriage, as a ritual sacrifice; the theme common to all these images is the theme of rebirth which made itself felt at the beginning of the *Ring* and will continue to do so to the end of it. Whatever the images by which it is evoked, this theme is bound to call up some intuitive response in us, because in one shape or another the experience to which it relates comes into any ordinary life-story. We are filled with grief when we hear Siegmund condemned to die, but there is never any likelihood of his death striking us as meaningless. This terrible scene in which we hear his death sentence is at bottom dramatically convincing because it is symbolically convincing. The theme itself is meaningful.

WOTAN CONFIDES IN BRYNHILDE

As Fricka departs, Brynhilde returns, the tonality of the music slipping gratefully from E flat minor to D major to welcome her back. She sees at once that Wotan has had to yield the victory to Fricka. His outburst of despair torments her. At first he will not even share his distress with her; but she soon persuades him that since she is really a part of himself, standing for his own true will, to give her his secrets is no more than giving them to himself. He then confides to her, and thus incidentally to us, that he is now in despair of ever getting free from the entanglements he has accumulated around himself. When the delight of young love faded for him, he became ambitious for power. He won it, but by wiles and bargains whose increasingly deceitful quality he hardly noticed at the time. His excuse is that Loge lured him on by lies, and then left him in his difficulties. But there speaks the Loge in Wotan, and in Wagner. It is quite typical of an ambitious ego to push and bully and get its own way without noticing how unscrupulous and dishonest its methods are becoming, and even when it does notice, to put the blame elsewhere.

The fading of the delight of young love can only mean the fading of the naïve illusion that falling in love is the blissful solution to every problem, instead of being, as it is, a new problem in itself. Love and the delight of love are enduring values, but the conscious and unconscious fantasies we weave round love in early youth have many elements which ought not to endure, and indeed the most callow of them seldom do. They did not in the case of Wagner; and because the hopes he pinned on them were exceptionally optimistic, particularly on the unconscious plane, he felt correspondingly disappointed, and made Wotan feel the same.

We have noticed already certain passages in Wagner's letters where he complains that true love has never come to him, although he certainly thought that it had, as we know, at the time, on a considerable number of different occasions. Here is a passage particularly relevant to the present scene: 'Not a year of my life has passed by of late without at least once bringing me to the brink of a decision to end my life. Everything in it seems so lost and gone wrong. An over-hasty marriage to a worthy woman, but quite unsuitable for me, has made me an outcast for life. For a long time the normal pressure of circumstances and my ambitious plans and desire to relieve that pressure by becoming famous enabled me to hide from myself the true emptiness of my heart. The fact is that I arrived at my thirty-sixth year before I fully realized that fearful emptiness of heart' (letter to Liszt, 15 Jan. 1854). That is a very near equivalent to the position in which Wagner has placed his Wotan here; and in view of this more than usually open element of autobiography, we can understand why Wagner once described this as 'the most important scene in the whole tetralogy' (letter to Liszt, 3 Oct. 1855).

Even when love's young dream had faded, Wotan continues, he still could not bring himself to give up love as the price of wordly power; it remained for Alberich to take that fearful step. Again we cannot altogether avoid the feeling that, in the sense already suggested in Chapter III, it was the Alberich in Wotan and in Wagner who is really being described. It is abundantly clear in Wagner's life-story how compulsively he was driven to live out the sides of his own character symbolized by

Loge and by Alberich. If ever there was a man compelled to live his shadow outwardly as the cost exacted for living his genius inwardly, that man was Wagner.

Next Wotan tells us how he stole the ring from Alberich, which in this condensed narration strikes us still more forcibly than it did at the time as tantamount to having let Alberich renounce love and steal the gold originally, only to take advantage of these dark deeds on his own account. But now he recounts how, at Erda's urgent bidding, he passed the ring on to the giants as the payment for Valhalla, where he could feel secure in his authority for a time. Her warning, however, that the end of the gods was coming so disturbed him that he subsequently sought her out in the depths of the earth, thus taking counsel with his own unconscious wisdom. In token of the value he set on her, he gave her his love, and she rewarded him by bearing him Brynhilde and her eight Valkyrie sisters, who have since gathered many dead heroes from the battlefield to reinforce the gods' defenders. It is possible that these dead heroes have to do with the genuinely courageous achievements of the ego in the ordinary give and take of life, which must leave some residue in the character to strengthen it. The undistinguished dead are not carried up into Valhalla, but linger rather nebulously in Hella, as if they stood for more neutral experiences which leave less mark.

The only real danger (but it is a serious one) which Wotan foresees to his authority will arise if Alberich succeeds in his unremitting ambition to get back the ring, in which case he will use it to summon up Hella's dead against the gods and even to suborn the very heroes who defend the gods, thus gaining the mastery of the world: here as elsewhere a symbol for mastery of the psyche. Because he still has the strength which he gained by forswearing love, Alberich can use the ring, if he gets it back, to usurp the authority of the ego; and this would be unquestionably a psychic disaster. At the best of times, the ego is all too prone to do unconsciously what the shadow prompts. To combat that, we need more conscious responsibility, not less; but the paradox is that we can only get it by yielding some of the ego's authority. In the long run, we can only prevent the shadow from encroaching on the ego's authority by allowing the self to do so in its own autonomous way.

Wotan assures us that only his bargains prevent him from seizing the ring back from the giant Fafner. We have already given some thought to these bargains in their aspect as the unconscious compromises with life by which we inhibit some of our potentialities in order to gain the confidence to let others develop. Wotan feels that he could not possibly attack the parent-image for which Fafner stands, because to do so would fill him not so much with fear as with guilt. But this is another of those forbidden acts which, fairy-tale fashion, above all things need to be done, as Wotan himself now knows. Not by Alberich, which would be a calamity; not by the conscious ego, which is too inhibited; but by the autonomous archetype of the free hero who may be called up in us by our need if it is great enough and if we can yield to it acceptingly enough.

The plan, therefore, which Wotan has already outlined to Fricka, and which he now explains more fully to Brynhilde, depending as it does on the aid of just such a free hero, is fundamentally the soundest on which he could have hit, and indeed the only one which can bring any lasting improvement in the situation. Unfortunately for what is left of Wotan's pride and ambition in the role of ego, its success hangs on his sacrificing still more of his own wilful authority. Sacrifice implies giving up voluntarily what was once a true value but in course of being outgrown has become a hampering burden. It is hard for ego to believe that. We need feel no surprise that there remained something half-hearted in Wotan's first attempt at abdication nor that it took Fricka's shrewdly hostile eye to detect the fact. Siegmund cannot quite function as an autonomous archetype. He is not fully independent of Wotan nor of Wotan's support. He is not fearless, nor is he unaware of his fear; he is brave, which is more human and harder. He is not innocent of convention; he defies it in the full expectation of having to fight his way out of the social consequences, though with his father's sword in his hand he is fully confident of doing so. But that is the trouble: it is his father's sword.

Wotan finally relates a further prophecy of Erda's, that when Alberich has a child by a woman not loved but bought by gold, the end of the gods is near. This child, now born, is Hagen. The birth of a child symbolizes the beginning of a new stage. The implication seems to be that this new stage, of which the psyche as a whole is in need, can only start in the shadow, where the conscious ego is least able to interfere. If the ego knew too much about the new start, its own fears and guilt and sheer reluctance to change might prove too much of an obstacle.

Hagen is the shadow counterpart to Siegfried, who though already conceived is not yet born. The relation between these two will be crucial to the events in *Götterdämmerung*, where we shall find Hagen making much the same ambivalent contribution that Alberich has made in *Rhinegold*. As Erda truly foretells, the outcome will be the end of the gods, in the very radical sense that command of the situation will pass from the control of the ego to the control of the self. The symbolism under which this happens is much more complicated, however, than the mere destruction of the existing order, and neither Wotan nor we must expect to understand the full significance of Erda's oracular utterances at the present stage. It is quite obvious that she does not herself. No oracle does, since the intuitive premonitions which it conveys only gain substance from the course of events.

In wrathful irony, Wotan utters his blessing on Alberich's son: an odd touch, which does just raise the question whether the blessing came from a deeper level in Wotan than the irony. He tells Brynhilde to give the victory to Hunding. She protests incredulously; and he breaks out into violent anger with her, to which she sadly yields. He storms off, and after briefly expressing her own misery at the turn events have taken, she also leaves the stage.

THE END OF SIEGMUND

The music takes up the agitated form of the motive (37) of Siegmund's and Sieglinde's love, which is also the second half of Freia's motive. Sieglinde enters in flight, with Siegmund behind her. He urges her to rest; she cries 'further, further!' He restrains her, but soon she breaks out again into terrified self-reproach, telling him to leave her tainted and unholy presence. Her joy in his arms, she sings wildly, had been a hallowed joy, with no thought but of him and her love for him; then had come the memory of Hunding and his unwanted embraces, and with that a torment of guilty remorse at having brought shame and ruin on her own brother and rescuer. Siegmund answers that it was Hunding who brought shame on her and shall pay for it when Nothung bites into his heart; but she quite loses her senses in a prophetic vision of terror. She cries out madly for Siegmund, unable to see him standing there; she can see only the forms of foemen and hounds; now she seems to glimpse him torn by the dogs; his sword splinters; the world ash-tree splinters too; she cries out 'Siegmund' and falls fainting into his arms. He sits, holding her head on his knees, where she remains in a deathly trance through the scene which follows.

If Siegmund is in essence a part of Wotan, Sieglinde, Siegmund's twin sister, must be a part of Wotan too; and this terrifying access of fear and guilt must stand for feelings which Wotan would be experiencing in person if he were able to let them up into consciousness. He would not be entertaining such feelings even unconsciously if his break with the sterile past, as represented in his entangling bargains, were really as abortive as his failure to set Siegmund free would appear to suggest. The truth seems to be that Wotan, and nobody but Wotan, has achieved a very bold defiance against everything that holds him back; he has succeeded to a far greater extent than he realizes; he has set something going which of its own momentum will take him farther than he can foresee. Although he does not yet grasp it, he is already well into that crucial transformation of character which is the underlying topic of the *Ring*. He is now in the throes of the inevitable reaction which is part of the distress accompanying all such transformations. He is racked by conflict over the fate of Siegmund, and knows it. He is assailed by fear and guilt, but has repressed his knowledge of that, so that they have to be expressed for him under the image of Sieglinde. As elsewhere, the dramatic effectiveness of this terrifying scene is reinforced by our intuitive sense of its symbolic truth.

As Siegmund gazes tenderly down at Sieglinde, out of their love motive (37) there blossoms one of the simplest yet most meaningful of motives: motive (84), in which is heard, quietly but inexorably, the very image of that power of destiny to which all men in the end must yield. With this, Brynhilde returns, directing on Siegmund a gaze of the deepest compassion. A further motive (83) is heard, longer than (84), but in the same mood, and ending with a phrase which actually is (84), so that the two motives, though used separately, are as intimately related to one another as they could possibly be. Motive (83) begins with the first four notes (all but the first inverted) of the 'renunciation' motive (76), whose deeper meaning we saw reason to take as the acceptance of destiny. Motive (83) is commonly known as the motive of Fate, and motive (84) as the Annunciation of Death: both good descriptions; but as with so many of the motives in which grief is an element, such as (76), (79) or (81), there is so profound an admixture of nobility that the grief itself is somehow transcended.

The force of the grief is not diminished by this; the nobility does not cancel it out; the two are fused into an emotion for which either grief or nobility alone would be an inadequate term. It has certainly to do with our awareness of mortality. It is an emotion which goes very deep into our hearts, with a suggestion of finality such as the acceptance of our mortal destiny must necessarily bring. But because the emotion is accepted, it reaches somehow beyond strife and torment, and carries a hint, not precisely of comfort, not precisely of resignation, but of ultimate reality. Mortals we are, and life is never so full of meaning as when we are able to hold on to our awareness of that fact, and of life's worth and beauty, in one deep act of acceptance.

Brynhilde quietly tells Siegmund that only men about to die set eyes on her, and welcomes him to the delights of Valhalla. He is at first incredulous, for he has his promised sword, and is not afraid of Hunding; next, when he learns that he must die indeed and that Sieglinde will not be with him, but only celestial wish-maidens, with an impressive gesture of maturity he refuses so infantile a compensation. His anguish at the thought of failing Sieglinde, his scornful rejection of Valhalla as a consolation, and his threat to kill Sieglinde outright, newly conceived baby and all, rather than leave her to anyone else's protection, so work on Brynhilde's susceptibilities that she decides on immediate rebellion against Wotan's decision, and tells Siegmund that after all he shall not die, for she will be at his side, and on his side. But as he hears the horns of Hunding's men and hastens away joyfully to the conflict, Sieglinde wakes from a nightmare about her traumatic experience when her mother was killed and she was raped away. From the front of the stage, she sees in helpless terror what now follows.

The night has grown dark with sudden thunder. A flash of lightning shows Hunding and Siegmund fighting on a rocky crag at the back. A longer, brighter flash, in which Brynhilde is seen protecting Siegmund with her shield. A great glare of red light between the combatants, and Wotan's spear intercepts a deadly stroke from Siegmund's sword, which splinters. Hunding kills the now defenceless Siegmund, but himself falls lifeless from a mere contemptuous wave of Wotan's hand. Sieglinde again faints when Siegmund is killed, but is carried away by Brynhilde on her horse together with the fragments of Siegmund's sword. Wotan's anger turns suddenly against Brynhilde, and he sets off in pursuit of her.

The stagecraft of all this is obviously tricky in the extreme, but succeeds admirably provided it is accurately timed to Wagner's music, in which every event is reflected with not a bar's margin to spare. It is extraordinarily moving, and in spite of the fact that it is all over so quickly, gives us the impression of being one of the great turning-points in the drama. Everything has been working up to it, but this is the moment of truth in which decisions become irrevocable. Siegmund is dead, so is Hunding, and there is no recalling them. Wotan might have decided otherwise; he might even have made a last-minute change of decision; but now he has acted, and is committed to the consequences.

THE CONSEQUENCES OF SIEGMUND'S DEATH

We have found a number of reasons why Siegmund was allowed to die; but it was Wotan who took the decision; and it is Wotan who has got to take the consequences. In the immediate future, these are not going to be at all pleasant for him, nor are his reactions to them going to be very pleasant to watch.

In so far as Siegmund stands for a part of Wotan which once was valuable but is now due to be outgrown, his death is a sacrifice which Wotan had to make. This aspect of Siegmund is the aspect which we noticed all along was too much an extension of Wotan himself quite to grow up as an independent personality. It was this aspect which the music suggested by the resemblance between Siegmund's motive (35) and the motive (73) of Wotan's spear, that is to say of Wotan's wilful authority in his role as conscious ego. Painful though the necessity is, this part of Wotan has got to die in order that the new part of his character can be free to go on growing. On this side, the sacrifice is positive, and represents a necessary death of transformation.

But that is not the only part of Wotan for which Siegmund stands: indeed he is a very complex symbol. On the one side, certainly, Siegmund stands for Wotan clinging to his wilful authority in a way that is ripe to end. But on the other side, Siegmund stands for Wotan trying his best to make over some of his authority to the autonomous psyche and the underlying purposes of the self. In so far as Siegmund is at least a first attempt at a free hero, Wotan's decision to let him die is a decision to give up that attempt. This amounts to a negative sacrifice of the forward impulse, in favour of the inhibitions represented by Wotan's bargains, and by Fricka in her adverse role as super-ego.

This will all sound considerably less complicated if we realize that what we are really talking about is a state of mind. There are bound to be some conflicting elements in any state of mind. Wotan half wants to go forward with his great scheme of abdication, and half wants to go back. Siegmund's symbolism has to do with Wotan's attitude both in the forward-going and the backward-going elements of it. Wotan has now realized, thanks to Fricka in her useful role as candid friend, that his attitude is too full of self-contradictions to see him through. He gives it up; and there are good and bad results of that. He will reap the good in the long run, but he will pay for the bad here and now. Things, as so often, will have to get worse before they can get better.

When Brynhilde told Siegmund that only those about to die set eyes on her, she was appearing in her most archetypal aspect. We all catch glimpses of archetypal reality in a great variety of more or less vivid images; but it is very seldom that we encounter an image which carries so powerful an archetypal charge as this vision which Siegmund had of Brynhilde. It is the nearest we can come to a direct vision of the archetype itself, and it is a tremendous experience to have. It speaks volumes for Siegmund's courage that he met it so fearlessly. It was a vision of the anima, and one of such exceptional intensity that it could only point to the imminence of a far-reaching inner transformation. This is the positive meaning of the Valkyrie's warning that only those about to die set eyes on her; for it is at the same time a promise. Those whom the Valkyrie summons do not merely drift vaguely down to the lower regions of Hella, into a dim misery of unconsciousness; they are brought up to Valhalla, where they will drink the mead of the gods and share in their higher level of consciousness.

But Siegmund would have none of it, since Sieglinde could not come with him. This may mean that he was not at a stage to experience the archetype of the anima in so numinous and collective an image as the great Valkyrie, to the exclusion of the nearer and more personal image of his own anima as he had so recently encountered her in his sister-bride. Like Wagner and most of us, Siegmund longed for and he needed a human carrier for his anima even more than he needed a divine carrier for the anima. This immediately called out the human side as opposed to the divine side in Brynhilde. She promised her help, but was unable to make it effective because of Wotan's decision.

On the unfavourable view, Wotan's decision can be seen as the over-violent reaction of a man who cannot for the life of him see what to do next, and who pushes the whole problem out of sight and out of mind by suppressing the promising possibilities and the unpromising possibilities of the situation in one harsh spasm of repudiation. He suppresses not only Siegmund but Hunding too; he would have suppressed Sieglinde if he had caught her, and we shall next see his attempt to suppress Brynhilde.

But all this is only on the unfavourable view. On the favourable view, all three deaths (Siegmund's and Hunding's already, Sieglinde's subsequently) are transforming deaths, so that what was lost in Siegmund returns in Siegfried, what was lost in Hunding returns in Hagen, and what was lost in Sieglinde returns in Brynhilde. As to what next happens to Brynhilde, and indeed to Wotan, we shall have more to go on in the following Act III.

CHAPTER IX

The Valkyrie, Act III

—————— ❊ ——————

THE VALKYRIE SISTERHOOD
AND THE RESCUE OF SIEGLINDE

Act III opens in prodigious excitement. The chief motive (47) of the Valkyries dominates the music, supported by figuration very close to some of Loge's fire music, e.g. (20C), and conveying a similar impression of demonic energy. The curtain goes up on a rocky, cloud-wracked mountain-top, where four of the Valkyries are standing in full armour. They break into imperious song to their further motive (22), of which the harmonic basis is the chromatically augmented triad; the orchestra intermittently writhes and slithers with sixth-three chords descending chromatically by semitones as at (22B), again related to the fire music as at (20B). We are into the famous Ride of the Valkyries.

The closeness of the Valkyries' music to Loge's fire music points to that aspect of these redoubtable war-maidens in which they stand for the sheer irresistible energy of life. In this aspect, they are libido symbols; but just as the libido shows very different characteristics according to the different channels through which it may flow, so its symbols, besides being extremely various in themselves, have a way of showing up differently in different lights. While the Valkyries are in their present mood, they touch on everything that is most potent and inexorable about the force of life. If we in the audience can catch this exuberant mood of theirs, and if the performance is a good one, we shall find the Ride of the Valkyries an exhilarating experience. If we feel resistant to its crude impetuosity, we shall dislike it however well it is being performed. A good performance will bring out its wild grandeur; a bad performance will make it seem a little vulgar; but the plain fact is that this is not tasteful music. The raw force of life itself is not in very good taste, and it is only in our more retiring moods that we either expect or want it to be so.

We must not forget, however, that the Valkyries are all sisters, including Brynhilde. It is part of Brynhilde's symbolism that she stands for something in Wotan. This something, as both she and Wotan have explained to us in Act II, is 'Wotan's will'. This does not, however, mean the conscious will by which he tries to impose the wilful authority of the ego; it means the will of which he is largely unconscious, but which holds more of his true desires than his conscious will. It was Brynhilde who insisted that Wotan really desired to save Siegmund, in spite of his furious insistence on the contrary course of action.

This wants a little sorting out. How can the same man have two wills at the same time? Is one of them merely a mistake, and no true will of his at all? Not so: it is perfectly possible to want contradictory things. But suppose that the ego is set on a certain course which is at variance with the true interests of the personality, because the time has come for it to develop beyond the present reach of ego's vision. Then it is the unconscious which must stand up for those true interests. For a man, it is his inner femininity which will play the mediating role (for a woman, her inner masculinity). Brynhilde is a representative of Wotan's inner femininity: his anima. In turning furiously against Brynhilde, Wotan has turned furiously against his anima, with whom he was already on bad terms in her guise as Fricka, and on uncertain terms in her guise as Erda.

The other eight Valkyries, as Brynhilde's sisters, are further representatives of Wotan's anima. Their present state of mind is therefore an indication of the state of mind in which Wotan is, not so much consciously as unconsciously. This indication is not altogether reassuring. There can be no possible objection to the Ride of the Valkyries on the grounds that it is not tasteful music: in that respect, it is true to the facts of life, and whether we like it or not is of no particular relevance to anyone but ourselves. There is, however, another element in the music which is relevant to the entire situation. This is a certain hysteria which is partly concealed by the genuine robustness of the music, but which is more and more borne in on us as the scene proceeds.

When we are being more than usually blind and stubborn with regard to our own inner promptings, the vast power of life, which is in no way reduced by our reluctance to let it flow freely through us, is apt to manifest itself in a harsh and potentially destructive fashion. Wotan at the moment is in a blind and stubborn mood of anger against Brynhilde. He is, in fact, estranged from his inner femininity to an extent which suggests pronounced schizoid tendencies, now operating to cut his ego off from his anima. There is considerable evidence that schizophrenia, which is one prominent pole in psychotic disturbance, has an unseen connection with hysteria, as an opposite but complementary pole; if one is visible, the other can probably be postulated, even if only in latent form.

Neither Wagner nor Wotan developed a psychosis. But there are psychotic dispositions, however slight, in every character; and, as his life-long conduct shows, they were by no means slight in Wagner. He often felt persecuted in the irrational way which we associate with paranoia, itself a schizoid symptom. Symptoms of hysterical tendency can also be pointed out. Since it was always Wagner's healing instinct to work out his deepest problems through his work, and since we have already seen how much of himself he poured into Wotan, we may accept the suggestion of the plot and the music here that Wotan has fallen into a temporary condition which is both schizoid and hysterical.

The element of hysteria is represented by these somewhat over-excitable young horsewomen, whose elation, intoxicating as it is, leaves us ever so slightly uneasy, as if we were witnessing the compulsive gaiety of a group of manic-depressives in their manic phase, which may at any moment swing over into the compensating depression. They sing to us about the dead heroes they have been collecting across their saddles. Four more of them arrive, leaving only Brynhilde, who soon follows, bringing no hero, but the almost lifeless form of Sieglinde. Brynhilde is in an agitation of fear, not elation. She asks her sisters to shield her from Wotan's wrathful pursuit. They collapse at once into impotent wailings: they will not even lend her a fresh horse. We have not had to wait long for the depressive phase to set in.

Sieglinde summons the strength to sing, but only of her desire to die in hope of rejoining her Siegmund. Brynhilde tells her that a still greater hero is to be born from Siegmund's seed within her, while the music floods with sudden ecstasy. Sieglinde responds immediately to the glorious challenge, and demands to be rescued. Since none of the Valkyrie sisterhood will provide a fresh horse, Sieglinde must escape alone and on foot, while Brynhilde stays to intercept Wotan's anger; and already the storm is to be seen and heard which heralds his approach. But to which direction can Sieglinde fly for safety?

The Valkyries answer this: to the East, where tangled forests spread and Fafner has hidden himself in dragon form to guard his treasure. Inhospitable territory; but Wotan shuns it.

The East is the quarter in which the sun rises, and is indelibly associated with the world-wide imagery of solar myths, of which the framework is astronomical, diurnal and seasonal, but the symbolism concerns rebirth. At each day's end the sun plunges into the circumambulent sea, to be swallowed, consumed, destroyed by the Great Mother. At each day's dawn, he is born again, as whole as ever he was, and in fresh radiance and vitality. His journey is the model for the famous 'night journey under the sea' undertaken by so many mythological heroes in their adventurous search for transformation.[1] The East is an appropriate direction for Sieglinde to take with her child-to-be.

Bynhilde tells her again of this child, who is to become the noblest hero in the world; and we hear the most heroic of Siegfried's motives, motive (78). She presses the fragments of Siegmund's sword into Sieglinde's hands, foretelling that they shall be newly forged; and she names Siegfried. Sieglinde is filled with an exalted rapture, to a motive (91) which makes comparatively few appearances in the *Ring*, but which always carries the highest significance when it does appear, and which has also the distinction of being the last motive to appear at the end of *Götterdämmerung*, holding as it does the image of redemption or transformation, and therefore summing up the underlying meaning of the entire drama. It is a wonderfully prophetic experience to hear it at this dark moment. As Sieglinde sets off on her courageous way, her last words to Brynhilde are equally prophetic: 'May my gratitude one day bring you a reward, and Sieglinde's woe be your blessing!' So it will prove in Act III of *Siegfried*.

WOTAN'S ESTRANGEMENT FROM BRYNHILDE

Wotan arrives in the red storm-cloud which continues to accompany him while he is in his present angry mood. After a not uncourageous attempt to conceal Brynhilde among them and plead for her, the eight lesser Valkyries wilt before Wotan's contempt; she steps voluntarily forward and they are at once reduced to insignificance. She asks to hear her sentence, and he replies, rather strangely, that she has already sentenced herself. By turning against his commands, she has cut herself

---

[1] The extensive literature includes C. G. Jung, *Symbols of Transformation* tr. R. F. C. Hull, London, 1956; C. G. Jung and C. Kerényi, *Essays on a Science of Mythology*, New York, 1949 (esp. pp. 60 ff); H. G. Baynes, *The Mythology of the Soul*, London, 1940 and 1949; Erich Neumann, tr. R. F. C. Hull, *The Origins and History of Consciousness*, London, 1954, and tr. R. Manheim, *The Great Mother*, London, 1955.

off from him, thus ceasing to be a Valkyrie, and becoming 'merely herself'.

This could hardly be a more double-edged remark. It is not Brynhilde who is cutting herself off from Wotan; it is Wotan who is cutting himself off from Brynhilde. Wotan is doing just what any man in his present blind condition is most likely to do: he is projecting his own hostile intentions on to the other person instead of seeing them in himself; this enables him to accuse the other person most self-righteously of the very offence he is himself committing. Brynhilde's intervention in the cause he would have liked underneath to favour has touched off all the bitterness which, if his state were less blind, he would be having to accept in his own person as the original instigator of the whole abortive attempt. But he is not yet ready to admit the failure of his wilful authority in the role of ego so openly. In the end he will be able to do so without blaming anybody, not even himself. At present his anger is opaque enough to conceal his incipient self-realization, which is no doubt why he keeps it at red heat for as long as he can, falling back on self-pity as a further recourse, and only returning more or less to an ordinary state of human openness by the end of the Act.

One of the ways in which we can describe a man who is in this blind state of self-righteous certainty at the very height of his own folly is by saying that he is possessed adversely by his anima. Something from the side of him which is most feminine and least conscious has taken over the effectual control not only of his actions but of his very thoughts and feelings. He feels absolutely convinced that he is acting as any reasonable man would act in his position. He is perfectly sure he is in the right. His blindness to the other side of the matter is astonishingly complete and impervious. His logic is as faulty as it appears to himself to be unanswerable. What he takes for obvious reason is to any outside observer obvious emotion; what he takes for justifiable anger is priggish vindictiveness. He is displaying the feminine mode of conduct not at its angelic best but at its diabolical worst. But so unconscious is he of all this lamentable unreasonableness that he cannot see what his anima is doing to him. That is precisely what enables her to do it.

It is just these moods of adverse anima-possession which so often disturbed the course of Wagner's relationship with his fellow men and women; and when he was in such a mood, his words and his actions could be really despicable. But before we start despising Wagner, or Wotan, for their despicable words and actions, we shall do well to recall that we are all subject to anima-possession (or animus-possession), and that we can none of us do very much to control our words and actions at such times. We are too swamped in unconsciousness. It is important to do what we can to summon up our scattered remnants of objective judgement, but it is difficult, and usually the best we can manage is to try and get out of our stubborn fit as soon as possible.

The difficulty comes first of all from the fact that we simply cannot see that we are in a stubborn fit. We feel particularly sure of ourselves. That itself is, in fact, one of the faint signs of something wrong by which we can gradually learn to take warning. Another faint sign is the sort of exaggeratedness in our protestations which Shakespeare noticed when he wrote 'methinks the lady doth protest too much'; and another is a curious uneasiness behind our own certainty. These are not necessarily faint signs to the outside observer; indeed they may be very blatant; but in ourselves we are lucky if we see them at all while the anima is still in adverse possession of our faculties.

Such anima-possessed moods range from a mere passing sulkiness or touchiness to much graver follies. Almost incredible as it may seem, Wotan's present intention is not merely to cast Brynhilde off, but to leave her exposed in magic sleep for the first stranger who casually finds her to possess with impunity. Casting Brynhilde off is tantamount to Wotan thrusting his anima out of sight; and leaving Brynhilde exposed to the first stranger to find is tantamount to Wotan leaving his anima at the mercy of his own shadow, since no part of the psyche is so strange yet so near at hand as our own dark component of unacknowledged disreputability.

All this looks very like an objectification of what is actually happening to Wotan. He has hardened himself against the best promptings of that inner femininity which is his anima. This has so outraged and alienated her that she has sided with all that is worst and darkest in him: she has sided with his shadow. It is through this unholy alliance that she has come to take temporary possession of his ego in so harmful a capacity. That is possibly the meaning of Wotan's contemptuous last words to Hunding: Go join your mistress Fricka. For we have always to remember that the unattractive Fricka is just as much a symbolical representative of the anima as the attractive Brynhilde, while Hunding is certainly a member of the shadow contingent. Wotan is himself behaving now exactly as if he were Fricka at her very worst. We might very well put it that Fricka, in that aspect of her which stands for the worst manifestations of Wotan's anima, has taken possession of him, so that he is doing his utmost to repudiate Brynhilde in that aspect of her which stands for the best manifestations of his anima. It is a dangerous situation; and it is a very lucky thing not only for Wotan but for the entire psyche to which the cast of the *Ring* adds up that Brynhilde is not going to let herself be disposed of quite so easily.

THE PARTIAL RECONCILIATION
OF WOTAN AND BRYNHILDE

After a final protest at Wotan's outrageous sentence on Brynhilde, in the disgrace of which, they complain, the whole family will be involved, the remaining Valkyries fly off in all directions, wailing to the last. The real argument between Wotan and Brynhilde can now begin.

Wotan has spoken a truer word than he realizes in saying that Brynhilde, by her independent action in standing up to him, has left her divine role as an archetypal Valkyrie behind her and become 'merely herself'. What Wotan means for a disparagement is more truly a compliment. Brynhilde has begun, though she has by no means yet completed, a transformation of her own, at the end of which we shall no longer find her acting only in an archetypal capacity, but also in a human capacity as a woman in her own right; while even the archetypal symbolism which she does at the same time retain will be found to differ in its emphasis.

She is still a little inclined to believe that the guilt Wotan is so unconsciously projecting on to her really is her own guilt; but she is by no means the docile 'father's daughter' whom we first encountered. With quiet tact and gentleness, yet firmly (85), she begins to reproach Wotan for his harsh reaction to her well-intentioned and in any case quite unsuccessful attempt to do for him what she knew he would have been only too glad to do for himself if he had felt at liberty. Quietly though she opens, it is a great turning-point, and the music responds with a new motive (90c) not very far distant from the second half (69) of Freia's music in its version as the love motive (37) of Siegmund and Sieglinde.

There is also another connection which has very interesting implications. The first dozen notes of (90c) are a descending major scale broken only by one upward leap of a seventh replacing a downward second (i.e. at the octave above). The first dozen notes of Wotan's spear motive (73) are a descending minor scale. There are less developed forms of both motives; indeed, (90c) itself comes in here in the minor. Between the fully developed forms, there is an essential identity of note-sequence made still closer by an identity of rhythm over the first few notes. The presence of the seventh, however, makes an emotional difference greater than the mere octave displacement might suggest. The change from minor to major makes still more difference; and when the motives are harmonized, as of course they usually are, the mood is more strongly contrasted than it is when they appear unharmonized. Essentially they are the same motive given different treatment.

This difference is all the difference between the hard wilfulness of Wotan in his entrenched capacity as ego and the compassionate responsiveness of Brynhilde in her developing capacity as that aspect of the anima which stands for warmth of feeling. Wotan needs that warmth of feeling as he has probably never needed anything in his life before.

In the bitterness of his failure over Siegmund, Wotan is trying to shut himself off from human feeling. He is trying to shut himself off from life itself in the attempt to shut himself off from the pain of it. He is trying to be uninvolved. Brynhilde will not let him spare himself the pain and will not let him be uninvolved. Brynhilde is his own warmth of feeling personified; and it is uncommonly interesting to find the music telling us that this warmth of feeling is nothing but the other side of his hard, cold will. It is uncanny how regularly a man's good qualities turn out to be the obverse side to which the reverse side is his bad qualities. Cold-hearted or warm-hearted, it is still Wotan's heart. Harsh as at (73) or compassionate as at (90C), it is still the same sequence of notes. Yet the difference between life and death is not wider than the difference between these two motives. Indeed it would hardly be too much to say that it is the difference between life and death, since a man who really succeeds in keeping his feelings uninvolved has made himself the enemy of life.

Wotan has, in fact, run into another crisis of the same order as when he wanted to keep his personal hold on the ring in Scene 4 of *Rhinegold*, and gave it up only at the oracular prompting of Erda. It is perhaps a measure of the progress he has made since then that his present experience of the eternal feminine is coming through Brynhilde, who is less impersonal and remote, more near and human than the great Earth Mother herself. But though he has taken a full turn of the upward spiral since last time, he has come round to confront a very similar choice again; and Brynhilde is not going to find him easy to win over.

She begins by recalling to him that she only carried out his original command and real desire. This does no good; he is all the angrier for being reminded of it. She says, with firmer insistence, that he was being false to himself; this does still less to improve his temper. She now goes on to describe a sight which she saw, but he did not; the sight of Siegmund taking so courageously the news of his coming death, and so touchingly distressed at being forced to fail Sieglinde for all his courage. You, Wotan, she says, placed this love for him in my heart; I was only obeying the dictates of that love in disobeying you. Ah, he answers, and do you think that love's desire can be so lightly gained? Did not I too desire to save him? Was not my heart torn within me when I was unable to? Since you find you can take life so lightly, you shall be free of me too and share no more of my thoughts and responsibilities.

Now she tries a rather different approach. I am of your race, she says; my shame would be your shame; my dishonour your dishonour. He merely answers: Since you are so taken with love, you shall take whatever love is forced on you. But not from a weakling, she pleads; and she adds, very pointedly, that the Volsung race will never produce a weakling. He reacts strongly and bitterly to this: has he not just destroyed the Volsung race in the person of Siegmund? Ah, but she reveals now that she has rescued Sieglinde and that Sieglinde will give birth to the new hero. Wotan instantly repudiates the unborn Siegfried: but he has plainly been touched. And Sieglinde has the fragments of the sword to hand down to him, she adds. He answers evasively, and formally repeats her sentence—to be sealed in sleep till the first man to stumble on her takes possession of her. In her desperation she has a wild inspiration. Surround me with flames, she cries, to burn up any weakling who dares to approach me, so that only a brave man, and a free one, can break his way through!

And with these words she finds the key to unlock his bitter, tortured heart. His anger leaves him and his coldness melts. He cannot bring himself to relent enough to take her back, but he has obviously been deeply moved. He draws her tenderly to her feet, and promises her such a torch for her bed as has lit no bridal yet. It will scorch any coward to flight, and she shall be freed as bride only by one freer than he is himself, god though he is. The music states plainly what free hero is in both their minds; here, and increasingly through the rest of the act, we hear the exuberant motive (78) of Siegfried's heroism. They are both sharing this thought, and Wotan must be adding to it his own prophetic vision of the day when his spear shall be shattered and his authority rudely ended by this young hero to whom, in all their interests, he will offer nothing but opposition.

THE PARTING OF WOTAN AND BRYNHILDE

Brynhilde's great thought and Wotan's great thought fit together like the two halves of a broken penny. When human plans fall into place as convincingly as this it is a reasonable assumption that they accord with the underlying purpose towards which the autonomous psyche is working. Wotan's anger furthered the underlying purpose of the *Ring* in preventing Brynhilde from remaining in her undeveloped state. Brynhilde's inspiration about the fire and the hero who alone could pass it confirmed Wotan's growing awareness of that underlying purpose. The ultimate rightness of these developments is further reflected in the poignant emotions which he and she now share, and which are wonderfully conveyed to us in the music (82).

He lays her gently on her rock-couch, already sinking into her magic sleep. The orchestra begins to glow and resound with the famous sleep music (16), with its slow chromatic drift and its modulations as elusive as the soft drift into sleep itself, when the sharp edges of consciousness begin to blur and fade. The hypnotically repeated motive (30) of Brynhilde's magic slumber is like a distant relative of (73) and (90c), but infinitely relaxed and yielding. It is warm enough, however, to convey to us that this is no sterile unconsciousness into which she is sinking. Her sleep, so long and so deep as to put us in mind of death itself, is like a womb from which she may be reborn. It is the gentler equivalent of a death of transformation, the result of which will be that when at long last Siegfried has grown to manhood, Brynhilde will have left enough of her Valkyriehood behind her to be ready for him as his human bride. The reader will hardly need to be reminded of her resemblance to the Sleeping Princess waiting in a hundred years' slumber for her Prince to pass through the hedge of thorns and wake her to womanhood.

As Wotan sings to Brynhilde his last farewell, we hear, for only the third time in the *Ring*, a full statement of the motive (76) of 'renunciation' which preceded Alberich's forswearing of love and accompanied Siegmund's acceptance of his tragic but heroic destiny as he pulled his father's sword out of Hunding's roof-tree. Wotan is not renouncing love; he is accepting something which requires just as much courage of him as both Alberich and Siegmund needed in their different ways before. Alberich accepted loneliness. Siegmund accepted love and death in profound foreknowledge. Wotan accepts the most creative future open to him; but it too involves a renunciation. The future which Wotan accepts is, in effect, to fade out altogether in the capacity he has so long clung to as the all too wilful representative of the conscious ego.

By the time Siegfried has woken Brynhilde from her magic sleep, Wotan's spear will have been cut in half by the very sword which he once left for Siegmund, and which will become Siegfried's in virtue of being re-forged by him. And that will be the end of Wotan's wilful authority. It is still a long way distant; but it is already implicit in the present situation. This situation is chosen quite deliberately by Wotan, under Brynhilde's inspiration, and in choosing it he knows what it involves. He will never see Brynhilde alive again, for the profound reason that he will never again represent primarily the ego in relation, among other inner figures, to the anima. When next he appears, in *Siegfried*, he will already have taken on the function of the Wanderer or Wise Old Man, and in that function he is a symbol not for the ego but, at the least, for psychic consciousness, and perhaps, indirectly, for the self.

Thus while Brynhilde is preparing to take on a less archetypal and more human role, Wotan is moving symbolically in the opposite direction. But all this symbolism is, as usual, being expressed through characters who are also presented to us as persons in their own right. As a person, Wotan is indeed making a costly renunciation in letting both his wilful authority and his beloved Brynhilde pass to the as yet unborn Siegfried. But the cost in grief is the price he has to pay for moving on to the next stage of his own development. Seen in terms of personal development, this means that by accepting his loss he is ultimately going to regain more than he loses, and the warmth, the feeling, the aliveness which Brynhilde represents for him will remain with him for the very reason that he has braced himself for the sacrifice. We are not far here from Matthew, x, 39: He that findeth his life shall lose it; and he that loses his life for my sake shall find it. Meanwhile, Wotan's grief at losing the delight of Brynhilde's familiar companionship is deeply moving to us. He is not losing the power to love, as we were at first afraid; but he is losing a dear object of his love, for the second time in one opera.

There is a very complete and impressive statement of the spear motive (73) as Wotan raises his spear-point to summon Loge in the shape of fire. It is by this action that Wotan sets his own destiny in motion. It is virtually his last action in the role of ego; and it is in itself an act of acceptance. The only thing which ego can really do to help destiny on is by accepting it freely; but this acceptance is an important and indeed a necessary contribution. We see the spear being used here in the most favourable manner, so that the link between its motive (73) and Brynhilde's motive (90c) becomes still more understandable.

At the end of the invocation by which Wotan binds Loge to his task of surrounding Brynhilde's sleeping form, he thrusts the spear-point three times into the rock, and the great flames break out, to be directed by the spear-point in a full circle. It has been suggested that this fire, being as magic as the sleep itself, has no power to burn, but only to scare away those who are not fearless enough to put it to the test. This, however, is not what Wotan and Brynhilde have described; they both spoke of the flames biting and scorching, and not merely scaring. The magic has its usual meaning of psychic force. But the terrors sent up by the psyche are not imaginary terrors; they are real terrors from the inside as opposed to the outside. They may not scorch the flesh, but they scorch the spirit. Loge is no mere master of innocuous fireworks.

The fire has its usual significance of the burning, compelling force of life itself. But there is a medieval tradition that paradise is surrounded by fire which is heat for the wicked, and light for the good. The wicked in this context may be taken to suggest those who obstinately, or fool-hardily, or merely inadvertently stand out against the underlying purpose which life has for them, and get burnt out by the inexorable force of it as a consequence. The good may be taken to suggest those who are able to let life blaze through them, and really find out something of its point and meaning as a consequence. Light signifies consciousness.

The underlying purpose of the *Ring* requires that Siegfried, and Siegfried alone, shall find his way through to Brynhilde. Thus for Siegfried, and Siegfried alone, the magic fire holds no danger provided he is not afraid of it. In his role as free hero, truly independent of Wotan this time, Siegfried is not going to be afraid of it. On the contrary, he is going to welcome it as a beacon to light him on his way, and the flames as he passes through them are going to set his heart alight with desire for his waiting bride.

Like the sleep music into which it now so skilfully blends, the fire music (20–21) has a long, low sweep to its modulations. There is a flicker of rising flames, and beneath that a steady, roaring glow of intense heat. There is the same suggestion of the boundaries of tonality melting away: for Brynhilde, into gentle oblivion; for the fire which guards her, into an inferno. Through it all, there strides the great motive (78) of Siegfried as the victorious hero. Wotan's mind is obviously full of him; and his final words show his new understanding of what is due to happen. He sings prophetically: 'Who fears the point of my spear passes not through the fire.' With that, he makes his exit, leaving the stage clear for Loge and the orchestra.

CHAPTER X

Siegfried, Act I

———— ❀ ————

MIME AND SIEGFRIED

It is some time since the events of the *Valkyrie*, and the overture to *Siegfried* gives a certain impression of a new start. It is almost as if we were taken back again to the primeval condition of affairs at the beginning of *Rhinegold*. This is not quite the case; but in a sense, Siegfried does represent a new start, and his strange upbringing does recapitulate the racial emergence from animal unconsciousness into human consciousness.

We hear a motive (9) which depicts a kind of elemental brooding. It made its appearance in *Rhinegold*, Scene 2, where Wotan described Loge's hidden depths of cunning; in *Rhinegold*, Scene 3, it accompanied Mime's lament over his brother Alberich's cunning in dominating the Nibelung dwarfs by the magic of the ring. Its material is an uneasy sequence of thirds low in the bass, and separated by a diminished seventh. It sounds like the slow, preliminary rumination of some thought which has not yet taken definite shape. And who at the moment is having such brooding thoughts? Not Wotan, not Alberich, not any of the great protagonists, but shifty little Mime, Alberich's weaker brother. We hear his two main motives almost at once. There is the crisp, pleasant rhythm which is his smith's hammer on the anvil (50); and we know, from the sound of that, the better side of him, for after all he is a smith, and a good one. But it is soon joined by the little grace notes followed by a descending second (71), which give his fidgety, treacherous side—unfortunately the dominant side. He really is a rather nasty piece of work.

Next comes a very different motive, the motive (8) of the ring itself. Meeting it in this context, we may notice again how strangely cornerless it is, and how elusive in its tonality. We may further note a connection between the ring motive (8) and the brooding ruminative motive (9) at the start of the overture. The ring motive is also a sequence of thirds, but in this case there are four down and three up again, with an interval of a third between each. If we take the two outside thirds and ignore the two in the middle, we actually have the brooding motive. One aspect of the ring's symbolism is the underlying purpose whose gradual emergence in the psyche shapes the basic plot from beginning to end. Evidently the brooding thought contributes, however obscurely or even paradoxically, to the purpose.

Up goes the curtain, and there is Mime at his anvil hammering away at a sword (45) which he is on the point of finishing. We soon learn that he is in despair because he cannot, with all his undoubted skill, make a sword strong enough for his nurseling, whom we have no difficulty in identifying as Siegfried even before Mime mentions him by name. Mime makes a good sword by any normal standard, and then Siegfried just comes along and snaps it to pieces.

And why is Mime so anxious to make Siegfried a worthy sword? He tells us. Siegfried is strong enough, as he is not, to kill Fafner (57) and win the ring, which Mime then feels confident of being able to trick somehow out of Siegfried's possession. Oh, it is a bold plan, a cunning plan, a plan which does credit to the clever, scheming, ambitious little dwarf he is; but unfortunately it depends on one thing, and that thing he cannot for the life of him accomplish. It depends on producing Siegfried a worthy sword. Mime knows, too, what is the only sword that can really serve. This sword is Siegmund's sword Nothung, of which he has the pieces in his cave, but not the craft to weld them together again. He knows how to weld steel well enough; but not steel as magically hard as this. No wonder he sits brooding and day-dreaming and hammering away by turns.

The day-dreams are now shattered. In runs Siegfried (48), driving before him, of all things, a great, shambling forest bear. This scares the wits out of Mime; and we are both amused and impressed by the contrast of Mime's fear with Siegfried's fearlessness. It makes a good boisterous joke to open the opera with; but it is also extremely revealing of Siegfried's character. We could never imagine his father Siegmund taking dangerous animals of the forest as a joke. Siegmund knew fear, but mastered it: he was a truly brave man. Siegfried, we are quickly aware, is not as yet brave in that sense at all, but only in the much less real sense of literally not knowing fear. There is something missing in him here, and since nothing so fundamental to the human character as fear is ever really absent, we may ask where it has gone.

Who hereabouts has a double dose of fear? Little Mime, of course. Mime carries the part of Siegfried's shadow which holds his fear, his meanness and in short the unheroic side of him. Siegfried hates Mime. If Mime did not stand for unconscious attributes of Siegfried's own, Siegfried would not hate him; he would merely be indifferent.

Before we let that bear out of our sight (incidentally, it should be in our sight and not just left to our imaginations as in some productions) we may do well to remark that its primary symbolism relates to the Great Mother in her devouring aspect.[1] Part of its secondary symbolism is as one of the images for the *prima materia* or raw material in alchemy, the dragon being another. This raw material prior to its transformation represents very unconscious and very dangerous psychic force, and we may feel that Siegfried, in treating the bear as if it were a tame and spiritless pet animal, is taking an unconscionable risk. But being without knowledge of fear, he is unaware of the risk; and the bear humours him as powerful beasts do at times humour children. The entire episode is reminiscent of a child playing, and by means of its play preparing itself for what life will later require it to do in earnest. The baiting of the bear is a playful foretaste of the fight with the dragon.

Having thoroughly frightened his little foster-father, Siegfried turns the bear out into the forest again, snatches the newly-finished sword and tests it by bringing it down as hard as he can on to the anvil. The anvil suffers no damage; it is the sword which shatters.

In the lively quarrel which results, two main accusations are exchanged, but never really come to grips. Mime keeps saying that he has done everything for Siegfried from a baby up, and that the boy owes him something better than furious ingratitude in return. Siegfried keeps saying that he may have done a lot for him and taught him a lot of lessons (both of which he very certainly must have done) but that the one lesson Mime seemed most eager to teach, how to love Mime, has failed. Siegfried's boisterous motive (53) and Mime's sly counterpart (51) are prominent here.

Mime is rash enough to insinuate in reply that all forest creatures love their parents, so Siegfried must love him: does love him, really, beneath this boyish frowardness. But Siegfried has seen something of such love in the forest; he has noticed, too, that offspring resemble their parents as he is quite confident of not resembling Mime. Where is your wife, Mime, that I may call her mother? We hear motive (38A), standing here for the mother's love which Siegfried has never known. It is merely

---

[1] J. J. Bachofen, *Urreligion*, Leipzig, 1926, I, pp. 138 ff. (from 'Der Bär in den Religionen des Altertums', 1863); C. G. Jung, tr. R. F. C. Hull, *Symbols of Transformation*, London, 1956, p. 316 and p. 322.

infuriating that Mime pretends he was Siegfried's father and mother in one, and he gets a sound shaking for his pains. Terrified once more, he brings out the truth at last, or most of it. And so Siegfried learns that his mother had been found by Mime in the forest, at the end of her strength. He brought her to his cave and cared for her; but she died in bearing Siegfried. And then, of course, Mime starts all over again his whimpering song (72) about how he brought Siegfried up, did everything for him, and so on and so forth. In the intervals of this, Siegfried extracts a little more information: that his mother's name was Sieglinde, that she had told Mime to call him Siegfried, and that his father died in battle, though for some reason Mime will not reveal his name, which he knows perfectly well (but it is quite traditional for heroes not to know their true parentage). And when Siegfried, who has heard lies from Mime before, wants some visible token that his new story is the truth, Mime presents him with the fragments of the sword Nothung as proof of the tale.

It is one of the test signs of a mythological cult hero that his birth and upbringing are not those of other men.[1] He may be supernaturally begotten, sometimes in what is called a virgin (symbolizing psychic) birth: Siegfried's begetting was natural, but the circumstances were highly exceptional, and one of the meanings of its incestuous character is that no mere human procreation was in progress, but a heroic mystery. Frequently the hero is exposed at birth, or abandoned, or orphaned, or lost, or in some other way separated from one or both parents: Siegfried was doubly orphaned. It is thus usually a foster-parent or foster-parents who bring the hero up: Siegfried was brought up by Mime in a cave reminiscent of the many womb-like caves, often treated as sacred, in which gods or demi-gods or cult heroes were born or tended by nymphs or country folk or animals.

These traditional features further emphasize the symbolic significance of the hero's life. He is not an ordinary mortal, growing up in the love and security of an ordinary family. He is a deprived child, compensating for his deprivation by growing up to do desperate deeds to which he is driven by his own inner necessity, but from which the world is the gainer. We have already seen this depicted in the case of Siegmund, and compared that case with Wagner's own. For such characters, there has been no average allowance of mother's love and there can be no average

---

[1] Otto Rank, tr. W. A. White, *The Myth of the Birth of the Hero*, New York, 1914; C. G. Jung, tr. R. F. C. Hull, *Symbols of Transformation*, London, 1956, pp. 321 ff.; C. G. Jung and C. Kerényi, *Essays on a Science of Mythology*, New York, 1949, p. 39.

achievement in the way of adult independence; it is all or nothing in lethal conflict with the inner mother-image. The hero's physical orphaning becomes a symbol for a psychic orphaning, out of which the possibility of a psychic rebirth arises. His parents in the flesh are not there to comfort him; his foster-parents (like god-parents) stand for the archetypal parent-images in the psyche, by cultivating which he may, if he succeeds at all, reach a more than average level of psychic consciousness. We are again reminded of John, iii, 8: That which is born of the flesh is flesh; and that which is born of the Spirit is spirit. Thus in a very roundabout way there is a sense in which Mime actually is, as he claims, Siegfried's father and mother in one. He is neither, biologically; but at a certain level in the symbolism, he is both. This level, however, lies far too deep for Siegfried even remotely to perceive. His need is to rebel; and rebel he does.

Siegfried (Sigurd) is by general consent the most notable of all the many notable heroes whose stories run through the Eddas and Sagas in every variety of style and detail. His courage was phenomenal; but there is no suggestion in Wagner's sources that Siegfried did not know the meaning of fear. Wagner, however, knew fairy-tales in which the hero tries to get himself taught this elemental human experience by every variety of terrifying adventure without success, until at last some unexpected trick is found which pierces his unnatural confidence and gives him the first conscious fright of his life. In one tale a bucket of ice-cold fish is poured over him in his sleep; the fish give him an immediate and sensuous (not merely intellectual) feeling of what his own inhuman coldness in this matter is really like, and he knows on the instant what he really fears but has never faced. It is his coldness itself, which is cured by being faced. Another such inhumanly fearless hero is cured by having his head put back to front by an obliging magician. That gives him a sudden vision of the back or shadow side of his own character which he has never seen before, but is what he is really afraid of without having known that he was. He, too, is terrified into an immediate cure by the shock of this realization, and on having his head replaced the right way round, becomes ordinarily human in that he is capable of knowing fear.[1]

These tales of the boy who does not know the meaning of fear appear to have held a prolonged fascination for Wagner, and he successfully

[1] See Grimm's *Fairy Tales*, tr. J. Scharl, London, 1948, pp. 29 ff., and J. Bolte and G. Poluska, *Anmerkungen zu der Kinder-und Hausmärchen der Gebrüder Grimm*, Berlin, 1913–32.

grafted the essence of them on to his conception of the hero archetype. Like Wotan himself, Wagner fastened almost unlimited hopes on to the symbol of which Siegfried is made the carrier. Some of these hopes were excessively naïve. Wagner actually thought that a new kind of human being could be called into existence (primarily by the influence of Wagnerian music-drama), and that this new being would be free alike of moralistic inhibitions and of calculating duplicity. The State (projected on to Wotan) would wither away; Society (seen as the free and independent 'folk') would come into its own.[1] Taken literally as a doctrine for the outside world, this line of thought is unreal to the point of absurdity; taken inwardly as a symbol for developments within the psyche, it is visionary enough. It is the ego whose wilful authority may wither away in the end, and it is the autonomous psyche whose leadership may come into its own.

The hero stands for the part of us which may be able to turn the perennial downwards pull of the Great Mother to advantage. He may be able to turn regressive incest (a symbol for being swamped by unconsciousness) into regenerative incest (a symbol for lapsing temporarily into unconsciousness as the matrix for renewed and greater consciousness). He may be able to overcome the Great Mother as Siegfried is being brought up by Mime to overcome the dragon.[2] To work, Mime! cries Siegfried; Forge the sword anew! And rejoicing in the thought that he should soon be free of him (56A), he rushes into the forest again, apparently quite satisfied for the moment that the little craftsman he so dislikes and thinks he so despises can achieve this essential task on his behalf.

Mime knows better, and falls back into his previous despair. And now comes one of those scenes in which we are most acutely aware of the characters as parts of one another. The conversation which follows can serve very little purpose except as an exchange between one part and another of the same character.

MIME AND WOTAN

We hear a motive (17) of quiet strength and dignity which at the same time contrives to suggest an exceedingly numinous awe and mystery.

[1] This idea is developed with particular fullness in Wagner's *Opera and Drama* (1851).
[2] The term 'regenerative incest' is applied to the cult hero's fight with the dragon by Erich Neumann, tr. R. F. C. Hull, *The Origins and History of Consciousness*, London, 1954, p. 154.

It is the Wanderer's motive. The Wanderer is Wotan himself, thinly disguised as an old traveller of no great importance, but belying this disguise by his own incontrovertible air of authority. He wears a long, dark blue cloak: i.e. of the colour traditionally associated with the Virgin Mary, and bearing the same significance of belonging to the spirit rather than to the flesh (but the Virgin's robe is red inside, to show that the spirit, too, is passionate in its inward way). The Wanderer's hat is broadbrimmed enough to fall down over one eye—a clue in itself to his identity, since most of us know when and how he plucked out this external eye as the willing price of inner wisdom, at the well of knowledge. He still carries, as a staff, his own spear carved with the runes and treaties which are the symbols of his authority. He is still, we realize, the mighty ruler of the world, though he knows something of his own weakness now, and has learnt an acceptance and resignation which were only just beginning to emerge when we saw him last, at the end of the *Valkyrie*. His sanity is very thoroughly re-established: the music alone is enough to tell us that.

In the earlier part of life, a man normally lives so fully and so absorbedly in his upper and more conscious layers that he has no need to suspect that he has lower layers where work is done and decisions are taken without his conscious knowledge. His main interests turn outwards, and his life's purpose fulfils itself through his natural energies and instincts. But in later life his natural energies will normally take a more inward direction. He will be brought into more immediate contact with his deeper layers and his underlying purpose.

Wotan has been finding this transition into the second half of life as difficult and as disturbing as many others do. He does not quite know what is happening to him; but he has formed this admirable habit of anonymous wandering. He is somehow aware that it is no use visiting his lower layers in all the proud and wilful authority of ego; he must wander in humble guise to see what he can see and hear what he can hear of his own underside and the quiet promptings of the self. Paradoxically, this increases his real stature. Henceforward, in his role as Wanderer, Wotan is a symbol less and less for the ego, more and more for psychic consciousness. As the Wise Old Man of myth and fairy-tale, he grows more and more closely related to the self, whose unresisting intermediary he is at last learning to become.

He has, of course, chosen his moment for the present visit. Not only does he catch Mime alone; he catches him in a very distracted and unguarded frame of mind. He gives Mime a courteous greeting, which is returned with an ill grace. But by wagering his head on his ability to answer any three questions that Mime likes to put to him (which is equivalent to setting the greatest value he can on the interview) he gains the little dwarf's attention.

Mime asks three elementary questions about the disposition of forces in the underworld, the surface world and the heavens above. Wotan replies. In the depths of the earth dwell the Nibelungs, black spirits ruled by black Alberich, who drove them to win him gold by means of which to master the world. On the earth's wide surface dwell the giants, ruled jointly by Fasolt and Fafner until the curse of the ring led Fafner to murder Fasolt. On the cloudy heights dwell the gods, light spirits ruled by light Alberich, namely Wotan, whose spear-shaft, torn from the world ash-tree, bears the runes and treaties which give him dominion over both dwarfs and giants. The ambiguous (14), so close to (13), is heard.

It will be noticed that Wotan makes no mention of the human race as among the inhabitants of the earth's wide surface. This confirms what we should in any case suspect, that we are not being given a lesson in natural geography, but in the geography of the psyche. No doubt the advanced geography of the psyche is complicated; but this is elementary geography and is not difficult to understand. The underworld is the unconscious; the surface world is the border territory; the heavens are consciousness. And we observe with interest that the blockage represented by Fafner's hold upon the ring occurs in the border territory where conscious and unconscious meet, and is thus evidently a crisis in communications between the two.

As Wotan ends with immense impressiveness both dramatic and musical, he lets his spear strike the ground as if by accident, and an answering growl of thunder gives Mime a considerable fright—still without suggesting to the silly fellow who this knowledgeable visitor really is. But we cannot help noticing that Wotan himself has been carried away by his own not unjustifiable sense of grandeur. The grandeur is absolutely genuine in so far as it is rooted, as it now fundamentally is, deep within his own character. But it does not in fact extend to dominion over the dwarfs and the giants. He cannot command Alberich; he cannot command Fafner; he could not command either Fricka or Brynhilde, nor will he be able to command Siegfried or Hagen. He cannot, in short, command the other partners in his own psyche.

He cannot command them, but he can get to know them better, which is getting to know himself. It might at first be thought that Mime's three questions had served no useful purpose, since they were all questions to which he and we already knew the answers. But in the psyche, it is not so much a matter of knowing the answers as of knowing that you know them. At a deep enough level we may know the answers; but that does not help us much until they can be brought up to a level at which they can be appreciated in the language of symbols if not of words.

In answering the third of Mime's questions, Wotan has, in fact, put into words a piece of knowledge about himself towards which he has certainly been feeling his way for some time, but which he has previously shown no sign of knowing that he knew. This is the realization, to which we, in this book, have given some previous consideration even if he has not, that he and Alberich are as close and necessary to one another as the obverse and reverse of one coin. The casual way in which this new piece of self-awareness has slipped out at him off the tip of his own tongue is typical of the invaluable tendency for gains in consciousness to bubble up of their own accord when we engage in this sort of conversation with one of our own inner 'characters'. We often do it in our dreams, and we can do it in waking fantasies and active imagination too if we can learn to give these valuable aids to self-discovery free scope.[1] Wotan is shown engaging in the mythological equivalent to active imagination; and while Mime may be none the wiser, Wotan is, and that is the advantage gained from his having sought this otherwise somewhat inexplicable interview.

Having now won his wager, Wotan has earned the right to ask three counter-questions in his turn. They are by no means so elementary, but Mime answers the first two readily enough. What is the race which Wotan loves best yet treats most harshly? The Volsungs: Siegmund, Sieglinde and their hero son, Siegfried. What sword shall serve Siegfried to kill Fafner at the bidding of the dwarf who has nurtured him in the hopes that he will win him the ring? Nothung, left by Wotan in an ash-tree (like the world-ash itself from which Wotan's spear was torn) for Siegmund, who broke it on Wotan's spear into the fragments which Mime has safe. But who shall make these fragments once more into a sword?

Ah, but now Mime has come to the end of his knowledge indeed. Who shall re-forge Nothung? That is the one question he most needs to answer and can answer least. It is the one question, as Wotan gently points out, which he should have made most sure of asking while it was

[1] See Michael Fordham, *The Objective Psyche*, London, 1958, Ch. V, and my Bibl. *s.v.* Jung.

still his turn to ask. But he was too busy scoring off Wotan: and now he has neither learnt the answer nor saved his head from the wager. Wotan quietly returns him both head and answer: Only he that knows not fear shall forge Nothung again. To him that knows not fear, he grimly adds, as he leaves the stage, shall Mime's head pay forfeit.

Terrified already, Mime hears these last sinister words in an extremity of panic. He begins to see things in the quiet air around him. The flickering sunlight grows harsh and threatening. Flames spring out at him; they gather together into a grotesque shape, a hissing, roaring monstrous shape. It is Fafner! It is the dragon! It is coming after him!

Certainly we hear Fafner's clumsy, growling motive (57) in the orchestra. But still more do we hear a fantastic distortion of the fire music (20–21), its harmonies twisted and its orchestration thinned to a harsh scream fit to burst the brain. It is nightmare music to a nightmare vision.

Yet however distorted, the fire music still stands for the compelling force of life. It is experienced by Mime as a torment because he is not accepting it but trying to oppose it. In a sense it is Wotan's nightmare, too: a warning seen on his behalf by the sly little Mime in him; for nightmares are one of the ways in which the psyche brings unrecognized dangers into the open.

THE FORGING OF NOTHUNG

Siegfried's return is as exuberant as his departure had been and as disconcerting to Mime, who whatever else he may be doing is certainly not getting on with the re-forging of Nothung. He is, in fact, hiding behind the anvil, mumbling to himself Wotan's last fateful words. Siegfried pulls him out and he elaborately explains that he was thinking out a new lesson unaccountably overlooked: how to fear. It has now become of urgent importance that Siegfried should learn to fear, so that Mime's own head should not pay forfeit to him; yet not too soon, or Nothung will not be forged nor Fafner killed—it is all really getting most complicated. Mime describes the flickering lights of the forest, the sound or fancy of pursuing animals, the shaking of the limbs and the pounding of the heart. But Siegfried, though he has seen the lights and heard the sounds, knows nothing of the shaking and the pounding, and thinks they might be a treat worth experiencing. How he will actually learn fear, from a sleeping woman, is movingly foretold for us by (30).

Here Mime has an inspiration of genius. Siegfried shall kill the dragon and learn fear in the very act of doing so. In the highest of spirits, Mime does not at all mind admitting now that he lacks the art to re-forge Nothung, and that this essential preliminary will have to be carried out by Siegfried himself. Siegfried falls to with a will. He horrifies the conservative craftsman in Mime by rejecting the solder and making no attempt at welding. Instead, he files the fragments of the sword down small enough to melt, pours them into a mould and casts it with a tremendous hissing of steam into a pail of water to cool off. All this is set to music of prodigious extroverted energy (43, 52). Fearless indeed! Mime is impressed against his will. But the awful thought has come to him that if Fafner frightens Siegfried enough, he will prevent Siegfried from killing him, and that if Siegfried kills Fafner without getting frightened, Siegfried will have Mime's head instead of Mime having the ring.

Meanwhile the bellows blow, the fire roars, the anvil rings and the preparation of the sword is going on apace. Mime decides to do a little preparation on his own account. Siegfried notices him fussing round with his pots and pans at the other side of the fire, and asks him what he is doing. Thirsty work, killing dragons, replies Mime; I am getting a nice drink ready for you. Siegfried, out of sheer instinctive distrust of the little fellow, lets us know in an audible aside that he will drink nothing of the kind, which is just as well, since the plan is to drug him to sleep and kill him with his own sword. Each proceeds with his task in high delight, so that the last scene becomes a counterpoint of Siegfried's glorious forging with Mime's unholy brewing.

The same fire serves for the forging and the brewing. The force of life will flow indifferently, it seems, into plans holy and unholy; but its own plans are the only winners in the end.

The Act finishes as it began, with Siegfried furiously testing his sword on the anvil. But this time it is not the sword that splinters. The anvil itself is split into two. That is in the first place a miracle of steel on iron; in the second place a symbol of differentiation (not for nothing have the opposites, fire and water, played their part in the forging); in the third place a reminiscence of the psychic birth of Athena as Zeus' head was split open, of the witch in the *Mabinogion* who had to be split down the middle and similar legendary parallels; above all, in the fourth place a triumphant demonstration that Siegfried has indeed forged his manhood keen and strong. Mime, who has already been seeing the ring and all its power as his own, is shaken once more out of his ridiculous complacency. The curtain comes down on his dismay and Siegfried's exaltation.

CHAPTER XI

Siegfried, Act II

ALBERICH AND WOTAN

Act II opens in different and darker mood. We may guess that Fafner is not far away now; we hear the pounding rhythm of the giants' motive (58), but what was previously a perfect fourth is here turned into an augmented fourth now that Fafner has become a dragon. The change is startling. We used to think of the giants as stolid but forthright, a comparatively straightforward pair of characters. This chromatic alteration, slight though it appears, adds a restless uncertainty which was not there before. Something has happened to take the sharp corners off Fafner, and to make him a more complex and interesting symbol. This tends to confirm that in killing Fasolt, Fafner assimilated him and his gentler inclinations, with progressive consequences ever since. Fafner is certainly going to behave in the coming scene with a depth of insight he has not previously displayed.

The next motive here is a new form of (57), first heard in *Rhinegold*, Scene 3, when Alberich turned himself into a snake-dragon to impress Wotan and Loge. This reminds us that Fafner to guard his hoard is now in snake-dragon form. We have considered the manifold meanings of snake symbolism in connection with the snake-markings in the Volsungs' eyes (*see* Chapter VII), and found them, as so often, ambivalent as between positive and negative associations. It is not only his destructive capacity but also his healing capacity which Fafner has increased by his voluntary transformation. He is potentially more formidable than before, but also he is wiser, and as events will show he is even in some strange manner milder. Above all, he is ready for the further stage of transformation to be symbolized by his death at Siegfried's hands.

But now we hear a motive from *Rhinegold* whose import is darkly obsessive. This is (15), the urgent syncopation of which, a mere rhythm in itself, is allied to brooding harmonies fit for the darkest character and the most obsessive of all: black Alberich himself. Sure enough, as the curtain goes up there he lies, in a scene of gloomy wildness and magnificence. The motive (8) of the ring confirms that the object of his obsession is still the same as it always has been since it was first stolen from him.

It is night, and we can only just see either him or his surroundings; but we can make out well enough that we are in a natural forest clearing and that at the back of the stage there is the opening to a cave. This is Fafner's lair, which Alberich is watching because he knows prophetically that the day about to dawn is Fafner's day of destiny, when Siegfried will kill him at Mime's prompting. Alberich has no objection to this excellent scheme; but he is going to do his utmost to see to it that he and not Mime falls heir to the ring.

With a forerunner of strange blue light in the heavens (blue again, like Wotan's robe—his cloud was red in the *Valkyrie*, when he was so insanely angry) and to the sound of his quietly imposing motive (17), Wotan the Wanderer strides in. This Wanderer disguise means nothing at all, however, to Alberich; he merely recognizes his old enemy, and snaps out at him in fury and bitterness. On his side, Wotan has not come to quarrel with the carrier of his darkest shadow, but to converse with him, as he has already conversed with a weaker part of his shadow in the person of Mime.

Alberich taunts Wotan with the treaties and runes on his spear, which prevent him taking any direct action against Fafner. He taunts him with the fear that once he had, namely that Alberich will again have the ring and by the power of it lead Hella's dead to overthrow Valhalla. Wotan points out that it was not the treaties that subdued Alberich, but the naked power represented by the spear itself (as a symbol of the ego's wilful authority). And Wotan is no longer afraid. To all the taunting he returns soft answers, merely announcing platitudinously, yet somehow enigmatically, that he who gets his hands on to the ring will be the ring's master. Alberich thinks at once of Siegfried, but Wotan replies that only Mime knows of or is interested in the ring, and adds, to Alberich's considerable astonishment, that so far as he himself is concerned, Alberich may work freely for his own ends. Wotan can only say this because he is beginning to realize that the fates themselves have this matter well in hand, and that to take any action to help Siegfried would merely be a disastrous interference. All this he makes quite plain to Alberich, treating him persistently as a colleague and not as an enemy.

Alberich cannot altogether believe this, and remains not only suspicious but actively hostile. It is part of the fates' arrangements that he should; he and his dour son Hagen have still the villain's function to carry on. But Wotan has achieved something more valuable than Alberich's direct co-operation. He has achieved increased awareness of the darkest side of his own character.

In further proof that he is no longer ill-disposed towards Alberich, Wotan wakes Fafner and suggests that he should give Alberich the ring so that Siegfried shall have no need to kill him. There is no real possibility either dramatically or symbolically that this might happen. As Wotan tells Alberich in this very scene, things happen as they have to happen. Fafner does not believe that anyone can kill him, and goes to sleep again after merely remarking that he is glad to hear his next meal is on the way.

Wotan, who does not expect Alberich to understand his motives, adds the friendly warning that Mime, more after Alberich's own kind, is about to arrive. His last words before disappearing into the forest are that Alberich will nevertheless soon learn some things he does not yet understand. As Wotan disappears, we hear a beautiful phrase, picked out by being scored for trumpet, and significantly indicative of Wotan's state of mind. This is (82), which was prominent at the end of the *Valkyrie* when Wotan was bidding Brynhilde farewell. Now (82) belongs to the same group of motives as (4), (76), (79), (81), (83), (84) and (85): motives in which a falling semitone—linked to the falling semitone of grief (68)—tends to be prominent, very often falling from the minor third of the scale. Grief permeates this entire group; but in many contexts, though not in all, the nobility of the progression tells us that the grief is in some way accepted, and the nobility and the acceptance mingle with the grief in most moving fashion. Such is eminently the case with (82). The essence of Wotan's farewell to Brynhilde at the end of the *Valkyrie* is his acceptance of the need to surrender her to Siegfried and his own wilful ego-authority to the underlying purposes of the self. The essence of Wotan's farewell to Alberich in the present scene is his acceptance of his own shadow-side, once more in the interests of the self. The self is the totality of the psyche, and its interests require us to accept as much of ourselves as we can, not least on the shadow side.

No less radical explanation seems to me adequate to account for the remarkable character of the present scene. On any less radical level, Wotan's change of front would scarcely be explainable. It is, indeed, commonly agreed that Wotan has come by now to accept the inevitability of his coming downfall. My point is that he has come to accept it not simply because it is inevitable, but because it is creative: and creative for himself, not solely for humanity at large. It grieves him, as creative sacrifices do, but in some deep part of himself he knows now that he wants it. He wants it for Siegfried's sake, admittedly, and he wants it for humanity's sake, if we are to believe Wagner's account of the matter. But far more than all this he wants it for himself. It is this point which is most commonly overlooked.

Wagner wrote (letter to Roeckel, 25 Jan. 1854): 'After his farewell to Brynhilde, Wotan is in all earnest a departed spirit; true to his high determination, he must now leave events to themselves, and renouncing all authority over them, allow them to go their own way. It is for this reason that he is now simply the Wanderer. Take a good look at him, since he resembles us at all points. He stands for the full total of the Intelligence of the Present, while Siegfried is the man we of the Future so dearly desire and long for. But we who desire him cannot shape him; he has to shape himself and through our annihilation.'

But, of course, Siegfried is not the man of the Future: not even in the *Ring*, where he soon comes to an untimely end. The man of the Future is a symbol for our own state after a sufficient growth in our character has taken place; and he is shaped, if at all, not by our annihilation but by our transformation. The annihilation of Wagner's intuitive forecast is a symbol for the transformation. Wotan's growing appreciation of this reality is what enables him to loosen his hold on his own wilful authority, even to the extent of encouraging his shadow Alberich to do his worst. Alberich's worst will include, with the help of Hagen, the murder of Siegfried, but not even this will prove unnecessary to the underlying purposes of the self. On this level, admittedly a deeply hidden level, Alberich's worst will prove Alberich's best, and the present scene makes it clear how close Wotan is now coming to an acceptance of this bitter, healing secret. Hence, I believe, the appearance of (82) in the orchestra.

With that, Wotan is gone, leaving Alberich somewhat unsettled, but adamant in his own harsh determination to make an end of the gods so soon as he can regain the ring's magic power. He too slips away, into a cleft at the side of the cliff.

SIEGFRIED AND THE FOREST MURMURS

As the day dawns, in come Mime and Siegfried. This is where Siegfried is to learn fear, in course of killing the dragon, whose appalling offensive armament—his vast devouring jaws, his poisonous spittle, his crushingly heavy tail—Mime now describes in detail. All Siegfried wants to know is: Has he a heart, and is it in the normal place? On being told that Fafner's heart is indeed in the normal place, he promises to thrust Nothung into it, and asks: Is this what you mean by fear? Mime goes on again about the fainting senses, the faltering limbs, the quaking heart. Siegfried's loathing wells up afresh for this poor creature whom he sees actually nodding and shrinking and blinking and slinking in front of him. It seems clearer than ever that this loathing is the measure of his revulsion from the cowardly aspects which he has, like everybody else, but which he is more than usually incapable of recognizing as his own. Unable to endure the sight of Mime for a moment longer, he drives him off-stage, on the opposite side to Alberich.

We now appear to have reached the climax of the action. Fafner will come out; there will be a vigorously staged fight; Nothung will prove its worth, and the dragon will be killed. But just as we expect all this excitement to begin, Wagner takes a different turning. He gives us a passage, and a very long passage it is, of the most tender quality in *Siegfried*— more genuinely tender than the impetuous love-duet with which the opera closes. He gives us a sense of peace before the storm which carries the entire situation into a new climate. Contrary to expectation, Siegfried does not plunge crudely into action. He takes time for his inward intimations to mature before following them into outward activity.

As he sits down relaxedly under a tree, drinking in the quiet and beauty of the forest around him, he knows that he is independent of Mime's assistance now. He knows, too, that his father's face was not the face of Mime, but one like his own. He cannot imagine what his mother's face was like, unless it was some soft doe. She died in bearing him, he recalls; and the noble, accepting motive (77) of the Volsung race comes to our ears. He longs for her, and we hear his longing in the music (38A). The murmurs of the forest rise and fall (29), until the very birds seem to be talking to him—surely about his mother? He cuts a little reed pipe from the side of a pool and tries to join in their song in the hope of understanding it. Too low: much too low. He shortens it once, and a second time. It sounds higher now, but he is no nearer conversing with the birds than he was before.

Meanwhile the orchestra is making a commentary of which the significance escaped me until Deryck Cooke drew my attention to it I had already noticed that the forest murmurs as at (29) and related versions have much in common with (28), which portrayed the glitter of the Rhine's water as the sun struck down on to the gold in *Rhinegold*, Scene 1; there is also a more distant reference to part of the fire music, as at (20C). I had noticed, too, the likeness of the bird-song (27) to the song of the Rhinemaidens as at (26). I had not noticed that the forest murmurs begin with a direct version of (2), the Rhine's own original arpeggiation; the minor version being, as we know, the notes of Erda's motive (3). Nor had I noticed that the resolving dominant ninths (31) which usually carry the Rhinemaidens' melting cry of 'Rhinegold! Rhinegold!' are later woven into the texture as an actual accompaniment to the bird-song as at (27A). These are all images to do with nature.

There can only be one interpretation for all this, and Deryck Cooke suggested it to me. We are witnessing an almost total regression to the situation in *Rhinegold*: the situation of largely undifferentiated unconsciousness to which we refer as the state of nature. Earth (Erda) and water (the Rhine) are in the music. Siegfried is blowing air down his pipe and will confront fire from Fafner's jaws, which completes the four elements of basic nature. I had already thought of the prelude to Act I of *Siegfried* as the opening of a new cycle of the spiral, bringing us close to the beginning though at one turn removed. The scene now unfolding will determine whether we shall just slip down Snakes-and-Ladders fashion to the beginning, or continue with the upward spiralling.

The outlook at the moment is not entirely promising. Siegfried has cut his little reed pipe from the natural growth at the water's edge. In dream material, and equally in mythology, the symbolism attached to a musical pipe generally includes a reference to the phallus. I am not certain that such a reference is included here; but on a very unconscious level, I am inclined to think that it is. If so, the implication would be that Siegfried is trying to establish his manhood in general and his sexuality in particular, but by a misdirected attempt. In cutting his pipe shorter, he would be confirming the symbolism through which he is undoubtedly returning in fantasy to a state of infancy. There might be glancing references to the small size of an infant's penis, and to the self-castration of Attis, servant of the Great Mother. Siegfried is longing for his mother.

None of this lessens the tender beauty of this quite enchanting scene. The infant's longing for its mother is the start of all our longing, and is an *ingredient* in our adult mating. Siegfried is also longing for a mate, though he still thinks of this mate in childhood terms, as a playmate. He is on the verge of discovering the sexual implication, but has not yet done so quite consciously. His feelings are very strong within him, and under the play-activity of the little reed pipe he is experimenting with them. The play-activity is rather more than mere undirected fantasy; it almost amounts to what in analytical psychology would be called active imagination. But everything depends on whether this descent of his imagination into the infantile condition just leaves him there or takes him out and up again on the farther side. If the first should happen, the bird-song will be no better for him than the siren-song of the Rhine-maidens which it so closely resembles. If the second, the positive value in these creatures of nature will be at his service, and his own natural instincts can carry him forward on a flood-tide of early manhood.

It is perfectly true that the birds, the forest murmurs, the forest itself are all talking to him about his mother. In the intuitive language of symbols, all nature recalls to us our deepest memories of mother and behind these our innate knowledge of the mother archetype. Our love of nature is nothing so vague and colourless as mere aesthetic appreciation. Her fecundity is the very image of motherhood. Her swelling downs and her secret valleys evoke the very outline of woman. Her clear streams are invitations to rebirth visions. Her groves and forests are patterns of feminine reassurance and feminine mystery. We cannot love nature without secreting fantasies which in their forgotten origins are mother fantasies. This is not a mere figure of speech. Patient after patient brings up such associations in analysing dream and fantasy material. Our infantile emotions are disguised by layers of subsequent sophistication, but they are the strongest we have, and we owe to their strength the raw stuff though not necessarily the end-product of our adult loves and hates. But that is just the question here: will the end-product be infantile dependence or mature relationship?

Suddenly, to our relief, Siegfried grows impatient of reverie. He throws away the feeble little pipe; he raises to his lips his own hard silver horn, shaped like a crescent moon; he blows a gay tune (48), already heard in Act I, which tells us of the resilience of his character, so different from Siegmund's foredoomed courage. Fafner responds immediately to the traditional challenge, lumbering out of his cave to meet young Siegfried.

And Fafner, too, despite the apparent incongruity of sex, is part of Siegfried's mother-fantasies. The devouring aspect of woman *is* masculine; it arises from her animus, her inner masculinity, when that inner masculinity is in blind and savage mood. A dragon is a traditional symbol for our experience of this devouring element within ourselves.

SIEGFRIED AND FAFNER

Siegfried's libido has been turning inwards and pouring energy into the mother archetype. She is activated, and not only in her gentle, doe-like aspect. She cannot be evoked as comforter and saviour without also being evoked as ogress and destroyer. Nature proliferates and provides; but nature is also red in tooth and claw. Nature is birth and nourishment; but nature is also death and bereavement. The Great Mother is both good and terrible; and a human mother has that in her which reflects both faces of the archetype. There is no mother however good who does not first create her child in pride and joy, and then bind him when he should be growing away from her. Yet she is proud, too, when he breaks the bonds, which will not be too strong for him unless the mother herself is in bondage and has not been able to teach him by her unspoken example the meaning of inner freedom and real love. If the mother can give him enough real love, the child can become sufficiently independent of her. Sieglinde could give Siegfried no love at all after he was born, having died in giving birth to him. That is why, like Siegmund, he lives in search for it. Having no physical mother, he is driven back to the Great Mother. If he experienced her only as a sweet seductress, he would be a lost man, because the seducing is itself the devouring. But Siegfried does not lose himself in his reverie. On some deep impulse— still, as he tells us himself, in search of a playmate or sweetheart—he challenges Fafner, unexpected playmate though he certainly is; indeed this is no mere play, as the encounter with the bear had been. Whether Siegfried realizes it or not, this time it is in deadly earnest. In Fafner the dragon, Siegfried the hero meets the Terrible Mother. Being, however, the true hero that he is, he meets her on terms not of seduction but of mortal combat.

The mythology of the dragon and the dragon-slayer is so universal and has been so well studied that the situation which now confronts us is not doubtful. The dragon symbolizes a terrible danger from our mother-image. The danger consists in that paralysis of the personality which an unconscious fascination with this image may produce. The force of this fascination is incalculably great; as a seduction it could not possibly be more negative. As a challenge to combat, however, it can have an effect just as powerful in a positive direction. The same force which can swallow the personality if the challenge is not taken up can lead to its transformation in so far as the challenge is successfully accepted.

The dragon guards a treasure which stands for the access of rich life accruing when the fascination of the mother-image has been confronted and overcome. The treasure may be of gold, signifying libido released by an increase of consciousness; it may take the form of a rescued maiden, signifying the increase of consciousness. But in all cases the libido thus released is the same libido which was previously flowing towards the fascination of the mother-image; and the increase of consciousness is the reward of confronting that fascination without being seduced by it. In Goethe, Faust's journey down through the underworld 'to the Mothers' was the most dangerous he ever undertook; but he came back with Helen. He came back with his relationship to his own inner feminity transformed. He came back on new terms with the anima.

As human being, Siegfried needs to confront and overcome the negative attributes of his mother-image before seeking out his mother's successor in the person of Brynhilde; for if he does not do this, he will project these negative attributes (as well as the positive ones) so blindly on to Brynhilde that a real relationship will have no chance of developing. As archetype, Siegfried will show us that hero-image within ourselves which can confront and overcome the mother-image; and in this light, we shall see him not so much winning an earthly bride as winning a more conscious relationship with the anima, like Faust with Helen.

Fafner, with Fasolt symbolically inside him, has grown a little tired of his own sterile existence as jailor and prisoner of his unused treasure, and is not altogether unwilling to be relieved of life. After a perfunctory exchange of insults, Fafner, emitting fire from his mouth and nostrils, makes one pass at Siegfried with his poisonous spittle and another with his tail. In so doing he exposes his chest to Nothung, and is pierced to the heart. He seems more surprised than distressed, wants to know who is killing him (but Siegfried, not knowing his own origins, cannot tell him that), adds a solicitudinous warning against the instigator of the attack (Mime), recalls Alberich's curse as a prior cause, and to the baleful sound of the motive (13) of that curse, dies.

The positive meaning of Alberich's curse is that whatever element in the psyche is due for transformation will not be allowed to linger obstructively but will die in order to be reborn in its transformed condition. Fafner dead loses no time in reappearing as Fafner reborn. Even as Siegfried withdraws his sword from the still warm body, his hand is wetted by the dragon's blood. It stings atrociously, in the way in which new knowledge stings. He puts his hand involuntarily to his mouth, and thus swallows a drop or two: not much, but enough to symbolize his assimilation of his conquered opponent. The new knowledge is immediately apparent. He understands the speech of the birds which he was so recently attempting to understand in vain. The birds are in their traditional role as associates of the Great Mother. It is the Fafner now reborn within Siegfried which has this knowledge.

Fafner alive stood in Siegfried's path with the forbidding face of the Terrible Mother. Siegfried stood up to the terror, and Fafner integrated takes on the smiling face of the Good Mother. The mere taste of his blood puts Siegfried in touch with nature. But not in servitude. The call of his instincts now reaches him not in treacherous alliance with his regressive tendencies, but in full and innocent support of his real manhood. It is his confrontation of Fafner which has done him this inestimable service.

There is a rock-engraving at Uppland in Sweden which shows Fafner as a long ribbon of serpent almost meeting at the ends, and covered from head to tail with runes of inner wisdom. Sigurd (Siegfried) is thrusting his sword into him. Opposite, Sigurd is shown putting his finger with Fafner's blood on it into his mouth, and listening to the birds with the wisdom thus newly assimilated. Thereupon he is seen cutting off Regin's (Mime's) head for a reason to which I shall shortly turn.[1]

For Siegfried to thrust his sword into Fafner is on one level a veiled symbol for phallic penetration. Since the penetration is of his mother-image, this amounts to a psychic incest. That is why the symbol has to be veiled; incest, even in the psyche, is too dangerous a topic to be lightly uncovered. No further back than the *Valkyrie* Siegmund was sent to his death in requital of it. The finest of margins separates its constructive from its destructive implications. But the offspring of constructive incest in the psyche is oneself reborn.

The rebirth is never final, and may need to be experienced repeatedly; but it is never without significance. That some such experience of rebirth is now happening to Siegfried at this momentous meeting-point of his vanishing childhood with his emerging manhood may be thought more probable in view of the advice which the birds now give him through his new knowledge of their speech. They advise him to go into Fafner's cave and investigate the treasure. On the same level on which his sword-thrust was phallic, his entry into the cave is his entry into the mother's womb, like all the other mythological heroes who enter the

---

[1] See the reproduction in Larousse, *Dictionary of Mythology*, London, 1959, p. 261.

bellies or cave-dwellings or labyrinthine lairs of monsters in order to be reborn. We are still within the influence of rebirth symbolism.

No sooner has Siegfried vanished into the cave than Alberich and Mime come trotting out from their respective hiding places on opposite sides of the stage, to quarrel over the booty on which neither of them has yet set his hands.

ALBERICH AND MIME

In course of this quarrel, Alberich so cowes Mime that Mime suggests a bargain: the ring to Alberich, Tarnhelm to Mime. But Alberich is not going to leave Mime with the power to render himself invisible and steal the ring unseen. No: he will not leave him with so much as a nail. Stung to renewed fury, and with the courage of desperation, Mime declares that he will not share, either; he will tell Siegfried to kill Alberich, and he will keep both Tarnhelm and the ring for himself. Keep! The truth is neither of them has the slightest real prospect of getting these treasures, let alone of keeping them. Meanwhile, their quarrel seems fairly pointless and ridiculous.

Possibly it is ridiculous; but it is not pointless. It has a meaning somewhere, connected with the fact that the shadow side itself is showing every sign of splitting up. There have always been Alberich, the baleful, and Mime, the spiteful. While Alberich had the ring, they worked together, however unwillingly on Mime's part. Now for years they have been at daggers drawn; the shadow is at war within itself. Siegfried at present has Mime for the carrier of his shadow; so, in part, does Wotan, as we have seen in the previous chapter. But Alberich carries a more significant part of Wotan's shadow. Later, in *Götterdämmerung*, Siegfried will appear with two distinct aspects to his shadow, carried by Hagen and Gunther, as well as two distinct aspects to his anima, carried by Brynhilde and Gutrune.

We may be tempted in all this complexity to imagine that the symbolism has become confused; but this is not the case. The symbolism is clear and logical; it is the situation reflected by the symbolism which is confused. If the psyche throws up images of splits and quarrels, that is because parts of it are split and quarrelling. It often happens that isolated complexes of intense activity hive off in the unconscious, or have never been effectually in contact with the centre. Their autonomy is formidably entrenched, and their influence over our conscious actions and opinions is as potent as it is invisible. They are often connected with schizoid and hysterical symptoms, both of which are to be detected in some of the more irrational and violent passages in the story of the *Ring*.

It is an element in the growth of character to integrate our split-off part-personalities as far as possible, and we shall find this happening increasingly later in the story. At present the tendency is largely towards division. That in itself may have its positive as well as its negative implications. To see everything as one amorphous mass irrespective of its true differences is infantile; differentiation is an advance on undifferentiation. It is not possible to reconcile the opposites until they have been seen apart. Moreover, the present tendency is not only towards division. Siegfried has not only seen the two faces of the Great Mother; by standing up to the terrible face, he has taken a first step towards accepting the hard truth that both faces belong together. This truth was always there, but Siegfried had not got it into his possession until he killed the dragon, and in killing it assimilated to some extent the inner reality for which it stands.

Mime, at any rate, will not be in a position to quarrel with Alberich again. Siegfried comes out of the cave, in subdued mood, having seen mysteries greater than he can yet understand and treasures richer than he can yet put to use. He brings only the ring and Tarnhelm, which the birds advised him to secure, nor has he yet grasped their vast potentialities. They are just pretty gold still to him, as they were originally to the Rhinemaidens, which is perhaps why we later hear the motive (31) unforgettably associated with their 'Rhinegold! Rhinegold!' The birds now have a further piece of urgent advice for Siegfried: Put no trust in Mime, but through the virtue of the dragon's blood listen not to what his tongue is saying, but his heart.

There follows the highly comical scene in which Mime, in tones of deepest flattery and affection, puts into words his heart's murderous intentions, at last inviting Siegfried to drink the drugged refreshment and be killed with his own sword. In a spasm of repugnance, Siegfried jabs Mime instead, and he immediately falls down dead. Alberich's mocking laughter is heard from his rocky cleft at the side; but he knows better than to try conclusions with Siegfried himself, and is seen no more in this evening's opera.

Siegfried throws Mime's body into the cave on top of the treasure he had so anxiously coveted. In the cave's mouth he sets Fafner's body, moving it with a mighty effort. This suggests that he returns the Mime in him as well as the bulk of his new-found treasure to the keeping of his unconscious. So far as the treasure is concerned, this may be a wise move, since he has taken hold of the psychologically active elements of it in the ring and Tarnhelm, and the remainder is probably not yet ready to be brought into consciousness. But it is not clear whether he is so wise to have disposed of Mime in this peremptory fashion.

Siegfried has never really confronted Mime. So long as Mime was alive, Siegfried saw in him all his own unavowed cowardice and shabbiness. He only saw them in projection, without realizing that they were his own, but at least he saw them. It would be encouraging and not impossible to believe that by killing Mime at this crucial point, Siegfried had assimilated this part of his shadow just as he has undoubtedly assimilated part of his mother-image in the symbolism of Fafner. But the turn of events taken subsequently in *Götterdämmerung* makes it probable that this is too optimistic an interpretation. So far from assimilating it he seems just to have repressed it, on the well-tried principle of out of sight, out of mind. He has not yet learnt the meaning of fear: that is to say, he has not yet become conscious of his unheroic side.

SIEGFRIED'S FOSTER-FATHER

The significance of the dragon is not obscure. It is the same in Wagner as it is in the Eddas and the Sagas, and indeed in all versions of this basic symbol throughout mythology. The significance of Mime is by no means so clear, and there are considerable discrepancies between Wagner's treatment and that of his traditional sources. There appears to be rather more of interest hidden here than at first meets the eye, and it may be worth comparing the events of *Siegfried* with the very striking version found in the Völsunga Saga.

The Völsunga Saga is based in substance on the Elder Edda, and includes poetic passages quoted from it (to which the translators of the edition here cited[1] add further such passages by way of amplification).

Sigurd (Siegfried) is described as the legitimate son of Siegmund by a marriage of his old age to Queen Hjordis. Ripe in years and experience, Siegmund in his last battle is confronted by an old man with a bill-hook, on which his magic sword, the gift of Odin (Wotan), breaks. What Odin gave, Odin takes away: not prematurely, but in the fullness of time. Siegmund accepts his destiny, will not be tended, and dies on the battlefield in his pregnant wife's arms. She allows herself to be taken on board a passing fleet, and presently to marry its commander, King Hjalprek, at whose court Siegmund's son Sigurd is born and given every care and

[1] *Volsunga Saga*, tr. E. Magnusson and Wm. Morris, London, n.d., Ch. XIII ff.

sustenance. He is allotted a foster-father, the king's cunning smith, a man (not a dwarf) named Regin; and it is this Regin who takes the corresponding role to Wagner's Mime.

Regin teaches the lad a great variety of skills, just as Mime does. Presently Regin prompts Siegfried to ask the king for a horse; and the king offers him his choice of the horses in a certain wood, where an old man (the same old man, of course) advises him to drive all the horses into the river, and to choose that one which does not turn back to the land in fear; this horse, says the greybeard, is descended from Sleipnir (the eight-legged horse of Odin); and Sigurd calls him Grani (Grane). 'Nor was the man he met other than Odin himself.'

Regin is Sigurd's father in the spirit, as Siegmund was in the flesh. The physical father belongs symbolically to the mother world, since his biological function is a part of nature; the foster-father stands for those forces which draw the hero into conflict with nature, and through that conflict into greater consciousness. But nature herself is the origin and indispensable sustainer of all our development. Libido as a force of nature is represented by the horse, which is a widespread symbol for instinctual energy or animal vitality.[1] Instinct is nature, and in this sense feminine; it emanates from the Great Mother, but can be as useful to the masculine spirit as the horse to the rider. Sleipnir, Odin's horse, had for mother, remarkably enough, Loge the fire god, in his aspect as burning energy; he took a mare's shape for the purpose. Grani the descendant of Sleipnir stands for the positive instincts within Sigurd, and the test of it is that Grani is not afraid of the water (nor indeed of the fire, as the events of *Götterdämmerung* confirm). Regin and Odin together have done Sigurd this invaluable service, and it is thus clear that Regin is an executive of Odin, both standing for the father principle as the embodiment not of nature but of spirit.

This throws new light on Mime; and we may here recall that whereas Regin is a man and Wagner's Mime (Mimir) is a dwarf, the original mythological Mimir is a giant who keeps the well of wisdom at which Odin drank, so that one of Odin's poetic synonyms is Mimir's Friend. We begin to see more clearly why Wotan had that extraordinary conversation with Mime in Act I; and it also begins to seem that Wagner through the mind of Siegfried has been considerably under-estimating Mime's true stature and significance.

---

[1] C. G. Jung, tr. R. F. C. Hull, *Symbols of Transformation*, London, 1955, p. 396, p. 421; H. G. Baynes, *The Mythology of the Soul*, London, 1940, p. 86; etc., etc.

Presently Regin tells Sigurd a strange story, with Wagner's version of which we are already familiar. Regin is youngest brother to Fa.nir (not Alberich) and Otter (who spends most of his time fishing in the guise of that animal, i.e. bringing up dynamic contents from the unconscious). A corresponding trio of gods (Odin, Loki and Hoenir) while on an expedition together had the 'ill-luck' to get into the power of the three brothers and their formidable father, because Loki killed Otter; their ransom being to cover Otter's skin completely with gold. This Loki steals from Andvari (Alberich) by catching him in Ran's net at his waterfall residence. This gold is described in the Edda as 'water's flame'. To cover the last hair of Otter's muzzle, Andvari's ring is added to the ransom, whereupon Loki (not Andvari) prophesies a doom on all holders of the treasure. Immediately Fafnir kills his father (not his brother) and appropriates the entire treasure to himself; and Regin now wins Sigurd's promise to kill Fafnir and take possession of it on his behalf.

The differences here appear greater than they really are, and the fundamental significance of the story is the same as it is in Wagner. We may notice that Loge plays a part in some ways equivalent to that played in Wagner by Alberich; but we have already seen much in common between these two shady and ambivalent figures, both of whom share with Goethe's Mephistopheles the capacity to bring about valuable results by devious and seemingly evil means, and both of whom are essentially expressions of psychic energy. Such energy is in a moral sense neutral, morality being a concept not of the primary unconscious but of the conscious ego and the partially conscious superego (to use the valuable terminology of Freud).[1] Energy is energy and we should not expect it (though we often do) to have a moral bias either way.

On the other hand, the psyche is inherently predisposed to our advantage, in so far as we can give ourselves up to its momentum. Sigurd is now being guided into his inherent destiny by Regin (or Mime), not from any benevolence on their part but because the forces they represent are fundamentally of a positive order. Life always is fundamentally positive; life is its own purpose, and though its workings may be both ruthless and devious, they are never of their own accord directed against life itself. Our contribution is to let life use us; and that is precisely what Sigurd (or Siegfried) is doing in letting himself be guided by Regin

[1] Sigmund Freud, 'On Narcissism', 1914, in *Coll. Papers*, Vol. IV; *Group Psychology and the Analysis of Ego* (1921), London, 1922; *The Ego and the Id.* (1923), tr. Joan Riviere, London, 1927, Ch. III.

(or Mime). But for this guidance he would never have encountered the dragon.

Regin now forges two unsuccessful swords, and a third which is successful because forged from the fragments of Siegmund's sword, preserved by Sigurd's mother. Thereupon Sigurd goes to a certain Grifir or Gripir, who is his mother's brother and has foreknowledge of the future. Sigurd presses him to foretell his life and destiny, with which Grifir, though reluctantly, complies. This is interesting in view of the special position of the maternal uncle in mythology, where he stands (like the foster-father) for the archetypal father as opposed to the physical father, and is as a rule extremely helpful to the hero. The same special relationship still prevails among the Stone Age men studied by Layard[1] and others.

The next episode is Sigurd's vengeance on the sons of Hunding for his father's death: an episode which Wagner for some time planned to adapt, but eventually discarded.

Now comes the dragon-slaying. Sigurd, not for the first time in the Völsunga Saga, is (unlike Wagner's Siegfried) afraid of what he is up against. Regin wants him to dig a pit in the monster's path, get into it and stab from underneath. Sigurd thinks he may be destroyed by the blood flooding into the pit, and Regin taunts him with cowardice. But Sigurd is not a coward; he is aware of fear but can conquer it, and he gets braver as his story unfolds. So in truth does Wagner's Siegfried as he learns the meaning of fear in the next act of the opera.

However, as Sigurd digs his pit, the old man reappears, and turns Regin's deliberately bad advice into good advice by suggesting not one pit but several, so that the blood can drain off harmlessly. As the dragon approaches, Sigurd forgets his fear, and gives Fafnir his death-stroke. On being asked his name and kin, he tells Fafnir that he has neither father nor mother, which is literally a lie, as Fafnir loses no time in telling him, but is symbolically a true description of his heroic status as a man deprived of ordinary father's and mother's love in order that he may be driven back on their archetypal counterparts in himself more inescapably than most people. He then receives from Fafnir some wise counsel which he only half understands. This includes a warning to beware of deep water (rather as Odysseus was forewarned that his death would come from the sea—which it did, in the unexpected form of a fish-bone arrow-head). This deep water, however, is his own deep unconscious and cannot be avoided.

[1] John Layard, *The Stone Men of Malekula*, London, 1942.

Fafnir further warns Sigurd to leave the treasure alone if he wants an untroubled fate, which he answers by saying that he would forgo the treasure if that could save him from dying, but that since all men have to die he prefers, as true men do, to 'have his hand on wealth till that last day'. He is right here. The man who tries to avoid life's pains by running away from them does not escape death, he merely loses his life while still living it; the man who risks everything by letting life take a firm hold on him is alive all the time. The wealth is life and the troubled fate is life, and the two aspects are inseparable from one another.

Fafnir dies and Regin returns. Almost his first words are: You have killed my brother, and I am not blameless for the deed. This guilty feeling on Regin's part is Sigurd's guilty feeling projected on to Regin. Sigurd has just accomplished the truly heroic act of piercing his own mother-image in a murderous assault which is also symbolically an incest. There is thus a dual guilt inseparable from this act; and its heroism lies precisely in the courage needed to overcome the guilt and do the deed. Some reaction is inevitable when it is done.

It is interesting to find Sigurd using Regin to carry his own unacknowledged negative feelings, just as Wagner's Siegfried uses Mime. As Fafnir's brother, Regin is also connected with Sigurd's mother-image in its dragon shape. The same force which in the shape of Fafnir has to be combated, in the shape of Regin helps on the combat; and the same inner conflict which has been resolved in the killing of Fafnir arises again in the nagging of Regin. That is typical both of the fluidity and of the immortality of the archetypes. No archetypal conflict is ever won outright; no archetypal opponent is ever finally overcome. We are fostered and hindered, helped and frustrated by what is ultimately the same force working to harden and develop us: the force of life itself.

Sigurd is next asked by Regin to cook him the dragon's heart. Putting his finger on it to see if it is cooked yet, and then putting his finger into his mouth, Sigurd swallows a little of the blood, and at once knows the speech of the birds, who start by telling him that he should be eating the heart himself, and go on to advise him to avoid Regin's treachery by cutting off his head. He does so without a moment's hesitation. If Regin had cooked the heart himself, this would not have happened; he brought his own death on himself, in appearance inadvertently, but in reality because he too is symbolically part of the psyche, is due for transformation and is willing to let it happen.

How true is this of Wagner's Mime? I think the situation is basically the same. The basis of it is that a hero has to grow as independent as he can: independent even of foster-fathering. But whereas Regin in the Saga is presented in all his true ambivalence, Wagner has weighted our sympathies much more heavily against his Mime in the *Ring*. He has made him a singularly unattractive little criminal, hardly allowing us to realize that without Mime's positive qualities Siegfried could never have come to manhood at all. As a counterpart to this deflating of the powerful Regin of the Saga into the miserable Mime of the *Ring*, we find that Wagner has puffed up his Siegfried into something a little more buoyant than we can comfortably stand. Everyone, Wagnerian or anti-Wagnerian, finds Siegfried, at least until misfortune begins to overtake him, rather an unbearable young puppy in some respects. This unbearable element has to do with his being the boy who does not know the meaning of fear. Wagner admired him for that; but in the fairy-tales it is not something to be admired, it is something to be cured by any possible means. It is a grave deficiency, and nothing to be proud of. Wagner must have been proud of some unrealistic and inflated quality in himself which he identified with the boy in the fairy-tales. When misfortune begins to overtake Siegfried, however, he becomes more real and human, thus showing that the realist and the visionary in Wagner (these two are ultimately one) were more deeply rooted than the boaster and the illusionist.

THE BIRDS GUIDE SIEGFRIED TOWARDS BRYNHILDE

The two versions now substantially coincide. In the opera, it is midday. The light and heat are at their strongest, and Siegfried relaxes once more under the great forest tree. He envies the birds their free companionship, and asks them if they can find him a companion too to end his loneliness. And indeed they can; they can lead him to the fire-girt mountain where Brynhilde lies. In the Saga the birds volunteer this information unasked; Sigurd eats part of Fafnir's heart, keeping the remainder; he packs two great chests of treasure which Grani takes in his stride, and the rider too. In Wagner, Siegfried is unladen and as yet horseless. As his bird-guide describes the flames surrounding Brynhilde, he already begins to feel answering flames rising in his heart. After teasing him a little by pretending not to know which way to fly, the bird sets off firmly, with Siegfried close behind her as the curtain falls.

CHAPTER XII

Siegfried, Act III

———————— ❂ ————————

WOTAN AND ERDA MEET FOR THE LAST TIME

For the two scenes centring on Wotan which now follow, the Saga deserts us; but they are none the less interesting on that account. Their sources are in the Elder Edda, but have been greatly modified.

The music gives us (5), a motive from the *Valkyrie*, Act II, where it expresses Wotan's urgent search for a free hero capable of cutting a progressive way out of the gods' entanglements. The material of (5) is drawn from (3), Erda's motive, and (4), the inversion of Erda's motive which stands for the downfall of the gods, that is to say the replacement of ego's wilful authority by the deeper authority of the self. We may take it that (5) expresses here the same search for a progressive way out, though possibly in rather more general terms now that Wotan has become altogether more open-minded as to where and how this way out is to be found. We also hear (73), the motive of Wotan's spear and of the side of him which clings to ego's wilful authority; (17), his motive as the Wanderer, on that side of him which is already a willing servant of the self; (4), the actual motive of the downfall of the gods; (68A), which is a form of the falling semitone of woe attached more specifically to the power of the ring to bring grievous developments, however necessary to the ultimate growth of the psyche; and (16), the motive of the magic sleep, closely akin to (17), and like it an expression of the creative principle inherent in the fluidity of the deep unconscious.

All this prepares us for the strange and almost self-contradictory mood in which we are about to find Wotan in the ensuing scene. He seems to be abusing and repudiating Erda's wisdom in the very act of consulting her, perhaps because he is on the brink of yielding, and is putting up a last defiance and resistance. It is, however, also possible that Erda, in contrast to Brynhilde, stands for too primeval and matriarchal an aspect of the eternal feminine to serve the psyche directly at this stage in its development. The likelihood of this view is somewhat strengthened by the scene at the beginning of *Götterdämmerung* where the aged Norns are likewise dismissed and sent back to Erda the Earth-Mother from whom they came—immediately before Siegfried and Brynhilde appear together in a blaze of light.

At all events, we see Wotan as the curtain rises, in his now habitual guise of Wanderer, calling on Erda to wake her from her long sleep and dreaming. She responds by rising from the earth to half her height, glowing with strange green-blue light and inner mystery. All things are known to you, says Wotan: then give me counsel. My sleep is dreaming, she answers; my dreaming is purpose; my purpose is wisdom's work. But while I am asleep, she adds, the Norns spin what I know; why not ask them to tell you? Because, says Wotan, they only spin, and can change nothing; I come to ask of your wisdom how I can change the course of a turning wheel. My spirit is darkened by your own past possession of me, she replies; why not ask Brynhilde, our child? Because, he says, I had to banish her for rebelliousness. You, the teacher of rebellion? cries Erda; leave me to sleep again, you are not the strong, just man you think you are. He answers: You are not the wise dreamer you once were; and he assures her that he is a man becoming resigned to his fate, since it now seems unlikely that he can turn it aside. But he no longer leaves his heritage in bitterness for the race of dwarfs to seize upon; he leaves it to his own race of the Völsungs. Siegfried, of his unaided daring, has won the ring; because he knows no fear, Alberich's curse will fall upon him without effect; he and Brynhilde together will set the world and Wotan's spirit free (89). (This is still not a full anticipation of the course of events, since we shall find that Alberich's curse will not be without effect on Siegfried; but it is essentially right, and Brynhilde, Wotan and Erda's child, will make it so.) With that encouragement, Wotan sends Erda, finally this time, to her deep sleep again, and settles down quietly to await Siegfried's coming.

WOTAN AND SIEGFRIED

Siegfried's forest bird takes one look at Wotan, and flies off in a panic. Siegfried walks past the old man without seeing him, but turns back quietly enough when he hears him speak.

Wotan begins by asking Siegfried who he is, what he has been doing and what he is now on his way to do. Wotan and we already know the answers, and the point of these questions is not information. The point is to draw conscious attention to the situation, so that it shall not slip by either Siegfried or us without sufficient importance being attached to it. There are a number of such outwardly repetitive passages in the *Ring*, and most of them are necessary parts of the emotional and artistic structure. In *Götterdämmerung* particularly we are told in narrative much that we have already seen in action during the previous three operas; but this does not mean either that these operas could have been dispensed with, or that they make the recapitulatory narrative redundant. Myths themselves are full of such recapitulations, which are part not only of their form but of their technique for emphasizing the most crucial implications.

The implication of the present scene is that Siegfried, having grappled with the mother-image, must now confront the father-image in an equally formidable embodiment, so that it shall not hamper him unduly in the next stage of his development. Like the mother-image, the father-image has its terrible side and its good side. The terrible side includes all the restrictive elements in tradition and spiritual authority, the dead hand of the past, the weight of law and order, the far heavier weight of the partly unconscious super-ego with its plausible disguises as conscience and morality, the dry bones though not the living stuff of religion and philosophy, science and the arts: in short, everything that results from the masculine principle when taken negatively. Wotan has now to show Siegfried this negative aspect of the father-image, thus giving him the opportunity of standing up to it.

Says Siegfried: Show me my way forward, or if you cannot do that, let me pass. Says Wotan: Young man, honour the aged. Siegfried replies that he has had quite enough of the aged in the hated person of Mime, whom he has just disposed of, as he will rapidly dispose of this new aged nuisance if he persists in getting in the way. Commenting rudely on Wotan's great hat, he next notices the eyeless socket which it partially conceals: Mind I don't rob you of the other eye. To this Wotan quietly answers that the missing eye is looking at him at this very moment out of Siegfried's head. That shows great self-awareness on Wotan's part, since Siegfried is indeed Wotan doubly reborn; but to Siegfried it is the last straw in idiotic mystery-making, and he laughs roughly and impatiently. Wotan goes on to give him some more hints, which to us seem so plain that we are astonished to find that Siegfried still does not know who this stern figure is. But he has been deliberately brought up not to know, in his ego-consciousness. In psychic consciousness he knows well enough, and it is to this knowledge deep in Siegfried's psyche that Wotan is now pointedly addressing himself.

Suddenly Wotan has no more need to act his part as the resisting old man hindering the passage of youth in his and its own best interests. He lives it. He feels a great gust of anger and resentment, and bars Siegfried's way in real earnest. As Wagner put it to Roeckel (letter of 25 Jan. 1854): 'The god has now become so human that [in his] jealousy over Brynhilde . . . the desire for victory overcomes him, acknowledging though he does that victory could only make him wretched.' But this fury of jealousy was the most fortunate thing that could have happened. From now on there is no pretence, and no risk that Siegfried will not feel the full impact of these necessary events. Wotan roused is not a force that anyone could experience without being aware of it.

Siegfried at this is not only defiant, he is very much surprised. He asks outright: Who are you, that forbids me? Wotan rasps out: Mine is the might that called up the flames between you and the sleeping maid, and the man who wakes her up, makes an end of my might. As if in answer, the great flames begin to mount not far away; the magic fire is preparing to defend its prize. Now, says Siegfried, I know which way to go. Then if you do not fear the fire, says Wotan, fear my spear—on which your sword has already splintered once before. Siegfried cries out: So I have found my father's enemy; and he cuts the spear in two with a mighty stroke and a last potent flash of lightning from the broken symbol, the pieces of which Wotan quietly gathers together. Pass on, I cannot withstand you, he tells him; and disappears, bereft once and for all not only of his wilful authority but of any lingering desire to get it back again.

SIEGFRIED AND BRYNHILDE

The flames are the force of life itself, a formidable enough force to confront in any circumstances, but dangerous and truly terrifying only to a man who is either running away from life or opposing his own small will to life's greater purposes. Siegfried is not opposing the force of life in entering the flames; he is obeying it with all the very great courage and purposefulness of his own true personality. It is a splendid act, and we can glory unreservedly in his heroism. For it is heroism, even though he will not be burned nor so much as singed. There is nothing to show him that he will not. He may not know fear, but he knows all about fire. He was brought up in a smithy.

The flames quickly fill the stage, as Siegfried climbs through them up the mountain and is soon hidden from sight. With gauze curtains and cinematography this effect can be very well presented. When next we are able to see into the stage itself, the set has changed to an exact replica of *Valkyrie*, Act III. There is Brynhilde on her rock, to all outward appearances a mere heap of armour; and here is Siegfried climbing in from the back. His feelings begin to show in variants of (6), (38B) and (90A).

He pauses there in wonder; it seems to him, not without reason, an enchanted spot. But now he catches sight of Brynhilde's horse Grane off-stage—also asleep. For Grane is a magic horse, not a mere means of transport. He is akin, that is to say, to those horses and other helpful animals not uncommon in fairy-tale which speak to their owners and give them good advice, and sometimes end by demanding to be killed in order (though they never explain this in advance) to be transformed, perhaps into human shape. The symbolism of Brynhilde's horse is not so fully elaborated as this, but such horses stand for the life of the instincts, which may indeed need transforming at a certain stage (one of Athene's many titles is *damasippos*, tamer of horses). Being part of Brynhilde (rather than of Siegfried, as in the Völsunga Saga, though this difference is not fundamental), her horse fell asleep at the same time as she did.

The next thing which catches Siegfried's eye is the armour. His first thought is that it has perhaps been put there for him; but when he lifts the long shield, he finds that the armour is already occupied. By a man, as he assumes; and that assumption, on the face of it, is not very surprising. Women are not usually found in full armour under ordinary circumstances.

But these are not ordinary circumstances. Siegfried is not expecting to find a man inside the fiery walls which he alone can penetrate. He *is* expecting to find a woman. Why then is he so easily taken in? A charming, naïve touch, perhaps we feel. But there are no naïve touches in myth, in the sense of causeless touches without inward significance. If Brynhilde was left so concealed by her armour that there was every chance of his at first mistaking her for a man, then there is something to be emphasized in Brynhilde which has decidedly the qualities of a man.

That something is her animus. But since every woman has an animus, the emphasis which her armour, and indeed her whole warlike past history as a Valkyrie, lays on Brynhilde's masculine qualities must be a means of telling us that her animus is exceptionally prominent and strongly developed. Her subsequent behaviour in *Götterdämmerung* confirms this. Brynhilde is in all respects a strong personality: strong in destructiveness; strong in creativity. She is, in short, good human material, which does not mean that she has not got a bad side but that she is intensely alive and capable of development. She is good archetypal imagery, too, and all the better for being so ambivalent.

Siegfried now divests Brynhilde of her helmet and armour, cutting the iron with the magic of his sword as if (in the words of the Völsunga Saga) it were cloth. But this is no man! cries Siegfried; and all at once he is seized by every symptom of the fear which he could not learn from Mime or the dragon: his blood races, his eyes are dazzled, his limbs falter and his heart is faint. He cries for help to his mother, but falls on Brynhilde's breast. And so he learns fear, from a sleeping woman. Motives (30), (77), (80), (82) and (84) add their testimony to his mixture of emotions.

The strength of our desire and longing gives woman her power, and she may use it to destroy us or create us or both. At the back of her always lies the mother-image, two-faced, double-edged. Siegfried's fear is elemental and utterly genuine. But so is his courage in overcoming it: real courage this time, now that he has learnt the meaning of fear. He wants to wake her. Merely calling out to her is not enough; he must kiss her lips, though he should die for it. This is the traditional fairy-tale method, and it means that he is putting all his sense of value into the experience. Her eyes open; he rises to his feet; she sits up. As she greets, not Siegfried first, but the sun and the light (which in a sense he is to her since he has restored her to consciousness), a new motive (25) is heard. An E minor triad on the wood-wind; C major with arpeggio strings; semiquavers in contrary movement on the harps; a high trill in tenths on the violins, and we are in the most spacious of worlds, at the freshest of dawns. Hail to thee, sun, hail to thee, light, hail to thee, radiant day! He breaks in (90); Hail to thee, mother, who gave me birth. She echoes his words (which can be meant in two ways, one poetical, but the other literal) and they gaze at each other in wonder. As she tells him that she has known him and loved him from before he was born, he is more than ever sure that this is literally his mother returned to life, not from death but from sleep. She gently disillusions him, but goes on, to his still deeper bewilderment: 'If I have your holy love, I am your own self; what you do not know, I know for you; yet my knowledge comes only from my loving you.' The tender (89) comes in here.

Here speaks not the woman but the archetype. Holy love in Wagner—here expressed by the intimate-sounding motive (80)—is seen in contrast to sexual passion. This contrast is not found in the Eddas and Sagas, where sexual union is taken unsentimentally and naturally. But the real meaning which is implied in Wagner, although the unnatural sentimentality of the mid-nineteenth century prevented him from seeing it quite unmoralistically, is the same as that found in the Eddas and Sagas. The real contrast is not between chastity and sexuality but between the anima (or animus) and the actual women (or men) in our lives. Brynhilde's words at this point are spoken in her capacity not as mistress but as anima.

TO THINE OWN SELF BE TRUE

A man's anima has no particular objection to his being unfaithful to his marriage, but she has every objection to his being unfaithful to herself. This theme is developed in a great many myths and tales, of which the following from the Staufenberger legend is characteristic. A white-clothed maiden shows herself to the knight, over whom she has watched all his life in war and other dangers, but invisibly. She now unites in love with him, and promises henceforth to be with him visibly whenever he desires. He may make love to other women, but he may not marry one, under penalty of dying within three days. He ignores the prohibition; she is so angry that she stamps her foot through the floor; and within three days he is dead.[1]

Fidelity to the anima is not a matter of physical fidelity but of psychic fidelity. In the outside world, to marry is not necessarily to be unfaithful to the anima, and indeed the most usual way of serving her is to project her on to a wife and to cherish her indirectly in that projected form. But in this tale, marriage to 'another woman' is made the symbol of being unfaithful to the anima, who is the white-clothed maiden. Being unfaithful to the anima is being unfaithful to oneself. A bodily infidelity may or may not be of much psychic consequence. A transference of inner allegiance is of very great consequence indeed, and it is just such a transference by Siegfried that we shall find Brynhilde avenging later in the *Ring*.

In the Völsunga Saga[2] the emphasis during Sigurd's first encounter with Brynhilde, though it was physical to the point of their having a daughter subsequently mentioned, lies on the wisdom he asks her to give him; and the Edda[3] contains many verses which convey her wisdom. They comprise runes of war and seafaring and diplomacy and sound worldly advice, of which the last includes the necessary caution to be observed when making love to other men's wives. At a second encounter

---

[1] Cited by Jacob Grimm, *Teutonic Mythology*, tr. J. S. Stallybrass, London' Vol. I, 1882, p. 419.

[2] Tr. E. Magnusson and Wm. Morris, London, n.d., pp. 68 ff.

[3] Cited loc. cit., in verbatim quotation.

(which Wagner has not separated from the first) Brynhilde welcomes Sigurd as warmly as on the first occasion, but when he wants to marry her, she answers: 'It is not fated that we should abide together; I am a shield-maiden.' She is indeed an archetype, and a man does not marry an archetype, not even the archetype of the anima. The archetype is for all men, which is one of the reasons why the Great Mother (the fundamental figure at the back of the anima) is so often worshipped as the Divine Courtesan, with sacred prostitutes for the priestesses of her temple (another reason is her impartial fecundity). The complementary face of the Divine Courtesan is the Divine Virgin who is not touched by any man, but only by the impregnating spirit. There is no blasphemy in this; both attitudes are equally reverent and equally symbolical. The unconscious is incapable of blasphemy.

Sigurd thinks that his life will be without fruit if he cannot live with Brynhilde. She replies: 'I shall gaze on the hosts of the war-kings, but thou shalt wed Gudrun' (Gutrune). He swears: 'Thee shall I have for mine own, or no woman else.' 'And even suchlike spake she', at once says the Saga; he 'gave her a gold ring, and now they swore oath anew, and so he went his ways to his men, and is with them awhile in great bliss'.

This is a passage so condensed as to be positively breath-taking. Within these few sentences Sigurd has proposed marriage; has been refused on the grounds that his beloved is for all men ('the hosts'); has sworn that he will have no other woman; has been told that on the contrary he will shortly marry another woman; has nevertheless been accepted by the first woman; and has at once departed, alone, but 'in great bliss'. This all feels mythologically quite acceptable, and assuredly troubled its original hearers not in the slightest. To our modern sophistication, however, it is in urgent need of expansion if it is to seem comprehensible at all.

The key lies in the bewildering flexibility with which the actors alternate between their human and their archetypal roles. Sigurd meets his anima in the usual way, by meeting a woman on to whom he projects the archetype. The archetype (not the woman) replies that he cannot marry her, but that he can and will marry a woman. This reply separates the archetype from the woman; but since both look like women, there are now two of them, one being Brynhilde (momentarily the archetype) and the other being Gudrun (momentarily the woman). In ego-consciousness, Sigurd still mistakes his anima for a woman (Brynhilde), and in psychic consciousness, he knows that he cannot live without his anima. He says this to Brynhilde, who without a moment's hesitation agrees, and (as anima) joins him in swearing mutual and eternal fidelity. He departs alone in the sense of leaving this woman behind but not in the sense of leaving his anima behind: hence the 'great bliss', which is what a mutual understanding with the anima produces. Yet since all this is happening not in the outside world but in a myth, Brynhilde is no more nor less an actual woman than Gudrun, and never was. Sigurd is no more and no less an actual man. They are images one and all, carrying both our human identifications and our archetypal experiences. They do not even take these roles by turns. They are both at once.

Cumbersome as such an explanation is, I can find no better way of putting into concepts some part of what the myth conveys in its own direct and lucid images. The attempt may at least help us to realize what Wagner's Brynhilde is now trying, with no very obvious measure of success, to make clear to Siegfried. Her first statement, 'If I have your holy love, I am your own self' means approximately: 'if you value me not as a sexual partner, but as your anima, I am the part of you which is feminine'. Her second statement, 'What you do not know, I know for you' means: 'I can then mediate for you, as the anima may, between the conscious and the unconscious sides of your own psyche'. Her third statement, 'Yet my knowledge comes only from my loving you' means: 'the aspect of your own psyche which I as your anima represent burns with a desire for recognition just as eager as your need to get into relationship with that part of yourself'.

Brynhilde next sings that she had divined Wotan's thought before he did himself, this thought being that Siegfried should be her archetypal partner. Siegfried has been entranced by her voice but unenlightened by her words; he only knows what his senses are telling him, that he is mortally afraid, and that he looks to her to give him back his courage. Though indirectly expressed, she takes his meaning, and replies also indirectly, and also to the point. She shows him her horse, Grane, now grazing quietly in the background. It is the living symbol of her own awakening instincts.

He is feasting his eyes on her lips, and is thirsty to kiss them. She gestures to her discarded armour, the symbol of her discarded aloofness. He has come as defenceless through the fire, he says, and it has lit another fire in his heart. She must quench it; and he takes her in his arms. But with all her strength she flings him off. For if she accedes to her rising instincts as a woman, what is going to happen to her archetypal wisdom? Already her spirit sways and her knowledge ebbs. Siegfried reminds her that she has told him that her wisdom is the light of her love for him. But no, she is in darkness now, her light dies out, and she, in her turn, finds the meaning of fear.

Brynhilde's godhead is now melting away, as Wotan rightly predicted at the end of the *Valkyrie*. For the moment, we see a woman meeting her destined lover, and projecting her animus on to him as he has projected his anima on to her. They will share the fate of any human couple, seeing in each other at first only the goodness and fascination their mutual projections implant; presently reacting into as profound a revulsion while they project their own worst in place of their own best qualities; gradually, if all goes well, settling down into a more balanced appreciation of one another as they come to accept the real bad together with the real good. Things will not go well in this outward sense with Siegfried and Brynhilde. In an inward sense, things will go very well indeed, but from a symbolical rather than an overt point of view.

With the last of her resistance, Brynhilde compares herself to a clear stream in which he can see himself, and begs him not to break his own reflection by plunging in. But all he can see before him is a glorious rolling flood of unconsciousness into which he must needs plunge, as at his age it is only right that he should. With that, she is alight again, but the light is red with passion and no longer chaste. Are you not blinded by my blazing eyes, she cries, burned by the fire in my blood? Are you not afraid of the wild raging girl? And we hear, unexpectedly but logically enough, Fafner's growling dragon motive (57) in the bass, a clear reminder that even the most desirable of women still has an animus which can display a devouring and destructive aspect. Siegfried will suffer from that in *Götterdämmerung*; but he has naturally no thought of it at present. As his eyes cleave to hers, as his blood answers hers, his courage mounts and he loses the fear she first taught him. And so they break out into happy laughter and sing together of love's light. But also of laughing death.

On the face of it, we take this not for the solemn death of transformation, but for that other death which is the name poets have so often and so justly given to love's consummation: justly, if only because the inwardness of the experience is so largely unconscious, and none the less moving on that account.

But there is more here to this imagery of death than the poetic metaphor for love's consummation. Beneath the surface, the lovers have exactly the same kind of premonition as came to Siegmund when he pulled his father's sword out of the tree at the end of Act I of the *Valkyrie*. They know in their hearts that death in its solemn meaning is implicit in their union: death meaning, outwardly, the end of life; inwardly (since this is myth and opera) the transformation of the psyche. They have a detailed premonition of *Götterdämmerung*. 'Laughing,' they sing, 'let us die and go down into destruction; Farewell, Valhalla's gleaming world; Fall to dust, proud fortress; Farewell, the glittering pride of the gods; End in ecstasy, eternal godly race; Break, Norns, the runic rope; Twilight of the gods, grow dark and descend; Night of annihilation, come down.'

It is Brynhilde who foresees all this, just as it was Sieglinde who foresaw not only the death of Siegmund but the splitting of the world ash-tree ultimately implied in it. This is in keeping with the Sagas, which credited Brynhilde with particularly wide prophetic powers. But she carries Siegfried along with her here in her wild, uncanny mood, and the love-scene closes with the oddest mixture of carnal delight, Schopenhauerian gloom, and Buddhist expectation of Nirvana in the sense of an ecstasy of personal extinction (but does this perhaps mean ego-extinction rather than self-extinction? Though I am not familiar enough with Buddhist teaching to be sure, that is certainly what I should expect.)

It is not only Wagner's philosophical preoccupations which introduce a certain confusion into what is primarily a climax of naïve (at this stage, rightly naïve) young love. Wagner had other preoccupations of a more private kind at the time of composing this last scene of Siegfried. On 6 June 1869, Cosima, by whom Wagner had already two daughters, produced a son for him, and the event seemed to him of almost cosmic importance. He called him Siegfried; and he worked into the music he was then composing two themes which also make their appearance in the Siegfried Idyll, his romantic birthday and Christmas gift for Cosima (her birthday being on Christmas day). One of these themes is certainly and the other is probably taken over from the discarded relics of a string quartet[1] which Wagner had planned, but did not finish, in an earlier transport of emotion for Cosima, quite near the troubled start of their relationship, when the prospect of its happy development still seemed remote. Von Bülow finally divorced Cosima on 18 July 1870; Wagner married her on 25 August 1870; the Idyll was first performed on 25 December 1870.

The themes in question are motives (87) and (87A); and even if we knew nothing of their complex history we should notice their incongruity with the normal texture of the *Ring*. They are not only longer but less

---

[1] See Gerald Abraham, 'Wagner's String Quartet: an Essay in Musical Specu-lation,' *Musical Times*, August 1945.

flexible and adaptable than any others in the score, with the possible exception of Siegmund's Spring Song (86) in Act I of the *Valkyrie*. But that has clear affinities with other material, such as the Rhinemaidens' Song shown at (26); these two are hard to fit anywhere into the scheme. Perhaps (87A) might be regarded as having something in common with (6), and therefore also with (38); I can see no connections with (87) except possibly for (32)—both express delight by a rising scale.

The musical incongruity is not extreme; much less so than in the famous quotation from *Tristan* which Wagner brought into the *Meistersinger*. But that was to accompany a deliberate reference in the text to the *Tristan* story. This has no such artistic justification, and though the incongruity is slight, it has been very generally noticed, and it does have a somewhat disturbing effect. The effect is as if the mythological Siegfried and Brynhilde have become momentarily contaminated by the personal Wagner and Cosima.

There is nothing unusual and nothing objectionable in pouring a personal emotion into a work of art, if it can be fused with the archetypal situation expressed in that work of art. On the contrary, there is and should be a constant interplay between the more personal ingredients and the more collective. It did nothing but good when Wagner identified himself with Siegmund and Mattilde Wesendonck with Sieglinde during the composing of the *Valkyrie*; the private emotion passed through his unconscious and emerged generalized and universalized. Here the fusion is less complete, as may be guessed from the conscious use of pre-existing material, which is always dangerous for a composer, and was complicated in this case by sentimental considerations. The hero and heroine with whom Wagner here identified himself and his loved one were being seen by him in too one-sided a light to be wholly convincing.

We have already wondered whether Siegfried, until misfortune overtook him, was not inflated rather beyond his true stature, even as a conquering hero; and whether this reflected a corresponding inflation in Wagner himself, who had recently been taken up by King Ludwig of Bavaria with an adulation no passing estrangements seriously endangered. For Cosima to present him with a baby Siegfried at just such a moment was enough to bias, for once, even Wagner's sure artistic judgement.

Many people would agree that the end of *Siegfried* becomes slightly blatant. This is not due to the crude vigour of the motive (55) which conveys the frank yielding to instinct of the excited couple: instinct is crude, and there is not the least reason why it should be anything else. We do not grudge the couple their excitement or their happiness. But we do shrink from the faint suggestion of manic over-elatedness at the end of *Siegfried*. Most of Wagner's greatest music, and his happiest—notably the *Meistersinger*—was composed when he was unhappy and in distress himself. He could so seldom forget that suffering is the underside of joy; we may readily forgive him for forgetting it here, not in the text, which takes both sides into account, but in the music, which does not.

At all events, in a good performance the whole scene goes off with a tremendous swing, and we may well let any undercurrent of unease be swept away in the general impetuous flood of sound. We have every good wish for Siegfried and Brynhilde in this first happy riot of their romantic love; all the more so because those of us who already know their story know that their happiness is not fated to last. We are altogether with them as, not one moment too soon, the curtain comes running down on the imminent climax.

CHAPTER XIII

Götterdämmerung, Act I

— ❊ —

LIFE'S TWO FACES: THE LIGHT AND THE DARK

There is one advantage in the somewhat hypermanic end of *Siegfried*; the contrast to the beginning of *Götterdämmerung* could hardly be greater or more dramatically effective. We know at once that Wagner has recovered his full grasp of inner reality.

The music immediately underlines this contrast, and in a very unexpected way. We hear the same two chords (24; cf. 25) to which Brynhilde opened her eyes in *Siegfried*, Act III, Scene 3. For Brynhilde, they stood in E minor and C major: a radiant tonality for the sun and the light and for the joy with which she greeted them. For the three aged Norns or spinners of fate on whom the curtain is now about to go up in mist and darkness, they stand in E flat minor and C flat major; a veiled tonality at the greatest possible effectual distance from the other, since keys a semitone apart have, paradoxically, the least in common. Yet the chords are in the same relationship and the reminiscence is unmistakable. We could not be more directly assured that the mist and the darkness are the complementary opposites of the light and the radiance. We are now to be shown the underside to all that confident elation with which *Siegfried* ended. Betokening the dark and the light sides of the psyche, the two situations, one as clouded as the other was brilliant, belong inseparably together, and it is with effecting the necessary reconciliation between them that the remainder of the drama will be concerned.

THE THREE AGED NORNS

Where the strings in *Siegfried* were beginning their bright C major arpeggios, here in the second bar of *Götterdämmerung* (see 24) they embark (in their veiled C flat major) on a partly arpeggio and partly stepwise movement first heard (2) at the start of *Rhinegold* in E flat major, a tonality neither so bright as the one nor so veiled as the other, but midway between as befitted the state of undifferentiated nature there depicted. So there is a common background, too, for the three feckless, beautiful young Rhinemaidens and the three Norns, who are neither young, beautiful nor feckless.

Seventeen bars later, the innocent-seeming nature motive (2A) from *Rhinegold* is darkly cross-bred with (8) to yield (10). It is now in two or more parts, largely in contrary motion, to harmonies of the seventh and ninth diminished and otherwise, with a strong spicing of Neapolitan sixths, all on muted strings, and in a mood of such uncanny remoteness as to carry us right out of this world. The curtain rises on a scene of indescribable loneliness. The mists hang heavy, the light is murky; but we make out a gnarled fir-tree and around it the three Norns in their grey and shapeless drapery.

They are evidently in a state of distress over and above their habitual melancholy. As they take their turns at spinning the golden rope of destiny, and while spinning, singing that which they are spinning, we hear that once they hung their rope on the world ash-tree, in whose shelter the well of wisdom poured forth its pure waters, till Wotan came to drink there, casting one of his own eyes in as the price. Then he broke off a branch of the world ash-tree to make his spear, on which the runes and treaties of his authority were carved. But the wound slowly festered, until at last the tree withered away; the flow of the spring dwindled; and the Norns' once holy song grew dark and troubled. The fir-tree must serve for their rope now; for when Siegfried cut Wotan's spear in two, the lord of Valhalla ordered his heroes to hew down the withered ash-tree for firewood and pile it round the hall in readiness for a final conflagration; the spring dried up. Loge (21A) lies imprisoned in the shape of the fire round Brynhilde's rock as a punishment (we learn with some surprise) for trying to win his freedom by gnawing through Wotan's spear; presently Wotan will pierce his breast, using the splinters to which his spear is now reduced, and the flames pouring from the wound will seize on the shaft, which he will cast on the heaped-up ash-tree.

In great agitation, the Norn now singing breaks off with the cry: The Rhinegold once stolen by Alberich—what became of that? But her sisters cannot answer. Their entire information came out so piecemeal that we feel they have none of them a real sense of time or causation. Their refrain (23) is on the ambiguous tonality of the augmented fifth. They are timeless, like everything in the deep unconscious. They know, but they do not differentiate: hind-knowledge, present knowledge, foreknowledge is all one to them. And now their knowledge is abruptly at an end. Somehow the rope seems too short. They take it from the tree and wind it on a sharp rock, which frays its taut strands; it breaks. 'Down,' they cry, 'back to mother, down.' And they are gone, merged with Erda the earth-mother from whom they came.

This scene helps to put us back into the mythological picture which we might otherwise tend unduly to forget in all the overt activity at the end of *Siegfried* and through much of *Götterdämmerung*. The world ash-tree is one of the main cosmological symbols of the Teutonic North, and it has universal parallels. It is impossible to confine it either to mother symbolism or to father symbolism; in its vast scope it embraces both.[1] But mother symbolism comes before father symbolism, and the tree holds even more of mother than it does of father. In wresting off one of its branches for his spear-shaft, Wotan has wrested away from nature some of her primal energy and used it in the creation of culture. The tree has withered as that matriarchal order has withered in which our race began, and each individual of us at the nursery stage.

The fountain dwindled; and this was the fountain from which Wotan had himself drunk wisdom, paying for inner vision by the loss of an outward eye, in token of the fact that visionaries are often half-blind with regard to external affairs. Rivers have river-gods and are usually male;[2] but wells and fountains have nymphs, and are female (one of the symbols for the Blessed Virgin is a fountain[3]). The fountain of wisdom stands for that aspect of the eternal feminine which has to do with the anima; i.e. not in woman but in man. This is wisdom in the sense of Sophia who played before the Lord, and who keeps the father young and human, tempering his logic with intuition and his authority with waywardness and mercy. It is her absence which causes the living spirit to dry up into sterile convention and tradition to harden into reactionary or at best stationary repressiveness.

Whole civilizations have declined because their culture has grown too top-heavy to keep in touch with nature; and individuals are subject to the same decline. But nature has a way of flooding back, as the Rhine floods the last scene of *Götterdämmerung*. Terrible as the destruction may be, it can lead to new construction on a firmer foundation. Both as a

---

[1] Erich Neumann, tr. R. Manheim, *The Great Mother*, London, 1955, pp. 49–52, Ch. XIII, esp. pp. 251 ff., p. 259, p. 283, plate 110; C. G. Jung, tr. R. F. C. Hull, *Symbols of Transformation*, London, 1956 (see Index *s.v* tree); *Psychology and Alchemy*, London, 1953 (see Index *s.v* tree); etc.

[2] Erich Neumann, tr. R. Manheim, *The Great Mother*, London, 1955, p. 48.

[3] C. G. Jung, tr. R. F. C. Hull, *Psychology and Alchemy*, London, 1953, p. 69.

cosmological account of the racial macrocosm and as a psychological account of the individual microcosm, the *Ring* seems to lead up to just such a crisis.

Wotan, we have to remember, has cut himself off not only from Erda but from Brynhilde, his anima and erstwhile playmate. In so far as he has ceased to be in touch with the Eternal Feminine, his authority, which was originally fruitful, has become barren, and that is one reason why it has to be replaced. On another level, the reason is the need for ego to resign its ruling attitude in favour of the self during the second half of life. In willing his own downfall at the hands of the free and independent Siegfried, Wotan shows his virtual awareness of both these inner necessities. Events show, however, that it is no mere question of handing down his authority, as man to man, either to his son Siegmund or to his grandson Siegfried. It is a question of the masculine principle being sacrificed, and of the feminine principle redeeming it so that it can come to life again. None of this is yet to be foreseen, and least of all by the Norns, those aged relics of the matriarchal order which must have so long preceded even the beginnings of Wotan's authority. Their rope was severed by a sharp rock reminiscent of the dividing sword of patriarchal authority; the orchestra sounded Siegfried's horn motive (48), followed by the curse motive (13); they yielded to their destiny, and are seen no more.

There is a common factor in the breaking of the Norns' golden rope on the rock, the breaking of the Rhinegold away from the rock, the wresting of Wotan's spear-shaft from the world ash-tree and the wresting of Siegmund's sword from Hunding's roof-tree, and finally the cutting of the spear in its turn by the reforged sword. They are all assertions of masculine consciousness. But feminine unconsciousness will need to catch up with them. Loge as the fire of unconscious libido had already been trying to gnaw his way free through Wotan's spear before Siegfried cut it in two; and Wotan has now had the intuitive forethought to pile up the logs of the world ash-tree round Valhalla, where Loge can take hold of them when this present cycle of events comes round full circle at the end of *Götterdämmerung*.

THE JOURNEY TO THE RHINE

Day dawns to a quiet orchestral interlude which soon draws on Brynhilde's main motive as a loving woman (88). As the light and the music together grow brighter and more estatic, Brynhilde and Siegfried run out of their cave to the motive (65) of Siegfried's heroic achievements, not the least of which is his winning of Brynhilde. He has her armour on, and though we are not told how long he has been with her, it has been long enough for him to feel in need of new heroic adventures. As I love you, I must not hold you, she wisely sings. In a moment of irrational self-depreciation, she is afraid that he will despise her now that she has given him everything that she has to give. He is not so neurotic; and even if he were, that need not make her so unless she secretly agreed with him. No one, ultimately, can make us feel inferior but ourselves.

Remember yourself, she urges him, remember your deeds in winning me, our plighted oaths, the love we share, and I shall always be with you. The irony is that remembering himself in his true relationship to Brynhilde as his own anima is just what he is not going to be able to do; but this, too, is still hidden in the future. He gives her the ring, in token of the supreme value he now sets on her; she gives him her horse, in token of the deep instincts she stands for in him (which like the unconscious itself are feminine), while he in turn stands for her animus (which is masculine). They have a certain poetical awareness of being thus parts of one another. Both Siegfried and Brynhilde will be riding off together, they sing; both Siegfried and Brynhilde will be staying behind. On this exalted note he goes from our sight, the sound of his horn (48) still reaching us. A last wave from Brynhilde as he is momentarily visible to her again, and the curtain falls to conceal the change of scenery, while the familiar and magnificent music of Siegfried's Journey to the Rhine is heard in the orchestra. The 'Rhinegold! Rhinegold!' motive (31) reminds us that the real conflict has yet to be resolved. The music grows darker as the gold motive (44) itself is heard harshly in the minor, with (68), the falling semitone of woe.

THE GIBICHUNGS

This much has all been by way of Prelude. When the curtain goes up again on the first scene proper, we find ourselves in a different kind of setting from any so far encountered in the *Ring*. The nearest was Hunding's hut; that was supposed to be a human dwelling, but there was no one to be seen other than Hunding, Sieglinde and Siegmund, and humanity was the last quality we associated with the gloomy place. Here we are in a spacious and open palace with every evidence of ordinary human comings and goings. We can see right through it as far as the river, and out to the rocky heights beyond. It has a cheerful air of prosperity and normality.

At the moment, three figures are in the foreground. Two of them, the Prince Gunther and his beautiful sister Gutrune, certainly have the look of human beings. Gunther looks neither particularly strong nor particularly weak: a man who will get on very well in life, we feel, provided no unusually great strain is put on him, in which case he will prove hopelessly inadequate (it is, and he does). Gutrune looks above all things vulnerable. Again equal to the ordinary run of human situations, but not to the tempestuous conflicts in which she is going to get caught up through small fault of her own, she seems deserving of a better fate.

All this is confirmed by their music. Gunther's motive (67) matches his quite impressive exterior; it makes a considerable show of heroism, but the faint hint of weakness is there as well. Gutrune's motive (40) is among the most heart-rending in all music. The whole poignant tragedy of her entanglement in forces too great for her is foreshadowed in this most touching of motives, not strong, not very heroic, but deeply appealing. Closely allied to it, and as full of pathos, is a motive (41) which belongs to the Gibichung pair, brother and sister.

The third figure is that of Hagen, their half-brother, who is presented as only partly human. All three had the same human mother. The father of the first two was, we suppose, a worthy man of no particular importance; his name was Gibich. The father of Hagen was Alberich: not a worthy man, but of undeniable importance. Where the other two are weak, Hagen is strong. Where they are bright and resplendent, he is dark and sinister: dark in his hair and his colouring; dark in his armour; dark in his manner, and yet darker in his counsels. He sits there now like some harsh shadow on an otherwise sunlit and pleasant scene, with his powerful motive (61) in the music to match. He is still more darkly characterized when (61) takes on the fall of the diminished fifth C to F sharp in the bass (61A).

Gunther, it seems, is seeking reassurance from his formidable brother concerning his fame along the Rhine. Hagen answers dourly: Neither you nor your sister are married. He goes on to propose Brynhilde for Gunther and Siegfried for Gutrune. He has a magic drink which will obliterate Siegfried's memory of Brynhilde and set him aflame for Gutrune (who like Gunther knows nothing of his love for Brynhilde), whereupon Siegfried will be glad to serve Gunther by bringing Brynhilde through the flames for him. No sooner is this agreed than Siegfried's horn (48) is heard with the extreme promptness and punctuality of mythological events, which are not governed by time or distance but call one another up by inward necessity. Hagen, who is only interested in the ring, does not yet know that it is now on Brynhilde's finger; but events work out even better for him than he expects.

Siegfried must have had some dealings with human kind already, since he has acquired a boat. In answer to a hail from Hagen, who knows him at once, he calls back that he is looking for Gibich's son, and on being told that he has found him, leaps ashore, horse and all. (But this particular symbol is best left severely to the imagination; a circus horse does not always appreciate the purely symbolic significance of its presence on the stage, and can to say the least of it be awkward to control, besides making the scenery somehow look like pasteboard by comparison.) As Siegfried commends his horse to Hagen's keeping, we may wonder whether he is wise thus symbolically to place his instincts at the shadow's disposal. Gunther offers Siegfried his land and vassals to command (42); Siegfried offers his own strong arm, which he says is all he has. Hagen reminds him of the treasure hoard, explains to him the powers of Tarnhelm, and asks if he still has the ring safely in his keeping. Ah, that is in a fair woman's keeping, replies Siegfried. Brynhilde, Hagen cries involuntarily; but no one notices.

SIEGFRIED AND GUTRUNE

Gutrune hands Siegfried the drugged drink, and is thus not quite blameless for the consequences. He drinks to Brynhilde, but in the middle of the music (89) expressing his devotion to her, something goes wrong with the tonality of the trill: the semitone turns into a tone.

It is one of the most terrible moments in the *Ring*. The beauty of the love-music as Brynhilde comes to the forefront of his mind; the horror of the twisted harmony as the potion twists his brain; then a new motive (19) strongly reminiscent of an old one (18) which we know well from hearing it when Tarnhelm has been at work before, both of them eerie progressions which audibly spell magic; and it is all over. He returns the drinking horn to Gutrune with such a gaze of concentrated desire that her eyes fall. Why will you not meet my eyes, he cries to her; and again she does. In language all too reminiscent of his previous scenes with Brynhilde, he goes on: Veil them; they have set my heart on fire; my blood is scorching. He asks Gunther to give her him as wife, promising in return to help Gunther win one for himself.

When he learns that Gunther has indeed a wife in mind who lives on a mountain top, something stirs in him in spite of the magic. On a mountain top, he breaks in, with an astonished voice. Yes, surrounded by flames, Gunther continues. Surrounded by flames, repeats Siegfried, in fey tones, and we know that he is struggling to throw off the spell and recall these vital memories. It is almost unbearably moving. But he cannot. He pulls himself together (more truly, to pieces), and with excessive gaiety (übermüthiger Lustigkeit, i.e. manic over-excitement), he turns to Gunther, and proclaims that he is not afraid to go through the fire for him. The tragedy of *Götterdämmerung* is fairly launched.

SIEGFRIED AND THE MAGIC POTION

While Siegfried was a mere carefree boy, so innocent of reality that he did not even know the meaning of fear, so guileless that he did not know that the hoard, Tarnhelm and the ring were things that men would plot and do murder to get their hands on, Mime, being every inch guileful and every inch a coward, served him very well to carry his shadow. Now that he has become successful, popular, active and in full enjoyment of his activity, his opposite is no longer mean little Mime. On the one side, it is Hagen, who is not yet successful in his life's aim of retrieving the ring, will never be popular, is sluggish in everything which does not further his obsession, and is incapable of enjoyment. On the other side it is Gunther. Where Siegfried and in his own slow fashion Hagen are confident of their strength, Gunther is not confident at all. Where neither Siegfried nor Hagen care anything for appearances, Gunther is greatly concerned for his reputation. It seems that Siegfried's shadow is now split into two.

It also seems that his anima is split into two, since Gutrune is the opposite of Brynhilde: gentle instead of wild; vulnerable instead of formidable; appealing instead of masterful. Every projection and every desire which Siegfried first poured on to Brynhilde he is now pouring on to Gutrune. Ostensibly, this is the work of the magic potion. Symbolically, magic is any work of the unconscious which we do not understand. Sometimes it is more helpful than any conscious scheming could have been, and sometimes more harmful. It often amounts to possession; and whether possession is thought to be by the devil or by an autonomous complex in the psyche, it is still possession. A man possessed cannot ultimately be blamed for it; yet if he is sane in the legal sense of not being palpably hallucinated, we are mostly bound in the outside world to hold him responsible. In the theatre we can afford to be more compassionate, admitting that there but for the grace of God go we. Siegfried cannot help it, but Siegfried is doing it; and in feeling compassion for him we are feeling compassion for ourselves, so that we come away less censorious, less hypocritical, less hard on others and therefore on ourselves, and to that extent purged by pity and terror as Aristotle so well described the function of tragic drama.[1]

The anima can only be split up if she is also split off. When a man projects his anima on to this, that and the other woman in bewildering succession, so that the object of his love is continually changing, we say that he has a wandering anima. Not having established any stable relationship with her in psychic consciousness, he can reach no stability in his projection of her on to the women he meets. It is not, to be exact, the archetype which is split, but his image of the archetype; and in the same way, it is his image of the shadow archetype which may likewise be split, rather than that archetype itself. But for the victim of these schizoid tendencies the effect is that of splitting in his own personality. Hence the amnesia which obliterates Siegfried's memory of Brynhilde.

As drama, the magic potion is splendidly effective; and so is the oath of blood-brotherhood which follows it. Once more a little crude, perhaps; a little melodramatic. But where life itself is so often crude and melodramatic, is it for art to be unwaveringly refined?

THE PLOT AGAINST BRYNHILDE

The oath of blood-brotherhood consists in Siegfried and Gunther each cutting his own arm with his sword, and letting the blood drip into the same drinking-horn of wine (itself standing for the blood of life) held out to them by Hagen. Then, each with two fingers on the horn, they pronounce each other blood-brothers, after which they drink the wine together. If either betrays the other, let the blood now flowing in drops flow in streams to atone the treachery (11). Neither for a moment thinks that this is going to happen, but the irony here is that we, to our sorrow, know better.

Siegfried notices that Hagen, who also knows better, has taken no part in the oath; indeed he has now ceremonially cut the horn in two with his sword. But Hagen excuses himself by saying that *his* blood runs pale and slow and cold; he keeps away from such fiery bonds. Ah, let

---

[1] For the significance of a psychic quaternity as represented here by Hagen, Gunther, Brynhilde and Gutrune, with Siegfried as fifth aspect or quintessence, see esp. C. G. Jung, *The Psychology of the Transference* (1946), tr. R. F. C. Hull, Coll. Ed., Vol. 16, London, 1954, p. 203 onwards; and John Layard, 'Homo-Eroticism in Primitive Society as a Function of the Self', *Journ. of Analytical Psychology*, Vol. IV, No. 2, London, 1959.

the joyless man be, says Gunther. And now Siegfried wants to be starting. He is going to assume Gunther's form by means of Tarnhelm (it is his own suggestion—truly he is making progress in dwarf-like guile); press his way through the fire to seize Brynhilde; and with but one night's delay he will be back at the boat and hand her over to Gunther.

And this most heroic deed will be Siegfried's. Magic potion or no magic potion, schizoid amnesia or no schizoid amnesia, it does not show him in a particularly favourable light. So the hero, after all, has feet of clay like the rest of us. He does not yet know this himself, but we know it, and our interest in him increases with this evidence of our common humanity.

Hagen remains on watch. To music (68B) of dark strength and magnificence, he sings of Siegfried setting off to bring his own wife back as captive, and with her the ring—for Hagen. The orchestra carries on his thoughts with the curtain down, but changes to Brynhilde's music, prophetically troubled and distressed (90B), before the next scene, high on her mountain top with a storm blowing up. Her sister Valtraute arrives in exceptional agitation even for a junior Valkyrie, and with some difficulty persuades Brynhilde that she has not come from Wotan with a reprieve but on her own initiative in terror at the home situation. Valtraute should be a genuine well-chested mezzo-soprano, as Wagner intended, to give the necessary contrast with Brynhilde's dramatic soprano. Valtraute should sound distraught, rather than hysterical. Brynhilde should not sound distraught at all. The scene is a little long, but it has the important function of bringing the absent Wotan into the picture again. We learn that he is filled now with that longing for death whose underlying meaning is desire for the transformation of the psyche, though we must not overlook here the direct influence of Schopenhauer's 'renunciation of the will to live' on Wagner's imagery. We learn that Wotan will speak to no one, eats no more of Freia's apples, and is sunk in gloom (75). He has nevertheless so far stirred himself as to send his pair of ravens out into the world in the hope of hearing the only news which he would consider good; that Brynhilde has lifted Alberich's curse by giving the Rhinemaidens back their gold in the shape of the ring.

Brynhilde refuses violently to part with this token of Siegfried's love. The course of events cannot be precipitated, nor would it be in the true interests of the psyche that they should be. Valtraute is quickly sent home again. But now a fiery glow announces that someone is approaching not by flying horse but on foot. This can only be Siegfried, and we hear his music, as gay and heroic as ever. He appears. And his shape is the shape of a perfect stranger to Brynhilde.

His music is wrested painfully into a blend of the Tarnhelm magic motive (18), the magic potion motive (19), and Gunther's motive (67). The magic is twofold, since the potion took Siegfried out of his proper senses before Tarnhelm took him out of his proper shape. Brynhilde's feelings would be beyond imagination if the music did not share them with us so plainly. Her thoughts she tells us in no uncertain terms: Wotan has deliberately reserved her cruellest punishment till now, and his vindictiveness is past praying for. She resists her attacker, but not before he has revealed an unnecessary brutality which is not really in the character of Siegfried but of Gunther: a far from brave man, but he is not afraid of any woman.

The unconscious fantasy which the magic potion initiated and Tarnhelm confirmed has got the mastery of Siegfried just when he thinks he is using it so cleverly. It is not merely his shape that he has identified with Gunther but his personality. Contrary to what he supposes, the puppeteer is his unconscious, and the puppet is himself. We are learning still more about the underside of his character; for we have always to remember that it is Siegfried who is doing these shameful deeds. Hagen who instigates them and Gunther in whose shape they are done are only disguises for those parts of Siegfried himself which, because he would not like them if he were conscious of them, are being kept unconscious. The magic potion is a symbol for the unconsciousness.

The ring, Brynhilde's only remaining defence against Siegfried, is a symbol for the self. That has been my contention throughout; and in view of the antiquity and universality of this traditional implication of its golden circle, I feel quite certain that we must accept some such statement as our starting point. I call the ring a symbol of the self as the simplest way of stating the essential fact; but put like that, it is naturally an over-simplification. We have already seen that the significance of the ring varies with the intentions of the person using it. We must not forget that the self seems to have its intentions for us too. The self furthers its own intentions by furthering our intentions, in so far as these can be turned round directly or indirectly to serve the underlying purpose which the self seems to harbour for each one of us. For this reason, it may often appear as if the ring were merely a symbol for naked power. It is undoubtedly a focus of power. But we can learn something from noticing the circumstances in which the power visibly operates, and those in which it does not.

The most notable occasion so far on which the power of the ring has not visibly operated was the scene in *Rhinegold* where Wotan and Loge stole it from Alberich. He still had it on his finger; why did he not just raise it and blast his two attackers into grovelling submission, like his own slave-gang of miserable dwarfs? Because the total needs of the situation, as opposed to the needs of any of the individual characters seen in isolation, demanded that Freia should be ransomed with all that followed. Alberich was unable to keep it; Wotan was unable to keep it. Alberich was overpowered; Wotan was grudgingly persuaded; but not even Alberich could do anything with the ring to prevent it from passing on where the total situation was taking it. There is nothing to suggest that he expected to; nor did Fafner try to use the ring against Siegfried, though it is true he had no reason to, since he assumed he was invulnerable in any case.

As to occasions on which the power of the ring has visibly operated, there have not been any since it was stolen from Alberich. What has been visibly operative has been the power of the curse which Alberich set on the ring. But beneath the visible surface, the ring and Alberich's curse on the ring are operating as one and the same thing. Their musical motives (8) and (13) are versions of the same material. We suspected at the time that Alberich's curse must ultimately embody the underlying purpose, since it is so plainly the means by which that purpose is gradually effected. There is therefore another sense in which it would be truer to say that the power of the ring has been operating invisibly all along, both when it avails the immediate needs of the individual holding it, and when it does not. In all cases it is furthering the total needs of the situation seen as a whole.

The self is the totality. Hence it necessarily includes everything which we have in us of evil as well as of good. There is no question of evil being unreal or unimportant; it is both real and important, and so are our best efforts to resist it. But the evil and the resistance, the bad and the good, add up in the long run to a whole of which it is useless to say: this is bad or good. We can only say: this is what actually is.

One of the ways in which we seem able to picture the underlying purpose of the self is that it means us to grow towards a more conscious experience of what actually is. We shall find Brynhilde experiencing this growth of character in course of the long evening's work; but she would not do so if the ring now availed her to frustrate the evil designs which Siegfried undoubtedly has on her. She would frustrate them if she could, and seeing only the evil as she inevitably does, not the distant outcome, she is right to try. In a human situation, we can only act on what we do know at the time, including any clear intuitions, but not including any inner knowledge to which we have no present access. Brynhilde is for present purposes in a human situation; she has no present access to her old archetypal wisdom, though it will eventually return to her redoubled as the result of her sufferings meanwhile.

She holds up the ring in desperate defiance. Siegfried tears it off her finger, and the last of her resistance fails her. For a heart-rending moment, her inner wisdom pierces his disguise. 'Her unconscious look meets Siegfried's eyes,' says Wagner's stage-direction; and their love-music in the orchestra tells us that she has half-recognized him, just as he half-recalled her after drinking the magic potion, when Gunther described her on her fire-girt mountain. At such moments, we must especially think of them all as parts of one psyche, but parts which are out of adequate touch with one another: itself a symptom of our more unconscious states. When we are in a particularly unconscious state, we do sometimes have flashes of extraordinary clarity, in which it almost seems as if we see clean through our obstructive resistances and know very well what is the matter with us. But we cannot hold on to our knowledge, and it slips away from us, not to be recovered, perhaps, until many painful hours or days, or weeks or months or years afterwards. If it is recovered at all, it is not wasted; but there may be nothing we can do about it at the time.

There is nothing that Brynhilde can do about it now. She is at the mercy of Siegfried, and of a Siegfried so translated that neither can effectually recognize the other. The music makes its own shocked comment: we hear the driving syncopation and obsessive harmony of (15). This has so far been particularly associated with the evil plotting and scheming of Alberich, and of Hagen who now carries his plot on for him. The significance here is two-fold. From this point onwards, the iron enters into Brynhilde's soul. She returns evil for evil, hate for hate. She is caught up in the near-psychotic crisis, as we do get caught up in each other's near-psychotic episodes. Looking at it from her inner point of view, we can say that her animus (as represented by Siegfried) is in a mood both bad and unconscious. Or again, looking at it from his inner point of view, we can say that his anima (as represented by Brynhilde) has been outraged into blind hostility. It is this outrage which is the other significance of (15) here. The essence of the outrage is that Alberich and Hagen are the masters whom Siegfried is now serving without knowing that he is serving them. In so doing, he is not only serving his shadow, he is driving his anima into the service of his shadow too.

On this latter level of interpretation, we may for the time being take Gutrune for a flesh and blood woman with whom Siegfried has fallen so violently in love that he confuses her absolutely with his own anima, thereby forgetting the vital experience of his actual anima which he has already gained under the symbolism of Brynhilde. If a man has established a secure enough inward contact with his anima, he can fall in love with a flesh and blood woman without any infidelity to his anima, that is to say to himself: he will project the image of his anima on to his beloved, as we all do, but not to the point of losing contact with the anima herself. If, however, his earliest development was so disturbed by a lack of adequate mother-love that the inner image of his anima is insecurely established, he pours too much of it outwards on to the woman or women he loves, and loses what insecure contact he ever had with his anima herself. That is what infidelity to the anima seems to signify. Among the many dangers of this situation, one of the worst is that the anima in desperation may be driven, as here, into an alliance with the shadow. But even this may be the means to a desperate remedy, since matters will grow so bad that the problem will be forced to a crisis, and will either have to become very much better or very much worse. It is then a question of mend or mar, and we shall see which in course of the next two Acts.

Meanwhile, Siegfried drives Brynhilde offstage, into their own cave— which he should know so well; and with every appearance of impending rape—on his own true love. Before he follows her, he falls rather oddly and unconvincingly into his proper voice, assuring us (42A) that his sword Nothung shall lie between them: rather as we assure ourselves in most plausible imitation of our normal tones that everything is quite as it should be, at the very peak of our unconscious fit. We may perhaps agree that even at the very peak of his identification with the Gunther in him he would probably like to think of himself as the soul of honour, however little that side of him may know of the reality of honour. With regard to sexual rape we may therefore give him the benefit of the doubt, as the curtain comes down on this stupendous first act of the great tragedy.

With regard to physical rape short of the sexual there can be no doubt at all. Siegfried is abducting Brynhilde against her will. He is doing violence to his anima, and they will both pay a pretty price for it. Yet we should be quite wrong to dismiss the significance of the sword between them as a mere gentlemanly gesture to moralism. On one level, it is no better than that; but on another level, it carries a most valuable symbolism. The primary symbolism of a sword is phallic, but with reference to the masculine principle in general rather than to the male organ of generation in particular. The image of a hero and heroine lying side by side with a drawn sword between them in token of chastity is widespread. The inner meaning of the chastity is that the heroine is not a woman of flesh and blood for the hero, sorely tempted though he is to take her for such; she is his anima. The inner meaning of the sword is that his physical maleness will not possess her, but that the masculine spirit in him will. With this in view, the night now spent together by Siegfried and Brynhilde in their cave, with the drawn sword between them, is capable of a very positive interpretation.

The masculine principle is a principle of differentiation. In lying beside Brynhilde, at once separated in the flesh and joined in the spirit by the sword between them, Siegfried in his deep unconscious is differentiating out his relationship with the anima from his relationship with the women of flesh and blood. There is nothing he more acutely needs to do. But his conscious ego cannot do it for him, being far too distracted by his loves in the flesh. His conscious attitude has gone badly wrong, and the only means left to his psyche for restoring the balance is by trying to produce some sort of compensating attitude in his unconscious. What his ego cannot do, his shadow may have to do for him, with all its habitual violence and tortuousness and dangerous potentiality for disaster as well as for good emerging out of evil. That is the desperate remedy we are about to witness.

CHAPTER XIV

Götterdämmerung, Act II

---❋---

THE PERSONAL SHADOW
AND THE SHADOW ARCHETYPE

The brief overture to Act II makes it abundantly clear that we are still in the thick of the plotting and scheming; it recapitulates the main motives of Hagen's Watch, and we are not surprised to find that it is Hagen on whom the curtain rises. We can just see his massive bulk, looking blacker than ever, for it is night and the only light comes from the moon behind the clouds. He is still where last we saw him, at the entrance to the hall; but we are viewing the scene from a different angle and this time the foreground is the space fronting the hall, so that only the outside of the entrance is visible, right, while to our left the ground slopes away to the bank of the Rhine. Hagen is sitting with his back to a pillar, and is asleep.

Suddenly the clouds part and the moon shines out. And he is no longer alone. There is a second figure. Is this a mere apparition in Hagen's dreaming? Or a materialization out of the earth or the air? Certain it is that we now see the squat form of Alberich, crouching in front of Hagen and leaning on Hagen's knees. 'Are you asleep, Hagen my son' (his voice sounds more like dreaming than waking); 'do you not hear me whom rest and sleep betrayed?' Hagen's eyes are open, but he sleeps on as he answers, in the same dreamlike tones: 'I hear you, evil dwarf; what have you to tell my sleep?'

A scene follows between them which in its strange way is among the most moving in the *Ring*. It is an important scene; not so much for anything new which it tells us as because it modifies the balance of our sympathies. We are already more than a little alienated from the bright Siegfried; we have seen the brash side of his brightness in action, and not liked it; without perhaps quite knowing it, we are more open than usual to the subtle interdependence of good and bad, of light and shadow, of outer and inner, of the bright upper world and the dark underworld and the other complementary opposites which together add up to the sum of our human experience.

The bright side of life can be either genuine or counterfeit. The heroic face which Siegfried presents to the world is basically genuine, but no man is altogether heroic, and to the extent to which Siegfried is not heroic, his heroic face is counterfeit. As archetype, we might conceive him as pure hero; but as man, he is mixed and vulnerable like other men.

Like other men, he wears a mask to hide his vulnerability. This mask is what Jung has called the persona.[1] Partly it is conscious; most of us are aware that we have a public personality which we can up to a point put on and off at will. Partly it is unconscious; we are none of us fully aware of it nor fully in control of it. In so far as the mask is true to the genuine personality within, we wear it easily and convincingly; in so far as it is a conscious or unconscious counterfeit we pay for the help it gives us by the effort of keeping it in place and by the secret fear that it may slip off or be seen through in spite of this effort.

Every persona is to some extent a bluff, but a necessary bluff. It is a mask, but it is also a protection. If we exposed other people to the full impact of our fluctuating moods and impulses, and were exposed to theirs, we would never know where we were with each other, and would be excessively vulnerable to each other's projections. The persona enables us to present a sufficiently stable and acceptable exterior to make continuing relationships a possibility: our mutual behaviour is moderated even if our mutual fantasies are not. The persona is also more or less adapted to the collective ideals of the community, and helps us to comply with them.

When the persona grows too rigid and opaque, the opposite difficulty arises: we are quite unable to see what the real man is like behind his impenetrable exterior. Still worse, the man himself cannot see what lies behind his own exterior. Such a man as this is unduly at the mercy of his shadow, which may be enabled not merely to take cover behind his persona, but to take possession of it. Instead of the mask affording protection to the vulnerable ego, it affords protection to the scheming shadow, leaving the ego very little room in which to assert itself at all, though it still thinks it does.

Something of this nature has been happening temporarily to Siegfried. Gunther can on this level be regarded as the part of Siegfried's persona

[1] A good account will be found in the Coll. Works of C. J. Jung, Vol. IX, Pt. I, pp. 122–23.

which is both counterfeit and unconscious, so that the shadow has been able to take possession of it. Being outwardly presentable, it can work in the open and yet arouse no suspicion in the ego. It would be difficult for Siegfried to identify himself directly with Hagen, owing to the obvious incompatibility between the darkness of Hagen's scheming ambitions and the lightness of Siegfried's ego ideals. But it is easy for Siegfried to identify himself with Gunther, who not only appears to share these ideals, but actually represents them in so far as they are counterfeit. It is in this sense that we may regard Siegfried's shadow as split.[1] There is the part of his shadow which he would hotly repudiate if he once acknowledged it in its true colours; this is the dark Hagen. There is the part which he can incorporate openly in his own persona: this is the bright Gunther.

In so far as we remain too infantile to separate out any such opposites as light and dark, we have no conflict with the shadow.[2] It is when we begin to see the opposites apart that our ego ideals (the light in which we should like to see ourselves) cast a shadow (the facts we do not like to see in ourselves) behind the ego. These descriptions must none of them be taken too literally, since the contents of the unconscious cannot really be delimited. We do not even know that there are any entities corresponding to the names we use, but we do know that the psyche has modes of behaviour which we can describe as the persona, the shadow, the anima or the animus. Among these modes of behaviour, the anima functions for a man, and the animus for a woman, as the prime mediator between the unconscious and the conscious. That is a function, however, to which the shadow may also contribute indirectly, by means of catastrophic developments the potentially healing value of which may or may not be actually realized.

We left Siegfried engaged, at the instigation of his shadow, in preparing for himself just such a catastrophe. Having identified himself with the equivocal figure of Gunther, he was busy estranging himself, on every level except the very deep level represented by the drawn sword, from his anima in the shape of Brynhilde, for whom the much darker figure of Hagen is lying in wait. Here Hagen is, under the dim rays of the moon, Queen of Night and of unconsciousness. And here, urging him on to yet greater strength and sterner resolution, is Alberich.

[1] On the possibilities of a split shadow, see C. G. Jung, *Aion*, tr. R. F. C. Hull, London, 1959, p. 120. See also John Layard, 'Boar-Sacrifice', *Journ. of Analytical Psychology*, London, Vol. I, No. 1, 1955, esp. p. 8.

[2] Erich Neumann, tr. R. F. C. Hull, *The Origins and History of Consciousness*, London, 1954, p. 117.

What the primeval Erda is to the more differentiated Brynhilde, Alberich is to Hagen. If Hagen is to some extent a shadow personal to Siegfried, Alberich is here the representative of man's racial shadow. If Hagen is a dark villain, Alberich is the very Prince of Darkness. If man takes to devilry, this scene reminds us, that is because the devil is always there to urge it. But the devil's provocation plays its part in the growth of character, which largely consists in learning how inseparable (but not irreconcilable) good and evil are. The diabolical is the underside of the divine. At some deeply intuitive level we are aware of this, and our awareness opens us to the haunting beauty and significance of the present scene, in which two archetypal images, the one more personally and the other more collectively inclined, confront us and one another.

Be strong, says Alberich, as your mother bore you. Little joy have I had from being born, replies Hagen; old while still young, hating the happy—and we realize that Hagen as man has stifling neurotic difficulties to contend with, not of his own making, which give him a greater claim on our understanding than at first we thought. Hate the happy, returns Alberich, and love your unhappy father; then shall we two inherit from the doomed gods. Only Siegfried, he adds, is to be feared: possessed of the ring but recking nothing of its magic powers, and living for love alone, he alone is beyond the reach of my curse.

But here Alberich underestimates: Siegfried is not immune, since like each new holder of the ring he is fated to an outwardly untimely end. If Brynhilde should bid him return the ring to the Rhinemaidens that fate could in theory be diverted, and then, says Alberich, the ring would be lost for ever to the dwarfs. But fate in practice never can be diverted. Brynhilde is not going to give him any such advice; the underlying purpose will have to work itself out through the very plottings and schemings of the shadow camp. Fate cannot be diverted because fate is a name for that which is. Our fate lies in our character, which is for each of us the most important part of that which is; and not the least influential part of our character is its unseen shadow camp.

'Swear to me, Hagen, that you will be true to me,' sings Alberich. Hagen gives an even better answer: 'I will be true to myself.' 'Be true, Hagen, my son.' And so gradually that we cannot be quite sure when he has gone, Alberich disappears again into the darkness out of which he came. As he disappears the day begins to dawn, like hope dawning out of despair, to a warm and beautiful canon on the horns, the motive of which (49) is later taken up by Hagen's vassals in response to his grimly humorous side; for Hagen has decidedly a sense of rough humour, drawn by Wagner from the more attractive portrait of him in the Nibelung-enlied. Hagen now makes a convulsive movement, and has clearly woken; but whatever the nature of the scene which he and we have just been witnessing, we feel sure that he will not forget it, nor we either.

THE QUARREL BETWEEN BRYNHILDE
AND SIEGFRIED

With a great shout, Siegfried suddenly appears in the very act of taking Tarnhelm off his head, having used it as a means of instantaneous transport. Gunther and Brynhilde, he explains, are following at a more ordinary speed in the boat. As Gutrune comes running gladly out from the hall, Siegfried tells her that he has won her for his wife by his deed that day. Her first thought is that he has been in Brynhilde's arms; but he persists in denying it, she believes him, and the two go back happily into the hall together.

The gloriously noisy scene of the calling of the vassals immediately follows. With a characteristic piece of dour humour which somehow wins our appreciation, Hagen calls them together in language which suggests quite untruly that an enemy is at hand. 'Weapons! Weapons! Weapons through the land! Need is upon us! To arms! To arms!' And with commendable promptitude they come running in, at first by ones and twos, then in considerable numbers, until a full-sized operatic chorus is assembled. We have had as much concentrated, baleful music-drama as we can stand for the moment, and this gusty incursion from the extro-verted side of life is just what we need to redress the balance. The whole scene has an animal vigour and a clangour in the ears which restore our spirits tremendously, and refresh us for the further tragedy and intensity soon to follow.

We find that we are not the only ones to appreciate Hagen's little joke. The vassals react with hilarious approval (54). For Hagen to make a joke and summon a wedding feast and urge them on to drink until the drink has tamed them shows that he has a human side for all his habitual melancholy. And as the boat now approaches with Gunther and Brynhilde on board, Hagen and his vassals do everything musically possible to give the happy couple a hearty welcome.

The couple themselves, however, look anything but happy as they step ashore. Gunther introduces her manfully enough, but she is the picture of gloom. He draws her forward, saying that two couples shall this day

be blessed: Brynhilde and Gunther; Gutrune and Siegfried. As he utters
the name of Siegfried, Brynhilde, startled, for the first time raises her
eyes. And there is Siegfried standing straight in front of her.

So visible is her astonishment that it attracts general attention. Siegfried, with a courtesy in striking contrast to his unwonted harshness
when last we saw them together, asks her what ails her. Siegfried here?
she falters; Gutrune? With the same friendly politeness he explains that
this is Gunther's gentle sister, won by himself as she is by Gunther.
And with that Brynhilde blazes out: 'You are lying'; and she falls half-
fainting. As Siegfried catches her, she looks up with real bewilderment
into his face. 'Siegfried does not know me?'

Her bewilderment might have led her to ask quietly for an explanation
of the mystery; but as she catches sight of the ring on Siegfried's finger,
and not, where she thinks she last saw it under the terrible circumstances
of the previous night, on Gunther's, she loses possession of her senses,
and is indeed possessed by elements from the shadow side of her own
unconscious just as surely as Siegfried was when he drank the magic
potion, so that they act out of character while convinced that they have
never been more reasonable and justified in all they do. The only explanation she now demands is how the ring changed hands. Gunther, though
genuinely failing to guess that, it seems, is much embarrassed by the fear
that his cowardly deception in letting Siegfried go through the flames for
him will soon become clear to everybody. It is already clear to Brynhilde.
No one else seems particularly interested.

But now it is Siegfried's turn to be bewildered. His mind goes back
to his historic encounter with Fafner, and he declares that the ring came
to him then, and not from any woman. So his schizoid amnesia is blanket-
ing even the events of the last night. Literally understood, the magic
potion ought not to be affecting that; but psychologically understood, we
should expect the amnesia to extend in this way to everything that could
disturb the illusions needed for him to possess Gutrune with an untroubled conscience.

Hagen seizes his opportunity for making strife. Do you know this ring,
he asks Brynhilde, for the one Gunther took from you? Then Siegfried
has it by guile: he is a traitor. She fastens on the word: she is Siegfried's
wife, and she is betrayed, and so is Gunther's honour, since Siegfried
possessed her first. This he hotly denies, remembering his drawn sword
between them last night, but not the many other nights in the cave
before he drank the potion and the amnesia set in. His open manner
carries considerable conviction; but so does her vehement sincerity as

she breaks into a great outburst of grief, conveyed in an agonizing version of (37), and bringing home to us the full dramatic justification of her subsequent betrayal of him in her turn.

Each, then, shall take the oath on Hagen's spear, which shall bring death to whichever swears a falsehood. The irony is that Siegfried's oath is false to our knowledge but not to his own. It is a typical situation of myth and legend, where effects are made less by dramatic surprises than by dramatic irony of just this kind.

Up strides Siegfried, puts two fingers on the point of Hagen's spear, and swears his innocence. 'Let this be the weapon to pierce me, if her tale is true, and I have dishonoured my friend!' Brynhilde pushes him violently to one side, and seizes the spear-point from him. 'Spear, by your point may he perish for his false oath!'

Siegfried is quite unshaken. Gunther, look to your wife who is slandering you, he says, as one man of the world to another; let her rest until the demon departs from her; and you vassals, leave the women to their women's nagging; we men are all cowards when it comes to a battle of tongues. Then, turning to the women, he urges them to get busy with their preparations, and promises to be the gayest of them all at the wedding feast. They catch his infectious mood, men and women alike, and sweep off-stage after him as he draws Gutrune along in boisterous affection. The stage is left to Hagen, Gunther and Brynhilde.

THE ALLIANCE OF BRYNHILDE WITH HAGEN

Hagen's plot against Siegfried is prospering better than could have been expected if we did not realize that on a deeper view it is Siegfried's plot against Siegfried: the plot of the darkest forces in his character against the disproportionately bright and confident surface personality. It only remains now for Hagen to draw Gunther and Brynhilde into the conspiracy: Gunther, the other half of Siegfried's split shadow-image; Brynhilde, the deserted half of his split anima-image of which the ruling half is for the time being Gutrune. This is brought about in the ensuing scene.

We get a passing glimpse of the old, real Brynhilde as she wearily asks: 'What demon's craft lies hidden here? Where is my wisdom? Ah, I gave it all to him, I whom he now gives lightly away.' And with that thought, her sense of reality disappears again, and she wildly asks who is to lend her the sword with which to sever him from her. Hagen is already at her elbow: I will avenge you. On whom? she asks, as wearily as before.

On Siegfried, who betrayed you, he answers. On Siegfried? You? Her scorn knows no bounds. A single glance from his eye, such as reached me even through his disguise, would make short work of all your boldness. But, Hagen insinuates, mine was the spear on which he swore his falsehood. She rounds on him again: Honour and falsehood—you had better find something stronger than words to strike at the strongest of men. Hagen replies: the strongest in battle, yes, of course; but you, perhaps, have some cunning counsel ɪor me? Well, she has. Her own spells have rendered him invulnerable—except for his back, which he will never turn to the enemy. Says Hagen, well satisfied: That is where my spear strikes.

That Brynhilde (not really through spells, but through his unconscious projections on to her) has rendered Siegfried's front invulnerable but not his back is uncommonly interesting. A man's front is the part of himself that he can see; it stands for his conscious personality, and is indeed what he normally presents to other people too. His back stands for his unconscious personality. But that and not the front of him is where his own shadow can get at him to betray him.

There is no doubt that up to and including his mating with Brynhilde, Siegfried's progress into adult life was going well. His successful encounter with his basic mother-problem in the person of Fafner, and with his basic father-problem in the person of Wotan, freed him to carry the image of his anima forward into the normal condition of young manhood by projecting it on to Brynhilde. On the other hand, having failed to deal adequately with his shadow-problem in the comparatively innocuous shape of Mime, Siegfried is now being overtaken by this problem in the far more formidable shape of Hagen, with the added complication of its deceptive double in the shape of Gunther.

Siegfried's anima in the shape of Brynhilde did her best to protect him by sharing as much of her feminine wisdom with him as he was capable of absorbing. This wisdom includes and centres around the knowledge that however much a man may value and desire a woman encountered in the flesh, the highest value still belongs to the inner femininity within himself: that is to say, the ultimate object of his desire is his own anima. That he should project his anima on to an actual woman or a succession of actual women is valuable so long as he does not lose touch with his anima in her own right, as Anthony did when he not only fell in love with Cleopatra but lost his soul to her, and as a not surprising consequence lost the world as well.

But where does the anima go when we lose touch with her? Not

239

literally into the beloved, who is outside, whereas projections are inner events. The anima cannot literally be driven outside us; but she can be driven out of touch with the ego, deeper into the unconscious, which allies her with the shadow. This seems to mean that all the inner feminine sensitivity, tenderness, intuition, waywardness and temperament which so complement a man's outer masculinity desert his ego to aid and abet his shadow in its perpetual plottings. A woman's complement of masculine force, logic and reliability may likewise desert her ego when her animus becomes allied to her shadow.

Brynhilde as a woman not only hates Siegfried but turns to Hagen, thus dividing her animus-projections between a once-loved enemy and an unloved ally, and presenting a terrifying demonstration of an animus-possessed woman in the process. Siegfried as a man forgets Brynhilde but loves Gutrune, thus transferring his anima-projections from one love to another, and presenting an equally instructive demonstration of a man who has got out of touch with his anima. As an archetypal situation, this can all be seen through women's eyes as an alliance of the animus with the shadow; or through man's eyes as an alliance of the anima with the shadow.

All archetypal portraits of the psyche are true from both sex-angles, and Wagner's *Ring* is as valid a study of feminine psychology as it is of masculine. But since Wagner was a man, the masculine interpretation reveals itself more readily, at least to an interpreter who is also a man. Continuing, then, to speak mainly from a man's point of view, I am certain that the anima does not get outraged into an alliance with the shadow merely because the man forms an absorbing attachment to an actual woman and projects his anima largely on to that woman. She does not even get outraged if his projection is largely mother-projection, as it normally is. But if too much of it is mother-projection the anima gets very confused and upset indeed. She has no objection to our finding some of the comfort and reassurance of the mother in our sexual partner, but she has every objection to our falling right back into the mother every time we fall in love. Like all other manifestations of the eternal feminine, the anima has elements of mother, but she is not just mother. She is not just Aphrodite either. She has much more of Athena. She is a man's inner femininity.

We men tend to project on to the beloved woman not only the comfort of our mother-image but also the menace. By this we bring out the most domineering tendencies in the beloved's animus, and the more we cringe under her domineering tendencies the more she will nag and rule us.

That is one way in which the anima is outraged; all the more so since she knows that if we could only turn from our obsessive mother-image back to herself, she could give us the real strength and reassurance to live either in or out of a sexual relationship without infidelity to the anima.

Ernest Dowson's double-edged phrase 'I have been faithful to you in my fashion', meaning that in the ordinary fashion of the flesh I have been very unfaithful to you indeed while keeping a certain fond allegiance in the spirit, can also mean that I may project my anima on to one woman and remain faithful to that projection throughout any number of sexual fidelities with other women. Infidelity to the anima is in no way synonymous with sexual inconstancy. It consists in that deeper inconstancy of purpose to which sexual inconstancy may sometimes give outward expression. The anima may be as dissatisfied with compulsive sexual constancy resulting from unconscious mother-projection as with compulsive sexual inconstancy resulting from the same cause. Only genuine constancy, however expressed, can satisfy her: whether to a woman, a faith, a church, a divine image or her own unprojected essence. But no human being can experience the anima unprojected except in so far as he has first projected her and then partially—no more than partially—withdrawn the projection.

At the moment our projection of the anima is personified in Brynhilde. And the misfortune which has overtaken Siegfried in his estrangement from Brynhilde is infidelity to the anima.

THE TERRIBLE MOTHER AS INVISIBLE PARTNER IN THE PLOT

What so dazzled Siegfried that he lost sight of his anima was not at bottom Gutrune's womanly grace and beauty, real and valuable though these must undoubtedly have been. It was the radiant but unconscious vision of mother which he projected on to Gutrune's grace and beauty. We may remember that his first naïve impression of Brynhilde too (as woman) was that she was his mother come mysteriously back to life again. He is not so naïve now, and the thought of mother does not come to consciousness when he falls in love for the second time, with Gutrune. Not coming to consciousness, however, it cannot be contradicted by Gutrune as it was by Brynhilde, and its hold is stronger than ever. The result is a regression to a more infantile state of mind, such as we are all liable to fall into from time to time. It is the Rhinemaidens' insidious temptation all over again. In the music of Gutrune's voice Siegfried heard the Sirens' song; and he could not withstand it.

A comparison with the Völsunga Saga confirms this point. When last we consulted this version, we left Sigurd not actually living as man and wife with Brynhilde (which she would not allow on the grounds that she was a shield-maiden rather than a wife) but elsewhere with his men, 'in great bliss'. The bliss was the result of his having (by means of his encounter with Brynhilde as archetype) got into a good relationship with his anima with whom he *could* live, and was living, in the sense of having her inside him. In the next chapter Gunnar (Gunther), Hogni (Hagen), a third brother called Guttorm, and their sister Gudrun (Gutrune) are introduced. Gudrun is visited by disturbing dreams, which she takes for interpretation to Brynhilde, much as one part of the psyche may take counsel with another and more knowledgeable part. Since Brynhilde has already dreamt that Gudrun will come to consult her, the link between the two must be remarkably close, and indeed there is clearly a sense in which they are aspects of one another. (Another level of interpretation might be that they mutually carry one another's shadow projections.)

Gudrun's dream was of a hawk, with feathers of gold, who settled on her wrist, and seemed to her more precious than all her wealth besides. This hawk would seem to hint generally at the self, and more particularly at her own animus as her link with the self—a precious discovery indeed; but since all such images appear in projection to the tellers of a myth, the hawk is assumed by everyone to be Gudrun's future husband. After mentioning certain other heroes, Brynhilde gives Gudrun a full description of Sigurd (Siegfried); so full, in fact, that Gudrun at once knows that they have been lovers. She then comes to the point by telling Brynhilde not the dream of the hawk, but another to the same effect: a great hart with hairs of gold, which she alone could capture. But this dream went on that Brynhilde killed the hart, and then gave Gudrun a wolf-cub which killed her brothers. Brynhilde interprets: 'Sigurd shall come to thee, even he whom I have chosen for my well-beloved; and Grimhild shall give him mead mingled with hurtful things, which shall cast us all into mighty strife. Him shalt thou have, and him shalt thou quickly miss; and Atli the king shall thou wed; and thy brethren shalt thou lose, and slay Atli withal in the end.'[1]

Grimhild (Kriemhild) is the mother of Gudrun and her brothers. Although both Sigurd and Gudrun have had their destinies prophesied by Brynhilde, they can do nothing to avert them, and Sigurd in due time

[1] *Völsunga Saga*, tr. E. Magnusson and Wm. Morris, London, n.d., p. 89.

accepts the fatal drink from Grimhild. He loses all memory of Brynhilde; swears blood-brotherhood with Gunnar; marries Gudrun; goes disguised through the fire to win Brynhilde for Gunnar; at their wedding, spontaneously recovers his memory of Brynhilde, but says nothing and merely accepts the situation. Both couples continue happily married until a jealous quarrel between the two women brings to Brynhilde's knowledge the deceit by which Sigurd won her while disguised as Gunnar. In what follows, both the resemblances to Wagner's version and the differences are of fascinating interest, but although the Völsunga version is much longer and brings out the archetypal situation still more clearly, the two versions are essentially the same.

In what has just been related, one difference does stand out: the magic potion is prepared not by Hogni the brother (who in the Saga does his best to mend the quarrel, the actual murder being done by Guttorm) but by Grimhild the mother. It is this detail which confirms that the disaster overtaking Sigurd (Siegfried) was falling victim to the fascination of the mother-image. It was his own unconscious incest directed towards his mother-fantasies which betrayed him—not because his victory over them in the guise of Fafner had been in any way unreal, but because we are always liable to regression, and never more so than when we have just achieved a notable triumph but not yet come to terms with our shadow.

THE PLOT AGAINST SIEGFRIED

Hagen's next move is to bring Gunther into the conspiracy by playing on his sense of grievance. Brynhilde does her part here, by goading him with his cowardice in hiding behind Siegfried. Gunther then appeals pathetically to Hagen for help. There is nothing that can help, says Hagen, but Siegfried's death.

It is the first time these ominous words have actually been uttered, and Gunther is profoundly shocked. Besides, there is their blood-brotherhood. That has been broken by Siegfried, returns Hagen. How broken? Gunther wants to know. By his betrayal of you. Has he betrayed me? But here Brynhilde cries: He has betrayed you; every one of you has betrayed me; all the blood in the world could not atone for all this betrayal, but one death shall serve—Siegfried's. Hagen is quick to press his advantage by whispering to Gunther that he stands to gain materially, too, from Siegfried's death: for there is the ring to be won. Not that Hagen has any intention of letting Gunther win it; but it makes a good and apparently decisive argument, since Gunther sighs in return: Must this be Siegfried's end? It will serve us all, replies Hagen. But how, asks Gunther, can we face Gutrune, with his blood on our hands?

Another key-word, this, for the distracted Brynhilde. A flood of apparent light breaks in. Gutrune! So there was the magic which ensnared my husband—may ill befall her! We know that it was not Gutrune's beauty so much as Siegfried's schizoid susceptibility to it which produced the effect of magic on him. Much Brynhilde cares. She has fastened her hatred on to the other woman in the case, and has, if possible, still less compunction than she had before.

Hagen disposes of Gunther's last feeble scruple by proposing that Siegfried's death shall be disguised as an accident in tomorrow's hunt. Being all now agreed, they sing a conspirators' trio of a blood-and-thunder quality worthy of Verdi, and, it must frankly be admitted, just as ghoulishly enjoyable. Melodrama again, but melodrama justified by the situation.

Gunther starts with an echo of that sinister falling semitone (68) which has so often expressed passive woe or active evil, and has by now become strongly associated with Hagen. Brynhilde follows with a much completer statement of it; E flat, D, E flat, D. She has, in fact, identified herself with Hagen in the same sense in which Siegfried identified himself with Gunther—and without even the excuse of a magic potion to confuse the issue. The alliance of Siegfried's anima with his shadow is confirmed in the music.

This musical allusion may well have been deliberate on Wagner's part. But there is a further subtlety which was perhaps less deliberate. This is the resemblance between the semitone motive (68) and Mime's motive (71). True, Mime's version is preceded by fidgety little grace notes which greatly alter its effect, and it is most frequently accompanied by his rhythmic smith's motive (50), which resembles nothing in Hagen's music. Nevertheless, the crafty dwarf is also given this theme of a falling semitone to express his whining ambition, just as his nephew Hagen is given it, vastly reinforced in scoring and harmony, to express his massive ambition. And now Brynhilde, temporarily in Hagen's service as he is in hers, is given it to express her murderous intention.

The second Act is about to end; but before it ends, there comes a stroke of dramatic pathos which has no superior in opera. On to this scene of appalling malevolence, in which Siegfried has been doomed to a cowardly and treacherous murder, there breaks in the gayest of sights. Young men and girls run on, waving branches and flowers. Siegfried is carried high on a shield, Gutrune on a chair. It is their bridal procession. The music has changed on the instant to a passage so noble, so charged with joy, so compounded from the foredoomed vulnerability which is Gutrune's all mingled in with the brightness which is Siegfried's, that it turns the heart over. The irony is almost more than can be borne; but it is a moment of moments.

The only thing which can spoil this scene is perfunctory conducting. If it is taken at the rush, it is all over so quickly that we hardly have time to feel the impact. Certainly it is at a brilliant pitch of excitement, the very unexpectedness of which is part of the effect. But it must unfold convincingly, and with great exactness in the orchestral playing. The producer, who can hardly have kept the preceding scene too dim and conspiratorial, should now flood his stage with sudden light, so as to wring the utmost out of this last overwhelming turn of the ironic screw.

With a visible effort, the conspirators join the bridal procession, and the curtain falls.

CHAPTER XV

Götterdämmerung, Act III, Part 1

———————— ❀ ————————

SIEGFRIED ACCEPTS HIS DESTINY

As we settle into our seats for the third act, the glad sound of horns reminds us of what the day's business is to be. The hunt is up. The music rejoices our ears in spite of our sad knowledge (also reflected in the music) of what the main prey will be; and now it quietens down into a steady flow of harmony all on one chord (F major, this time) such as we have not heard for a long while. There is a little arpeggiation, at first singly, then in canon. We know it well enough; it is (1), the primary arpeggiation from which all the music in the *Ring* has ultimately unfolded, beginning with (2), which is the Rhine as the first slightly differentiated symbol of primary nature herself. There can be no doubt that this return to the beginnings is a deliberate reminder of what were the sources of all the subsequent development.

We are carried along now by the slow surge and eddy of the Rhine itself. And in a moment, still on a pedal F, we hear (31) the resolving dominant ninths of the Rhinemaidens' cry for their gold; another horn-call; then the lilting tunes (32, 33, 34) to which they weave their swaying dance and their seductive spell. Now the curtain is up, and there is the surface of the great river and the maidens three, swimming around happily enough although their song is of the gold which they have lost. The sun up here is bright, but we know that night lies under the waters, because there is no gold there now to catch the sun's rays. 'Rhinegold! Rhinegold!' And so their plaintive, beautiful trio runs on, with its liquid melody and its limpid harmony, until we would gladly plunge into the depths with them like any doomed sailor into his mermaid's arms.

It is the old enchantment, the familiar pull backwards into irresponsible bliss, the perennial unconscious fantasy of return to the mother's embrace. It is hard to believe that such a promise of delight can conceal such a lure of danger. We must once more remember that the delight and the danger are both real. All the joy and all the poetry in our adult lives are flooded through with emotions the undertow of which derives from what we felt as infants when mother was herself the source of life. So is the hate and the harshness; for she also inevitably frustrated us in part. What we stand to gain by going repeatedly back to this source is immeasurable, but only if we have sufficiently internalized and confronted it to bathe in it without drowning.

Having sufficiently internalized the mother-image means not being so liable to be dragged out of ourselves by perpetually but unconsciously projecting it too much on to other people. Having sufficiently confronted it means not being so liable to be swallowed up by the sheer nostalgia of our unconscious longing to be once more tiny infants. But the spontaneity of the infant and the unrivalled force and directness of its emotions are assets the more of which we can carry forward into adult life the more richly we shall live—provided it really is adult life. We are all right if we can plunge like pearl-divers into our infantile longings and come up with treasures of love and tenderness and art and religion, not getting caught up for too long at the bottom. The danger represented by the mermaid tribe is that they will not let go. They will hold us for ever at the bottom if they can. And by the mermaid tribe we must understand our own longings, personified as dangerously fascinating creatures who make us long for them.

In the opera-house, at any rate, we are held safely in our seats. Like Ulysses tied to his mast, we can hear the sirens' song, which is the most alluring in the world, but from the comparative security of our uninvolved role as audience. That is the advantage of an artistic experience; we pass through the gamut of human emotion, but not as literal participants. We learn from the experience without paying the heavy price which that lesson might cost us in a direct encounter.

But here is Siegfried, not by any means safe from the Rhinemaidens' enchantment. It seems they have been waiting for him. They tease him a little, and then ask him outright for the ring on his finger. He teases back: his wife might scold him if he threw away his goods on such as them! Is she such a terror, then? She hits him? The hero has felt the force of her hand? And with uncontrollable laughter they renew their dance. As they vanish beneath the water, however, Siegfried has a curious urge to end their mocking by giving them what they ask. Come up, he cries, and I will grant you the ring!

They may not have heard him. When they come up they have, for Rhinemaidens, solemn faces. They foretell to him, with a prophetic insight which comes from the positive side of their customary archetypal ambivalence, that the curse hidden in the ring will bring its holder to untimely death. Even as you killed the dragon, they sing, so shall you be killed, and this very day, unless you give us the ring back to rest for ever in the waters of the Rhine which alone have power to purge away the curse.

Siegfried has listened to them with quiet attention; but he refuses to be threatened. My sword, says he, once cut through a spear (which it did); if the Norn's rope has a curse woven into it, my sword shall cut through that as well (which could not be). A dragon once warned me of the curse; yet he did not teach me fear. A ring has won me the world's wealth; for love's grace it would have been yours, and still might be, but as for your threats to my life—see! And he lifts a lump of earth over his head and throws it away behind him. 'So I throw my life away!' At which they give him up for a madman, and after circling round for a time in great agitation, and prophesying that his heir this day shall be a proud woman who will hear their prayer, they vanish altogether, leaving him, not frightened, but a little regretful that he had not taken advantage of one of the pretty creatures while opportunity offered. He would have done, he says, if it had not been for his troth plighted to Gutrune.

The grace and charm of this scene and the irony by which it brings the feckless boy so near to reprieving himself (so near yet so far) combine to make it one of the most enchanting in the *Ring*. It is also, beneath the surface, one of the most crucial. For Siegfried to have remembered his plighted troth to Gutrune under the temptation of three new young women—and such young women—marks, with the lightest of touches, a turning-point. He did not remember his plighted troth to Brynhilde when he met Gutrune. He acted then with schizoid instability (under the symbol of the magic potion); but he is acting now with simple honesty. He does not even notice that he is being put to the test; yet he passes with flying colours. The test is whether this time he can hear the sirens' song without being seduced by it.

Siegfried's anima must be very pleased with his reaction. Double-faced like all archetypes, she doubtless arranged this encounter. She is both the temptation and the force resisting the temptation. On that side of her which merges into the archetype of mother nature, she is present in the Rhinemaidens. On her other side where she has to do with the growth of consciousness, she is present in the intuitive good sense with which Siegfried let the Rhinemaidens go unmolested. Like any other embodiment of femininity the anima has her flighty moods and her steady moods, yet will not respect a man who gives in to her flightiness and cannot stand up to her. A man who lets his anima control him will behave like a woman at her flighty worst, not at her steady best—just as a woman who lets her animus control her displays a caricature of masculine logic and firmness, not the genuine article. The anima will control a man if he disregards or despises her, and she will control him if he indulges and gives in to her. Above all, she will control him if he is so blind to her very existence that she remains excessively unconscious and therefore uncontrollable herself.

When Siegfried fell so fickly and naïvely in love with Gutrune, he outraged his anima in her steady self, but followed the promptings of her flighty self. Her flighty self encouraged the same unconscious mother-longings in him which distracted him from her steady self. It is an excellent example of the anima's capacity for giving bad as well as good advice. Siegfried's fickleness felt just as convincing to him at the time as his constancy had previously felt when he said good-bye to Brynhilde. This conviction in a man's feelings is the work of his anima, and it is always as well to scrutinize it with a certain scepticism if possible. Living by our feelings rather than by arid calculation is very desirable, but our feelings have this deceptive ambiguity. It is wise to be guided by the anima but dangerous to be possessed by her, and it is not easy to distinguish the two conditions at the time. A man should not listen to everything his anima is telling him. He needs his own masculine sense of discrimination to hold the balance.

For the Rhinemaidens to press Siegfried to give them back the ring in the unrealistic attempt to escape his own destiny is equivalent to his anima giving him bad advice. If he had taken it, he would have been possessed by his anima just as he was when he took the magic potion from Gutrune—which further opened him up to possession by the shadow. The ring, including the curse on it, is working out its own slow purpose of character-building, and it would spoil everything to repudiate it now. Yet we have to be given every opportunity of repudiating the underlying purpose, because it is only by accepting it through our own free choice that we can make it our own.

Our most crucial choices are often made when we least imagine that anything of importance is being chosen. Time and again we can look back at small changes of direction which prove to have been partings of the way. Siegfried does not seem to notice that his attitude has changed. But he is in fact not being seduced and not being cowed; he is being himself—no mean achievement. He is showing himself ready for the grimmer ordeal next awaiting him. He is willing to 'throw his life away'; which means that he is willing to accept the next stage of transformation which life has in store for him.

SIEGFRIED'S NARRATIVE AND SELF-DISCOVERY

On the enchanted beauty of this timeless, fairy-tale scene which Wagner has painted with music of such strangely bitter-sweet poignancy beneath its surface glitter and sparkle of dancing ripples and gleaming mermaids, there breaks in the menacing motive (13) of the curse, then Gunther's Gibichung motive (41) on his horn, followed by a distant hail from Hagen. Siegfried pulls himself with difficulty out of his day-dream; and so do we. He answers with a call on his own horn. The vassals are heard shouting, too, and then Hagen and Gunther come into sight. Siegfried calls them down to his cool resting place by the water's edge, and soon the whole hunting party is on the stage, complete with game, wine-skins and all the necessary provisions for an outdoor meal.

Siegfried admits to having had no success in the chase, although, he adds, he might have caught some strange water-fowl who sang him ill tidings, that he should be killed this day; whereupon Gunther gives a very guilty start. That would be an ill-fated chase indeed, says Hagen, if a wild beast were to kill the chaser. Siegfried says: I am thirsty; and so he is, but for more than wine. He is thirsty now for the knowledge about himself which can finally dispel his schizoid illusions and bring him to himself again. As Hagen's conspiracy against him approaches its climax, Hagen begins plainly to conspire for him too. It is Hagen who gives him wine and encourages him in his half-unwitting search for the truth about himself, asking: Have I been rightly told that you understand the speech of birds? Siegfried replies in some surprise that he has long ago given up listening to the birds. This is no surprise to us, however, since it is obviously some time since he was in the habit of letting his own feminine intuition give him advice. Yet he has just now understood the speech of the Rhinemaidens, which is of the same order of intuitive prompting.

Siegfried next urges Gunther to drink from his wine-horn, and hands it to him. Gunther excuses himself by saying that Siegfried has mixed the drink too thin—but then cries, with sudden horror, that he can only see Siegfried's blood there. Siegfried gives a great laugh, and pours from Gunther's horn into his own until it overflows. Then let our blood be mixed, he says, and make a libation to our mother earth! He asks Hagen: Is it Brynhilde who is getting on Gunther's mind? And Hagen brings him gently back again: If he could but understand her as you do the bird's song! Siegfried answers: Since I have listened to women's songs, I have forgotten the songs of the birds. Hagen presses on: Yet you once understood them? And with that, Siegfried turns to Gunther, and says: If you will thank me for it, I will sing you stories of my young days. I thank you for it, says Gunther; and the whole company settles itself comfortably on the ground to listen. There is a pregnant pause in the music and in the action. Then Siegfried's narrative begins.

This narrative has been criticized as repetitive. Psychic material, however, whether in myths or dreams, is repetitive; the same vital points are made over and over again. Art is likewise repetitive, or it could have no form; but the old matter is so brought back that it has a new effect. Every member of the audience is now conscious, though Siegfried is not, that these are the last few minutes of his life. Self-knowledge pours in on him, and it is this self-knowledge which gives meaning to his life as well as his death. His boyhood memories are knitting his life together at the closing of it. They make an idyll which our awareness of the circumstances frames in tragedy.

Mime, sings Siegfried, was a scoundrelly dwarf. He brought me up to kill for him a dragon who lay guarding a treasure; taught me to smith and forge; but the pupil had to master what the craftsman could not, the re-forging of my father's broken sword. With that sword I killed Fafner the dragon. And when my fingers burned with his blood, I put them to my mouth—and knew the speech of the birds, who told me of Tarnhelm and the ring.

As he himself tells us of these deeds, we hear them over again in the music, which takes us back even more movingly than the words. Here is the vivid scene now in front of us: the silent vassals, absorbed in the story; Hagen and Gunther, who know as the others do not know its imminent ending; Siegfried himself, more and more rapt, more and more immersed in these memories which are also realizations, this recapitulation which is also learning. It all looks quite normal and three-dimensional; but behind it there shapes this other reality, as if there were a second plane of experience not quite in focus with the first. It is uncanny how Wagner builds up this almost visible presence of the inner world looming through the outer world which in the ordinary course of events so effectually conceals it. He does so by using our ears as a second pair of eyes.

So now Siegfried sings the forest bird's very words and notes, to the same carefree accompaniment from the orchestra, in the same bright key. Tarnhelm will serve Siegfried for deeds of wonder—we know what deeds these have been and we have felt the wonder and much else besides. The ring will make him master of the world—we know that in these last moments of his life he is becoming the master of his soul. Trust not to the falsest of friends—even as we recall Mime, we remember with a shock that there is another false friend here and now, but no forest bird to reveal the murder that is in his heart. Or is he false?

'And Nothung paid Mime his wage,' ends Siegfried. As the laughing vassals press him to go on with his story, we realize that he cannot, having come up against the schizoid blockage in his memory; for the next part of it concerns Brynhilde. But the blockage is no longer firm now; it is nearly free. Siegfried has got his past life into his possession again, and he is ready to take up his own true story at the point at which he lost sight of it when Hagen drugged him with the magic potion. Drink from my horn, says Hagen his shadow; I have mixed you a drink to wake your memory. As it was the shadow who usurped power over Siegfried in his amnesia, so it is the shadow who will take the amnesia away now that Siegfried is ready to be his own master again. The shadow is an intermediary; the shadow is a potential bringer of new consciousness. The shadow can be a friend in disguise, and is no more false than we compel him to be by not accepting him.

Siegfried looks thoughtfully into the horn, and then as he slowly drinks from it we hear in the music (19) the magic working itself undone. From here onwards his rapt state is more marked than ever. The whole quality of his voice should change and become more inward. Now I know a glorious bride for Siegfried, he sings in the words of his forest bird: on a high mountain she sleeps, hedged around with fire, and he who breaks through it wakes the bride. And did you follow the bird's counsel? asks Hagen. 'Straightway I pressed through the fire, and found her asleep, and woke her with a kiss—ah, then like the fire enfolded me Brynhilde's arms!'

We are with him on that distant rock, and have hardly noticed the mounting consternation of the hunting party. But now Gunther springs to his feet: What do I hear? he cries. And suddenly Wotan's two ravens spring up, circle round Siegfried for a moment, and head off up the Rhine to tell their master that the end has come. Hagen breaks in: Do you know these ravens' speech? As Siegfried turns his back to watch them, Hagen thrusts his spear into him from behind, crying out in a great voice: They speak of vengeance!

The hero rounds on him; finds that his sword has been carefully put out of his reach; seizes his shield and aims it at Hagen with what is left of his strength. But even as he holds the shield above his head, he falls backwards on top of it. The vassals rush up to stop the deed already done. Gunther, now that it is done, shares in their shock and horror. But Hagen: as we first hear that pounding motive (62), punctuated by silences and by urgent triplet semiquavers, which is the main matter of Siegfried's funeral march, Hagen disappears quietly into the night now rapidly falling—the night to which he has always belonged.

SIEGFRIED'S DEATH

The impact of these events is harsh in the extreme. But we have to remember that the situation in the psyche for which they are the drastic remedy is critical in the extreme. This is so from whatever angle we look at it. Wotan has cut himself off from Erda and Brynhilde: the representative of fatherhood, masculinity and the spirit from the representative of fruitful motherhood and the representative of wise femininity. Siegfried has driven Brynhilde into a murderous alliance with Hagen against himself: the redeeming hero has put himself in urgent need of redemption. At the back of this crisis of the psyche portrayed in the *Ring* there may lie a crisis in the growth of Wagner's psyche: he may have identified himself too exclusively with the heroic strength and confidence he saw in Siegfried, thus unconsciously concentrating the opposite qualities of his own weakness on to Gunther and of his own unscrupulousness on to Hagen; and he may also have aroused some jealous resentment in his anima in course of his romantic relationship with Cosima. All the tension generated in these and other ways is here discharging itself in violent action. The discharge looks and feels like disaster, but it is happening in the same sense in which the psyche sometimes puts a man into a breakdown if there is no other way of breaking up an unduly rigid attitude on the part of ego. This may prove ultimately to his benefit if he can accept the breakdown as a healing opportunity, though not otherwise. Wagner personally had no need of a breakdown, since he was able to work the situation out in his operas. But there can be no doubt that we are experiencing an archetypal crisis in this tremendous scene of Siegfried's death.

We may suspect that the ravens were not at the scene of the tragedy merely to report it to Wotan, but to help bring it to a head, since it was they who caused Siegfried to turn round and expose his back to Hagen. The ravens are as black as Hagen, and know as much about the dark unconscious, which is why they are such useful news-gatherers for Wotan.

They are news-gatherers and messengers in various mythological traditions. Their swift flight suggests the flight of thought, and the names of Wotan's pair are Thought and Memory. They pick out the eyes of corpses both in outward reality and in folk-lore, thus symbolically acquiring insight. But they are not only spectators. In American Indian mythology there is a typical culture hero who is Raven, and he undergoes a typical night journey under the sea in the belly of a whale. Throughout the long history of alchemy, the raven was a prominent symbol of transformation. He is an associate of Mercury, for whom he sometimes stands, while at other times he stands directly for the devil. He shares to the full in Mercury's extraordinary ambiguity: in part, the base material from which the process of transformation starts; in part, the sublimated essence (philosopher's stone, elixir of life, divine child, differentiated as opposed to primordial hermaphrodite, etc.) to which it leads. In part, again, the substance to be transformed; in part, the transforming agent. Since this association with transformation is common to so much folk-lore and myth quite apart from its special application in alchemy, and since it is peculiarly relevant to the present scene, we have no reason to doubt here that it is subliminally operative.[1]

Gunther and the vassals are all one now in their stricken sympathy with Siegfried. As he struggles to rise, they hold him gently in a half-upright, half-sitting position. He opens his eyes, with Brynhilde's name on his lips. And as he opens them, we hear again, of all wonderful inspirations, the music (25) to which Brynhilde opened her eyes—how many lifetimes ago?—at Siegfried's kiss. She woke to greet the light, and the hero who became her light. Siegfried wakes to the light which is his own realization of himself, and with his last breath calls it by her name. What else could he call it? She is his anima and he has got her back. 'Holy bride, wake, open your eyes; who has locked you in sleep again? Your awakener kissed his bride awake, and now he wakes her again; Brynhilde's joy laughs for him; those eyes are open now for ever! Ah, the fragrance of her breath! Sweet passing, hallowed fear! Brynhilde gives me greeting!'

And so he is dead, and lives again. That is what these words which Wagner gives him state; and Wagner was not mistaken. Death in myth is transformation.

---

[1] For the above paragraph, see the indexes (*s.v.* Raven) of: C. G. Jung, tr. R. F. C. Hull, *Psychology and Alchemy*, London, 1953; E. A. Armstrong, *The Folklore of Birds*, London, 1958.

CHAPTER XVI

Götterdämmerung, Act III, Part 2

———————— ✼ ————————

THE DARK NIGHT OF THE SOUL

Gunther motions to the vassals, who lift Siegfried's body shoulder-high on his shield, and carry him off in solemn procession. The moon breaks through brightly for a few moments; but then the cloud closes in again, and the river mist rises to join it, so that the stage becomes invisible. While the scene is being changed, we hear the great funeral march, whose themes (36, 37, 45, 65, 66, 77, 78) recall the hero's high ancestry and bright glory, but in a setting so dark that pride and grief mingle on equal terms. Through it all the pounding motive (62) dominates the music with an overriding sense of shock, to which the motives of destiny (84)—heard as Siegfried died though not in the march itself—and of grief accepted (81) add their resigned commentary.

The funeral march is long enough for us to assimilate the sense of shock in full, and it is very important that we should do so. Death may be transformation, but we experience it as death, and the impact of so violent a death can neither be genuinely softened nor genuinely avoided. If it could, it would not transform. Sentimentalizing life's tragedies is one way of rendering them unfruitful. We may contrive to evade the pain; but there is a maturer happiness which comes only to those who have had to accept suffering and yet not been destroyed by it.

The situation now confronting us corresponds to that darkest hour before the dawn which the mystics and the alchemists recognized under the name of the *nigrado* (blackening) or *putrefactio* (dissolution), and for which, incidentally, the black raven was one of the symbols. It is an experience which no one having once passed through it will under-rate. Like so many of the realities in which mystics and alchemists have dealt, it is by no means out of the ordinary. There is nothing uncommon about the inner realities except that their intangibility makes them uncommonly difficult to describe. Besides being difficult to describe, however, the darker realities of our shadow side were actively resisted and played down by Christianity in the interests of reason, so that it was on the whole left to the unorthodox minority of Hermetic philosophers, alchemists and others to keep alive a more positive attitude to the daemonic element. Hermes (Mercury) was the ruling principle of alchemy precisely because he moves in the dark shadows with daemonic power and ambiguity.

Satan is likewise a Prince of Darkness, but his positive potentialities are not officially admitted, and this one-sidedness exacerbates his negative potentialities. The repression was a necessary contribution to the growth of consciousness, but it has tipped the scales so far against the claims of the unconscious that we are only just beginning to redress the balance by means, largely, of depth psychology, one of the uses of which is to help in taking up a positive attitude with regard to the underside of life in general and the problem of pain in particular. A necessary step to such an attitude is to accept that there is an underside, and to look pain in the face. Death is painful; so is birth. The death of Siegfried is shatteringly painful, and though there is an eventual rebirth implied in it, we have first to experience that dark night of the soul in which no glimmering of light suggests that there may yet be another dawn.

Grief such as we experience for Siegfried, however, is not the same as barren desolation, and is not destructive to the personality as desolation may be. Grief is a crisis of the emotions which has to be lived through to the full. If it is lived through, it can resolve into strength and not into weakness. Neither grief nor fear in themselves make anyone neurotic, though panic inability to accept them may. It is for this reason, and not from sentimentality, that our funeral rites do not stress only the terrible face of death but also his dark comeliness. We pile the grave with gay flowers not necessarily to escape our grief but to signify that any grief which is accepted as part of our common lot can flower again with new life. Grief is not only a negative emotion, but like everything else which is unhypocritically direct and human, contains values which are positive.

To some extent our experience of destiny (though not destiny itself) is what we make of it. We may experience destiny as cruel, senseless and capricious, but only in so far as we are out of touch with life as a whole. No primitive man experiences destiny in so exclusively negative a way. Jung has suggested, indeed, that the invisible pattern of the archetypes comprises not only the inexorability which we experience as destiny, but also the meaningfulness which is the positive part of the experience.[1]

[1] C. G. Jung, *Two Essays on Analytical Psychology*, Coll. Ed., tr. R. F. C. Hull, Vol. VII, London, 1953, p. 107.

The motive (84) which Wagner uses for the idea of destiny and of quiet resignation to destiny confirms that he did not conceive of Siegfried experiencing his fate as cruel and senseless. It is a motive of remarkable solemnity, at once tragic and serene. Here is a force which cannot and in the last resort should not be resisted; that is the implication of this brief but pregnant modulation, itself irresistible in its tonal force, so that the motive makes its own impression of inevitability.

The funeral march gives the violence of the tragedy full scope, yet tempers this violence by intimations of the dignity of human suffering. It is a genuine expression of grief because it suppresses neither the suffering nor the victory over the suffering. The essence of suffering, however, is that it really hurts; and though in the end true grief brings its own healing, that cannot be emotionally foreseen. This is the valley of the shadow of death, and this is us in it. While we are in it, there is nothing we can do about it except endure it.

Meanwhile, the violence is still continuing. When the mists again divide, we see the inside of the Gibichung hall, as in Act I. The moon is now uncovered, and at first the moonlight reflected up from the Rhine is the only illumination which reaches the interior. Gutrune comes out, sleepless with foreboding, and straining her ears for the sound of Siegfried's horn. No, that was not it. But she has heard, or dreamt of hearing, his horse neighing wildly, and a laugh as wild from Brynhilde, whose room, terrifyingly, she now finds empty.

Hagen's voice breaks in, a rough cry for attendants and lights. With harsh irony he tells Gutrune to greet Siegfried; and to her tortured questioning replies that a boar has killed him. It is a lie, but an appropriate lie, since a boar is a typical symbol for the destructive attributes of the Great Mother.[1] As Siegfried's corpse is set down, Gutrune falls on it, but knows at once that he has been murdered—by Gunther? No, says Gunther, by Hagen; and Hagen defiantly admits that his spear did the killing, since Siegfried's false oath was sworn on it. And with that he steps forward to claim the ring. As Gunther intervenes, saying that the ring is Gutrune's dower, the two men fight, and the stronger wins. Gunther falls dead.

During this fight for possession of the ring, the ring's own motive (8) is heard in a harmony which sounds really vicious. As Hagen kills Gunther, that terrible form (68A) of the falling semitone of woe is heard of which the specific characterization seems to belong to evil deeds done

[1] John Layard, 'Boar-Sacrifice', *Journ. of Analytical Psychology*, Vol. I, No. 1, London, 1955.

through coveting the ring, or what is the same thing from another angle, through the power of the curse placed on the ring. We could not be more forcefully reminded that the self is the totality, and that the totality includes every particle of evil as well as of good. It would not be the totality if this were not the case.

In our human experience both evil and good play tremendous parts, and it is quite beyond our power to reconcile them in anything but a more or less incomplete measure. Yet reconciling them is the only way ultimately of dealing with evil. The evil is not really the devil's responsibility, but ours, and is a part of ourselves however convincingly we paint up the devil to project it on. It is, moreover, a part of ourselves which conceals some of our best potentialities as well as of our worst, as the mythology of the devil in his innumerable manifestations has always recognized. It is no use rejecting a part of our very selves which can only be modified in so far as we can get on terms with it. Since it is part of us in any case, we have to know it better in order to have at least some success in relating it to our ordinary conscious values. The worst feature common to evil deeds is the extreme degree in which they are cut off from ordinary human values. They are unrelated, schizoid like the people doing them. If we were not cut off from ordinary values when doing them we should not be able to do them. The only cure for our own evil genius is to integrate it better by becoming less cut off from it.

If this murder in pursuit of the ring were done in outside life, the evil of it, as far as human judgement can see, would be stark and unredeemed: exactly as we hear it in the twisted harmony here given to (8) and the violence given to (68A). In the opera-house, however, while we are thus rightly reminded that murder is evil, we are well aware that murder is also a symbol. The music tells us that the symbol has to do with the ring. It is easy to see that the ring is the coveted object for which the murder is done; less easy to see that the murder may serve the underlying purpose towards which the ring itself, or rather the central principle for which the ring stands, has been working all along. Yet if Hagen's primary murder of Siegfried served the purpose of the self, his secondary murder of Gunther must do so too. Since Hagen and Gunther, on this level, have been acting as split-up components of the shadow, the probability is that Hagen in killing Gunther has assimilated him in the same sense in which Fafner long ago assimilated Fasolt. By this violent deed, the split in the shadow has been remedied, and painful though it may be, that is a step in the direction of better integration.

THE ETERNAL MASCULINE
AND THE ETERNAL FEMININE

Hagen stretches out to seize his prize. He is stopped by a force stronger than his own dour strength. The dead Siegfried raises his arm, with the ring on his finger, in the legendary miracle of denunciation. We hear the sword motive (45) ringing out in all its potent brightness and clearness. There is nothing ambivalent in the sound of that. Siegfried's manhood, once forged by him under the symbol of the sword, rings truer now in death than in his recent life. Wotan's great thought at the close of *Rhinegold* when we originally heard (45) is finally vindicated in this tremendous moment. The element in the psyche for which Siegmund was the first tentative symbol and Siegfried the second and more developed symbol was not destroyed when these heroes died. There is more power of life in one limb of Siegfried's corpse than in the whole of Hagen's living body. Behind this miracle of the flesh, however, lies the more ultimate truth that we are not really being shown bodily events at all, but psychic events under the appearance of bodily events.

The psychic event which we are being shown by the miracle of Siegfried raising his dead arm to refuse Hagen the ring is the climax of the whole long process by which Wotan, in his role as representative of the ego, made up his mind to yield to the superior power of the self. The climax of a psychic process has often this air of arising with dramatic suddenness; the process itself is long drawn out, with many a lapse and many a regression on the way. We see a vision as Wotan saw a vision at the close of *Rhinegold*. We see that we might, one day, really commit ourselves to being alive, with all that means of fear and pain as well as of hope and delight. We want to commit ourselves. The first time that really happens sets the process in motion; but it is an initiative which must be repeatedly renewed. It may first be foreshadowed in the womb; certainly not long afterwards. It is met by a force of regression so strong that the issue can never be quite decided. The siren-call here symbolized by the Rhinemaidens in their negative aspect sounds in our ears all our life. We are continually sliding down. That does not matter if we pick ourselves up again. And sooner or later the time may come when in our hearts we know that we are committed. We are not safe; anything may go wrong; but as far as a human decision can be certain, we have decided.

For the psyche portrayed by the cast of the *Ring* in its entirety, this is the moment of decision. The decision is as unambiguous as anything can be in this life. It may not last; and indeed we know that Wagner had still to go over the whole story again under another form in *Parsifal*. But it is not half-hearted. All Wagner's manhood stood behind the supreme gesture of faith which the miracle represents. All Wotan's manhood, all Siegmund's, all Siegfried's are concentrated into the power of spirit which raises the dead man's arm against his old enemy-friend, the dark spokesman of the shadow. It is for this reason that we hear not the archetypal ambiguity of the ring's motive (8) but the ringing confidence of the sword's motive (45). It rings with manhood.

But manhood, however confident, is not enough by itself. Wagner had an extraordinary intuitive grasp of this fact. He wrote to Roeckel (letter of 25 Jan. 1854): 'Siegfried on his own (man by himself) is not the complete man. He is not more than the half, and not until Brynhilde is with him does he become a redeemer . . . in the end, woman suffering and voluntarily sacrificing herself is the real and conscious redeemer; for indeed love is the "eternal feminine".' With this, we come to the remarkable last scene of the tragedy, in which the theme of redemption finally takes the stage: redemption by the voluntary sacrifice of a woman who is capable of uniting the eternal feminine to the eternal masculine by her own act of self-immolation.

If we cannot understand this final theme of redemption, we cannot understand Wagner. It was his life-long preoccupation, almost from the beginning. He told Roeckel (letter of 23 Aug. 1856): 'The period in which I have worked in response to my intuitions starts with the *Flying Dutchman*. Then came *Tannhäuser* and *Lohengrin*, and if in these works there is any underlying poetic theme, it must be looked for in the supreme tragedy of renunciation, the abnegation of the will, which is shown there as necessary and unavoidable and alone capable of achieving redemption.' Wagner's spectacles at the time were Schopenhauerian; mine are Jungian. I should put it that we have to renounce and abnegate the wilful authority of the ego. The deep growth of character culminating in what Wagner called redemption is what I have here called transformation.

I do not myself see the renunciation of ego's wilful authority as tantamount to personal annihilation. On the contrary, I see the ego as flourishing better after yielding to the superior authority of the self than ever it could while still unduly resisting. A flourishing ego is a very necessary part of the human psyche in this life, and when the ego, as often happens, is inadequately established, it is extremely important to build it up. This can only be done successfully, however, in relation to the self.

Wagner, when under the influence of Buddhist thought as transmitted by Schopenhauer, explained the fire in which Brynhilde is now about to immolate herself as the gateway to redemption in the sense of freedom from rebirth; even Hagen, though consigned to rebirth, was eventually to achieve redemption in this sense of personal annihilation.[1] We must, however, remember that one of the four questions which we are taught that the Buddha deliberately left unanswered was whether the emancipated still exist after death. I do not know, and I doubt if Wagner knew, what Buddhist thought really expresses under the symbol of annihilation. I do know that none of Wagner's images in the *Ring*, whatever his reason may have had to say about it, actually points to annihilation as our own Western thought conceives it. One after another of them points to rebirth in the sense of transformation.

Certainly the music now soars into a quiet elation by the use of the motive (4), which is an inversion in the major mode of the Earth-Mother Erda's primeval motive (3), itself a minor version of the still more primeval nature motive (2); and (2) is only one step from the utterly primitive (1), the upwards arpeggiation to which all the subsequent motives can in some measure, however indirect, be related. To return to the Earth-Mother carries mythologically and symbolically the meaning of going down into the unconscious as into a womb from which to be reborn. Going down into the unconscious nevertheless feels to the ego like annihilation. It feels to Brynhilde, as it seemed to Wagner, like self-immolation. Thus (4) means that the old order gives way to the new.

The concentration of the eternal masculine in the miracle of dead Siegfried raising his arm at once calls up the eternal feminine at her radiant best. Visibly transfigured from the evilly possessed creature as which we last saw her, Brynhilde reappears.

BRYNHILDE'S HOUR

A strange peace descends. All of us who have passed through experiences of bitter doubt and distress can recognize it. Unpredictably but blessedly the dark night of the soul is lifting. The valley of the shadow of death is opening out again.

The music becomes full of the grave motive (84) of destiny accepted. Destiny is not accepted without doubt and distress, but the more we can come to terms with the doubt and the distress, the more we can reap the astonishing rewards simply of being alive and human. The distraught Brynhilde we last saw plotting Siegfried's murder was rather less than

[1] See Ernest Newman, *Life of Wagner*, London, Vol. II, 1937, pp. 328 ff.

human, in the sense of having lost possession of (indeed being possessed by) her animus; she has very obviously regained possession of her animus now in the flood of illumination which must have broken in on her through the shock of realizing that she herself was a primary accomplice in that murder, just as Siegfried regained possession of his anima in his vision of Brynhilde as his dying eyes saw her so clearly.

The split in the shadow healed in the usual drastic fashion of myth when Hagen killed Gunther. The split in the anima now heals as drastically. To Gutrune's heartbroken accusation, Brynhilde gently answers with the truth that she and not Gutrune is Siegfried's original and only real wife. Where illusion is the disease, it is always the truth, however painful, which is the healing thing. But at this late stage in the drama, we shall hardly be concerned much longer with the separate characters; it is in the psyche as a whole that these violent yet healing transformations are taking place. 'My eyes are opened,' sings Gutrune, and she sinks down, it seems to die, and not even from a sword-thrust like Gunther, but from a broken heart, that is to say undisguisedly from inner necessity.

It is the following scene which Wagner first drafted as a somewhat moralistic explanation by Brynhilde, then recast in the light of Schopenhauer, and finally left almost entirely to the symbolic action and the music.[1] Works of art are never made clearer by incorporating explanations; they are only diluted. Poets and musicians learn to trust their images to make their own effect, by means which are the complementary opposite of reason. There is not even much verbal poetry left here; but the symbolic action is traditional, and the music is fully equal to the situation.

THE RETURN TO INNOCENCE
IN A MATURER STATE

Brynhilde orders the vassals to heap up a great funeral pyre by the water's edge. This at once puts us in mind of the logs of the world ash-tree piled up on Wotan's orders round Valhalla; we can hardly miss the deliberate correspondence between the terrestrial situation on the stage in front of us and the celestial situation above as described by the Norns in the Prelude to *Götterdämmerung* and by Valtraute in Act I, Scene 3.

Though the fire has not yet been lit, Brynhilde already seems to see light pouring from Siegfried towards her, just as she did when first she woke to his kiss in the last Act of *Siegfried*. Now, as then, we can take

[1] See Ernest Newman, *Life of Wagner*, London, Vol. II, 1937, pp. 328 ff.

this light as symbolical of the new consciousness arising as a result of their relationship.

Now that Brynhilde knows she is Siegfried's murderess, she can become Siegfried's redeemer. We hear a motive (90, 90B, etc.) which has been well called 'love as fulfilment', and which derives from the same second part (69) of Freia's music as does the love music (37) particularly associated with Siegmund and Sieglinde. The fulfilment which Brynhilde's love for Siegfried is about to find is a strange one from the literal point of view, but we shall find it a true fulfilment from the symbolical point of view. It is, however, only because she can now accept both the good and the evil in herself (and others), without either flattering or despising herself (or them), that she is capable of finding her fulfilment in becoming Siegfried's redeemer, and the redeemer of the situation as a whole.

Next she sends up a short prayer to Wotan, in which she shows her new grasp of the paradox inherent in the opposites of life: Siegfried, she sings, was the most faithful man who ever broke faith—that a woman might grow wise. She has grown wise enough to know that there are not two Siegfrieds, or two Brynhildes, one good and the other bad, one faithful and the other faithless. It is the same Siegfried who is both good and bad; the same Brynhilde. It is the same life which presents us with both good and evil. Life's opposites are like the two poles of the same electric current. Until we have learnt to distinguish them, they are in short circuit. When we have gone on from there to learn that though the poles are distinct the current is the same, they are in working circuit. The work is done by the tension of the opposites in relation to one another.

Not so much forgivingly as acceptingly, she bids Wotan rest in peace. Calling the ring 'accursed circle' (which it is literally in a negative sense, and symbolically in a more positive sense) she draws it quietly off Siegfried's finger, sets it on her own, and tells us how she intends to redeem the situation. She intends to rejoin Siegfried on his funeral pyre, the flames of which shall purge the ring of Alberich's curse, while the waters of the Rhine shall cleanse it as they flood over the flames. The Rhinemaidens shall take back their gold, which she advises them to keep more safely than before.

To purge the ring by fire means to bring to an end the present cycle of violent deaths, the necessary transformations having been achieved for the time being. To cleanse the ring by water means to regain a comparatively innocent relationship to the delights of nature. The ring is to be purged and cleansed, not melted down into raw gold again, which would represent a return to immaturity and a reversal of all the growth of character to which the intervening violence has contributed. The ring is to be kept safely, we may infer, not to prevent further growth but to prevent the shadow from having too much hand in the growth another time, because of the appalling disasters through which the growth has then to take place.

The implication of the *Ring* is that every heedless over-indulgence in unconscious mother-longings and every wilful obstruction to the under-lying purpose of our lives will be paid for by disasters until we either go under or are shaken out of our mother-bound and wilful state into going on. But it is only in so far as we remain in this state that the delights of nature are a danger. Some saints after long and rigorous asceticism have been told by their visions or voices that they can now go back to the ordinary indulgencies of good living. Once they are able to enjoy the delights of nature without being swallowed up by them, they have no more need of fasting and continence to keep their unconscious mother-longing within bounds. They have regained an innocence not of im-maturity but of maturity.

Innocence is the positive aspect of the Rhinemaidens. Their delight in playing with their regained treasure is going to symbolize our potential delight at being able to play with life and with the delights of life as freely as if we were infants again: but with all the difference between being sucked down into a compulsive infantilism and being enriched from a fountain-head of infantile spontaneity.

But first not only the ring but Brynhilde must pass through an ordeal or baptism by fire and water of which we must not under-estimate the bitter reality.

THE VOLUNTARY SACRIFICE
OF OUTWORN VALUES

Other characters in the *Ring* have accepted their destinies; but Bryn-hilde goes into hers with a voluntary and conscious courage. It is her deliberate intention to bring redemption not only to herself and Siegfried but to the gods. She is deliberately acting for the psyche as a whole.

Divine deaths by sacrifice involving immolation and commonly dis-memberment are the prerequisite of creation in the most widespread mythologies, including the Norse.[1] Rebirth, which is, for the psyche, like creation recapitulated, is similarly dependent on sacrificial gods:

[1] Mircea Eliade, *Myths, Dreams and Mysteries*, tr. Ph. Mairet, London, 1961, pp. 183 ff.

Osiris in conjunction with Horus; Attis; Adonis; Christ; probably Baldur. The rebirth may sometimes amount to a millennial reorientation of human consciousness, as it did with Christ. The doom of the Norse gods themselves was prophesied by the Eddas in the strange vision of Ragnarok, fulfilled historically when the Aesirs with Odin at their head gave place to Christianity.[1] The common element in every such myth is the realization that a new stage can only be bought by the sacrifice of values which were once precious and are still keenly prized. The sacrifice is a bitter reality.

Wagner's explanations on this subject were up to a point uncannily accurate. He wrote to Liszt (letter of 19 Oct. 1858) about the ending of his impassioned love-affair with Mathilde Wesendonk and her creative influence on *Tristan*: 'The pains and pangs of birth have their victorious issue now in all this wealth of beauty. The love of a tender woman has made me happy; she dared to throw herself into a sea of suffering and agony so that she should be able to say to me "I love you!" No one who does not know all her tenderness can judge how much she had to suffer. We were spared nothing—but as a consequence I am redeemed and she is blessedly happy because she is aware of it.'

The only serious failure in this account is that it fails to distinguish between a voluntary sacrifice made on Wagner's behalf by a woman of flesh and blood, and a voluntary sacrifice made by the feminine element in Wagner himself. When young people fall in love, they exchange mutual projections of the anima and the animus with a touching naïveness which is neither so touching nor so inevitable in later years. In 1858, Wagner was no longer so young as that. He was forty-five. He had reached a stage of life at which two needs are likely to have become pressing: to free the anima from the undue domination of the shadow by growing more conscious of our own inferior qualities; and to experience the anima more directly by withdrawing some of our projections of her from women of flesh and blood. We can no longer afford to be so naïvely romantic as young people can. That means in effect the sacrifice of some younger and naïver version of our image of the anima.

I cannot help wondering whether Senta had to plunge into the waves at the end of the *Flying Dutchman*, Isolde to sing of the flood of oblivion in her love-death at the end of *Tristan* and Brynhilde to go through fire and water at the end of *Götterdämmerung* partly in order to show us this

[1] The term *Götterdämmerung* (twilight of the gods) is discussed by John Corcoran in the Larousse *Encyclopedia of Mythology*, tr. R. Aldington and D. Ames, London, 1959, pp. 282 ff.

outgrown version of the anima returning to the native element of unconsciousness from which, like Aphrodite from the sea, she first arose. Through each of these unforgettable scenes Wagner was perhaps schooling himself to let go a little more of that immature element in his own inner femininity which was holding him back. The last of them, and perhaps the nearest to being consciously experienced, was Kundry's death of transformation in *Parsifal*: an opera which unlike the others goes on after the symbolical sacrifice for long enough to reveal something of the fruitful consequences.

It is obvious that Wagner's own redemption was connected with the burning integrity of his artistic aims, shining so radiantly through all the confusion of his outer troubles. He was driven on to achieve maturity in his artist's vision by the very agonies of neurotic compulsion and distress of mind which robbed him of maturity in his everyday contact with the world. He achieved his artistic maturity to the ultimate benefit of the world but at appalling cost to himself. This must have been another factor in his deep conviction that sacrifice was somehow demanded if he was to win through to his own true individuality. In this sense Wagner was his own sacrificial god, dismembered in order to be born again. The degree in which Wagner succeeded in sacrificing his friends and admirers to his own advantage was infinitesimal by comparison with the degree in which he was willing to be sacrificed himself to his inner task of creation and individuation.

The creation was only possible in the same measure as the individuation. At all costs to himself and those around him, Wagner had to go on being Wagner. That meant something more than being egocentric. It meant being centred increasingly on the self, whose purpose it was that he should achieve his creative work. We become more truly individual by becoming more at the service of the self, which is perhaps one of the meanings of the Christian paradox: 'In thy service is perfect freedom.'

A man outwardly proud may pay for it with inner misgivings. A man outwardly timid may be impelled by unconscious delusions of grandeur. A man who swings between extremes does not know how to take himself; nor does the world know how to take him. But in so far as a man can get into balance not like the swings of a pendulum but like the credits and debits of a balance-sheet, he may come to tolerate his bad side and believe in his good side. He may be content to be a human being: namely, himself. A man able to be himself can grow more integrated, since it is not our limitations which hinder the process of integration so much as our failure in living up to whatever potentialities we have. To live up to our potentialities means to let go our outworn values. That is the bitter sacrifice once again.

THE BAPTISM BY FIRE AND WATER

It is easier to stage convincingly a man being stabbed in the back than a woman being burned alive; and for this reason we need to call more heavily on our imagination, with less help from stage-craft, in order to respond in full measure to Brynhilde's heroism. There are, however, many subliminal associations evoked by the symbolism which work without our necessarily knowing it to help our imagination.

In the first place, we are carried back in a fairly obvious manner to the beginning of the *Ring* itself. Like the premonitory dreams which often anticipate so constructively the main lines of a long psychological analysis, the start of *Rhinegold* has already anticipated this culminating scene of *Götterdämmerung*. The fire is still as it was then the blazing energy of life; the water is still the illimitable unconscious. The Rhinemaidens' gold blazed like fire under the water to symbolize an impregnation of the feminine darkness by masculine illumination. Presently the fire surrounding Brynhilde entered Siegfried's heart as his desire to possess her; and he brought her not only love but light. The same desire which burned then as outward sexuality burns now as inward longing. This longing can at last be interpreted directly for what it has always indirectly represented. It can be interpreted as the longing for rebirth.

There are plenty of further associations to point in the same direction. Ordeal by fire was part of the rebirth ritual in the Eleusinian initiation mysteries of classical Greece. A ritual quenching of old fires and lighting of new fires puts the old year behind and brings in the new year in numerous ceremonies, all of them directed to rebirth in the spirit as much as to renewal in the calendar.[1] The custom of Suttee by which Indian widows sought to rejoin their dead husbands through the funeral fire has not long been obsolete. Stone-age primitives still survive whose dead are believed to reach immortality by crossing the water to an actively volcanic island.[2] The Irish hero Cuchylain in his first transforming adventure grew so preternaturally hot that three tubs of water were necessary to cool him, of which the first burst, the second boiled, and the third merely became hotter than most men could bear;[3] this may remind us of the

[1] Mircea Eliade, *Patterns in Comparative Religion*, tr. Rosemary Sheed, London, 1958, Ch. XI.
[2] John Layard, *Stone Men of Malekula*, London, 1942.
[3] Mircea Eliade, ibid.

creative or incubating heat described in the Hindu Upanishads. One of the fairy-tales collected by Grimm[1] relates how the Lord and St. Peter, when staying with a certain smith, took pity on an old incapacitated peasant and put him in the smith's fire to make him young again, cooling him off in the quenching tub; the smith later tried it on his old mother-in-law, but she howled so (without getting any younger) that she frightened the smith's wife and daughter into giving birth to the first apes. Siegfried, we recall, re-forged his father's sword and thus forged his own manhood in the smith's fire, hardening it off in the quenching tub; Siegfried himself had to pass through fire in his search for his inner femininity under the personification of Brynhilde. I am reminded of another typical hero described by Rydberg as entering a paradise surrounded with flames, as a result of being swallowed Jonah-like by a dragon, and in this paradise encountering a heroine who stands for his anima just as Brynhilde stands for Siegfried's anima.[2] Siegfried passing through fire to join Brynhilde foreshadowed Brynhilde passing through fire to rejoin Siegfried. An ordeal by fire leading to renewal or rejuvenation or rebirth Phoenix-fashion, or to union of the male and female principles, or in still more direct imagery to a revelation of truth, has always to do with an increase of consciousness under whatever variety of symbolism. It is not a rare theme, and still less is it a theme unique to *Götterdämmerung*. It is among the basic themes of mythology.

St. Anthony, the patron saint of swineherds, traditionally controls the holy fire surrounding Paradise. He can send some of this fire down on men as a punishment, but can also be moved to extinguish it again. He is the most prominent exorcizer of demons in the Catholic calendar, as befits a saint particularly associated with pigs. On Judgement Day all creation shall be conducted through this river of fire surrounding Paradise; the fire brings purification and salvation, since what it consumes is evil. St. Thomas wrote of the Fall that 'only he who has been purified by fire can thenceforth enter Paradise. For the way of purgation comes before the mystical union, and the mystics do not hesitate to put the purification of the soul on the same plane as the purifying fire on the way to Paradise'.[3] We are brought very close to Brynhilde's ordeal by this archetypal imagery of the purifying fire.

---

[1] Grimm, 147, 'The Old Man Made Young Again'.

[2] Victor Rydberg, *Teutonic Mythology*, tr. R. B. Anderson, London, 1889, pp. 208ff.

[3] Mircea Eliade, *Myths, Dreams and Mysteries*, tr. Philip Mairet, London, 1960, p. 69.

THE SACRED MARRIAGE
AS THE UNION OF OPPOSITES

The mystical union of which St. Thomas speaks is the sacred marriage, a symbol which has already been adumbrated by Wagner in the incestuous mating of Siegmund and Sieglinde. The union can in one aspect be described as a union of the complementary masculine and feminine principles within the psyche. Wagner knew enough about this aspect to be able to write to Roeckel (letter of 25 Jan. 1954): 'Now a human being is both man and woman, and it is only when these two are united that the real human being exists.' Wagner's reason could not quite help taking this for an outward union, so that he added: 'It is only in the union of man and woman, by love (sensuous and supersensuous) that the human being exists.' But his intuition was basically of an inward union. Siegfried and Brynhilde are not going to be reunited outwardly through the fire and the water, but inwardly. Not even the most literal-minded of spectators goes home thinking merely of a damp little pile of mingled ashes by the river's edge. We are all aware that the cremation and the flood are significant in virtue of their reconciling symbolism. Brynhilde is not expecting to consummate her literal marriage, which she did long ago; but she is expecting to consummate the sacred marriage which Siegfried's infidelity and her own revenge have previously postponed, or more truly prepared.

The association of fire and water with the sacred marriage is particularly clear in alchemy, where the fire has an incubating function again reminiscent of the Upanishads, while the water is represented by the fluid contained like amniotic fluid in a womb-like retort. The retort is often replaced by a trough or bath of water, commonly in the shape and sometimes in the likeness of a coffin, which is another symbol for a womb inviting a descent into death as a channel to rebirth. (Can it have been some such inner premonition which an Indian woman recently misapplied to the outer world of a London suburb by soaking her sari with paraffin and burning herself to death—in the bath?[1]) There are, again, many accounts and illustrations of an ever-flowing alchemical fountain; and any alchemical water could be regarded as partaking paradoxically of the nature of fire.

Jung reproduces[2] from the *Rosarium philosophorum* (Frankfurt, 1550)

[1] *The Times*, London, 9 Feb. 1960.
[2] C. G. Jung, *Psychology of the Transference* (1945), tr. R. F. C. Hull, Coll. Ed., Vol. 16, 1954.

a series of alchemical representations of the sacred marriage in which the brother and sister Sol and Luna, each carrying appropriately symbolic objects, approach one another, get into a stone bath full of water, embrace there, and by the heat of that embrace fuse into a hermaphrodite of which the body is male on one side but female on the other, and has two heads of opposite sexes (perhaps, as with the two-headed eagle, one head is for looking towards the outer world and the other for looking towards the inner world). The hermaphrodite dies and its soul flies out as a small child (sometimes there are two, a girl for the soul and a boy for the spirit). An agony of obliteration and unknowing (the stage of putrefaction, which is sometimes distinct from but sometimes equivalent to the blackening) ensues; but at last healing water in the form of the dew or rain of grace descends, followed by a further (or the same) child to signify the spirit descending, once more as in a baptism, from the father-principle. The hermaphrodite then rises up again, surrounded by symbols of its reborn condition.

The point of the sacred marriage is that it symbolizes the union of opposites which have previously been differentiated. The state of nature is not a differentiated state; it is the pristine state out of which human consciousness has to grow by means of differentiation. It is this state of nature prior to human consciousness which is referred to in the familiar Greek myth related by Plato[1] of man's primordial unity as a spherical hermaphrodite comprising male and female in perpetual embrace until the gods in envy divided the two halves, which have ever since gone in search of one another. The sphere stands, as usual, for wholeness, but the primordial unity consisted in the undifferentiated wholeness of our unconscious state of nature before any awareness of life's inherent opposites had brought the creative pain of inner conflict into our experience. That more or less corresponds to the situation at the start of *Rhinegold*.

There is, however, another myth, told in its Hellenistic form by Ovid,[2] of Hermaphroditus, son of Hermes and Aphrodite, who was beloved against his conscious wishes by the nymph of a fountain, in which he nevertheless made so bold as to bathe; whereupon her prayer that they should be united was answered more conclusively than she had bargained for by their emerging transformed into a hermaphrodite. This is not the primordial unity of unconscious nature, but the differentiated unity reached in the human psyche as a result of the long and difficult search for each other by the halves first divided when consciousness

---

[1] *Symposium*, tr. W. Hamilton, London, 1951, pp. 59 ff.
[2] *Metamorphoses*, IV, ll. 285 ff.

began to make us something other than the animals. Notice that it is the feminine element which takes the initiative. It is some such differentiated union as this which Brynhilde, in the role of anima, now seeks with Siegfried, in the role of animus.

In the Völsunga version[1] of the cremation, Brynhilde, having mortally stabbed herself, asks to be burnt next to Sigurd (Siegfried) with a drawn sword between them (again standing for psychic as opposed to physical union) so that they 'may have the name of man and wife'. Other corpses, not all of whose causes of death are made clear, are to be arranged 'so that all is shared equally' in a rather striking four-sided pattern which can only, I think, have reference to the mandala. The mandala is a highly traditional pattern which many people (whether in touch with traditional knowledge of it or not) tend to produce, under a great variety of detail, in their dream material or analytical drawings (or under other circumstances in religious images, or again in other mature works of art) whenever they are inwardly engaged in an active phase of individuation. The pattern itself is one of mankind's fundamental symbols for this process of individuation, with all that it implies in the way of reconciling and integrating tendencies. It is in many respects a visual counterpart to the sacred marriage.

The main impression visually conveyed by a mandala is of a circle squared. The square may be contained within the circle or the circle within the square. The square may conceivably refer to the ego, with which we stand four-square to the world; the circle unquestionably refers to the self, in which we have our centre. The combination of square and circle adds to the suggestion of totality, and also suggests the union of opposites. The whole may be quartered by a cross; smaller circles may appear in each quarter; there is no limit to the detailed possibilities. The quadripartite orientation suggests the four points of the compass, the four winds, the four elements, the four humours of the body and therefore the four human functions of thought, feeling, sensation and intuition first analytically defined (like the dual polarity between extroverted and introverted attitudes) by Jung.[2]

The even numbers are traditionally feminine and passive, in contrast to the uneven numbers, which are traditionally masculine and active.[3] This tends to confirm that our three Rhinemaidens and our three Norns,

[1] Tr. E. Magnusson and Wm. Morris, London, n.d.

[2] C. G. Jung, *Psychological Types*, tr. R. F. C. Hull, Coll. Ed., Vol. VI, London, 1953.

[3] C. G. Jung, *The Psychology of the Transference*, tr. R. F. C. Hull, in Coll. Ed., Vol. XVI, London, 1954: esp. p. 207.

like the three Graces, and our nine Valkyries with Brynhilde at their head, like the nine Muses, are primarily conceived by male poets like Wagner as images for something embodied not in woman but in man. Brynhilde has the shape and some of the symbolism of a woman. But primarily she is not a woman; she is a man's experience of womanhood, both external and archetypal, as focused in his inner femininity. Primarily Brynhilde is an image for the anima.

REDEMPTION AS TRANSFORMATION IN THE PSYCHE

It is as anima that Brynhilde is now fulfilling her proper psychic function as an intermediary between conscious and unconscious, a reconciler of conflict, a uniter of opposites. She is by now beyond praise or blame either for herself or for Siegfried or for Wotan or for Hagen; she is in some paradoxical but quite real sense beyond good and evil; she is magnificently tranquil. The serenely beautiful motive (91) of redemption, that is to say of transformation, first becomes prominent in this closing scene. We have not heard it as (91A) since Sieglinde was told by Brynhilde that she was pregnant with Siegfried. Sieglinde's mother-hood brought her own death, so that she was herself a redeeming sacrifice, though less consciously and therefore less effectually than Brynhilde: nothing quite like it has happened in between to call out (91A). We can think of Brynhilde now as pregnant not literally but symbolically with the future of the psyche. Everything rests with Brynhilde now.

She throws a lighted torch on to the pile of logs, which blaze up with a rapidity eloquent of her longing to pass through the flames to the trans-formed life on the farther side of them. She has, however, no intention of leaving her human instincts behind her. Life can be transformed without becoming disembodied; the need for austerity may actually grow less. At all events, she calls to the symbol of instinct, the magic horse Grane: 'Do you know where we are going together? Does the fire's light which is Siegfried's light draw you to it too? Siegfried, Siegfried, see how your holy wife greets you!'

She rides into the flames, which spread everywhere until they bring down the hall in ruins. We are shocked and shaken. The music surges on through a vast range of relentless modulations which complete our sense of disintegration. But it is disintegration with a purpose. The music is just as much purposeful as it is relentless. It brings in Siegfried's most triumphant motive (78); it brings in (4), the motive of the transformation of the old order; it ends with (91A), the motive of Brynhilde's redemption of that old order. It is shattering music, but with the shattering upheaval and creative pangs of rebirth. One small touch must not escape us: Siegfried's motive and Brynhilde's motive are not, as might well be expected here, contrapuntally combined, perhaps because it is a paradoxical but essential feature of the sacred marriage that a man should not be merged with his anima, but should see her as an entity more distinct from his conscious ego than he had ever before realized.

The Rhine floods its banks; the funeral flames die down. The Rhinemaidens swim to the pyre, and Hagen plunges in madly after them, crying: 'Away from the ring!' There speaks our old unregenerate shadow, who is certainly not going to be silenced on this side of eternity. However, he will share according to his measure in the general transformation, which is no more complete than human transformation ever is, but which is nevertheless extraordinarily comprehensive as human transformations go. As he utters this last word which is also the theme-word of the *Ring*, two of the Rhinemaidens draw him down into an embrace of death. The third holds up the ring for us to see before following them with it into the depths. The waters subside after her.

But at the back of the stage, high up and far away we see an answering blaze. It is Valhalla, in whose burning interior Wotan waits quietly with his old order for whatever future the transforming fire may bring.

T

Appendix of Music Examples

————————— ❋ —————————

How many musical motives are there in the *Ring*? That all depends on what we call a motive. At one extreme, the motives dwindle into mere fragments of figuration; at the other extreme, they pass into passages of development or even tunes; but neither dividing line can be sharply drawn, and no attempt has been made to do so here. Most but not all of the following examples are motives on any showing. Not all of them have been included for the same reason, but they are all illustrations of my text, at the points indicated in the text by numbers.

There is no motive in the *Ring* which cannot be traced either directly or indirectly to the simple arpeggio figure (it is scarcely yet a motive) with which *Rhinegold* opens. Some of the remoter motives have undergone many transmutations before reaching their extreme forms; but similarities can be noticed, I believe in every case, which lead from one motive to another until the extremes are reached. Some similarities have always been familiar; some others are so conspicuous that the wonder is they have not yet become familiar; some again are not conspicuous at all, and might fairly be doubted were it not that the entire fabric of the *Ring* shows such clear signs of holding together. A merely casual and undetermined motive is almost inconceivable in such a context.

Great craftsman though Wagner was, he could not have deliberately planned all the underlying similarities which give the *Ring* its almost unfailing unity. The more obvious were certainly deliberate, and no doubt a number of the less obvious; but many more must have arisen as part of the deep shaping of the work by his artist's intuition. Some of these he must have noticed afterwards with delight, and further developed; others he will have not even have noticed, nor his commentators either, which of course includes myself. Up to the moment of going to press, I was still noticing new ones, or having others pointed out to me by Deryck Cooke, and apart from the limits of Faber and Faber's already most generously extended patience, there seemed and seems no particular reason why this discovery of hitherto unnoticed subtleties should ever stop.

Since Deryck Cooke has carried his discoveries further than previous commentators, I recommend the reader to his book, and confine myself here to the bare lines of growth. Thus it is familiar knowledge that, using my system of numbering, (1) leads directly on to (2) and (2) to (3), the common factor being the idea of nature in different aspects. Of these, (2) in the major and (3) in the minor show an upward stepwise trend of which echoes can be found as near at hand as (5) and as far afield as (83), or with chromatic inflexion at (6) and at (38).

It is also familiar knowledge that (4), which is a motive associated with the return to nature as events come full cycle (subsequent further rebirth from her symbolic womb being implied), is an inversion of (3). Because such a creative return comes with the acceptance of destiny, (79) is a close relative, and since yielding to love can be part of destiny, (80) is just as close, while the enigmatic (76) is not far away, with (81) and (82). Here the thread leads us to the very elemental (68), and on to (69) which is another form of (37), with (75) only just round the corner as a kind of parallel by opposites. At this point a group of motives may be assembled which includes (70), (73) and (74), reflected in a lower plane of tension by (71) and (72), but also on a higher plane by (84), (85) and (90), and in a more innocent vein by (26), (27), (31) and indeed (30). With these stand (28) and (29), also (32), (33) and (34), together with the bass of (39).

Again, (78) has the same affiliation, the first bars of it being a variation of (76), thus confirming that the enigma of (76) really has to do with the acceptance of a heroic destiny rather than with mere negative renunciation (for which see my text, Ch. II etc.). But (78) is also strongly connected with a further primary element, the element of arpeggiation found at its purest in (1), but also underlying the stepwise element in (2), (3) and (4) together with their derivatives (5) and (6) and to a lesser extent (83), not to mention the latter portions of (26) and (27).

One direction taken by this arpeggiation is diatonic and cheerful, often glorious. There is an entire group of leaping motives expressive in their different ways of abounding energy, and including (43), (44), (45), (46), (47), (48), (49), (64), and with an eerie chromatic twist, (22). Diatonic again are (7) in its joyful mood, (63) in its grander fashion, and the heroic (65). But the weaker (67) and the more tragic (66) belong in the same quarter, though the direction has a little changed. Not far from here lie (40) and (41) with their depth of pathos; and (42) has obvious links with (41). Nearer to the original arpeggiation, but in the same poignant vein, comes Sieglinde's tender (36) so often found in contrapuntal union with Siegmund's (35), which is close to (70) and (73), and which links with (77), whereby also with (91). Also near to the original arpeggiation, but chromatically veiled and softened, lies not only (10), which gives the Norn's relationship to nature's wisdom, but another main group centring on the ring's own tonally ambivalent (8), and its upwards, spaced-out equivalent, the curse (13). Here fall (9), which is the two ends of (8), and (11), (12) and (14), which are aspects of (13); (15), too, is like a harmonic and rhythmic compression of (8) and (13). The harmony of (61) is on the same lines; but the bass-part is related to (3) and (5); (61A) links back to (8) and still more clearly to (13).

Diatonic tonality, from its comparatively uncomplicated character, tends to innocence or openness. Chromatic harmony is suggestive of hidden workings, of ambivalent potentialities. All the basically chromatic motives stand in some relationship to the central (8), and thus to the elemental material of (1), (2), (3) and (4). In a dream-like or mysterious rendering, they include (16), (17), (18), (19) and (23); allied with demonic energy, they include (20), (21) and (22), and in a very ponderous form, (57). The ponderousness of (58) and (59), however, is heavily diatonic; they relate to (70) and (73). The pounding of (60), and more tragically of (62), as also this element in (61), have something in common with (58) and (59). A lighter pounding—more of a zestful tapping—marks Mime's (50) and (51), but there is weight again in Siegfried's (53) and (55), while the vassals' (54) is very close to (53), and (52) links (56) with the same (53).

There are points in common between (86), (87), (88), (89), (90) and (91), and this group has certain links with such basic elements as (2), (4), (6), (7), (8), (63) and (73). The mediant modulations in (24) and (25) are identical, the one proceeding to (2) and the other to material drawn from (2).

For readers who do not wish to follow up all these suggested indications, a clear view of the principle may be had by tracing the lines of force, in the order stated, through (1), (2), (3), (4), (79), (26), (31), (68), (70), (73), (35), (69), (37), (84), (76), (78), (36), (44), (45), (48), (65), (63), (8), (13), (15), (77), (88) and (91). The lines are not always continuous through these numbers, but they all connect back with the original group (1) to (4), and these connections are not only of a relatively obvious character but are typical of the workings of the principle. I suggest making at least these comparisons, and preferably also the more detailed comparisons from the preceding paragraphs.

I   The depths of the Rhine as undifferentiated nature

(N.B. the diatonic stability and the undisturbed persistence of the tonic harmony)

2   First stirring under the Rhine as a premonition of consciousness

(Developed from 1)

3   Erda the Earth-Mother as ancestral wisdom

(Minor form of 2)

4   The downfall of the gods (full cycle back to Mother Nature)

(Inversion of 3)

5 Further comments on the downfall of the old order

(70)

(5a)

p   *cresc.*   *f*   *p subito*   *etc.*

(Developments of 3 and 4, with 70)

6 Freia as young love

(Related to 2: but N.B. the slight chromatic element)

7 Freia's golden apples as the joy of life

(A complementary opposite, in the major, to 4, in the minor, and also to 76, in the minor; 4 is an inversion of 3, which is a minor version of 2; and 76 is the source or the twin of 79)

8 The ring as the underlying purpose of the psyche (more specifically, as the self)

8a

8b

(The basis is, I believe, 4, but with chromatic modification; and it is this chromatic modification which gives 8 and its derivatives such as 13 their special character. Taken diatonically, however, the material of 8 produces 63; and in this aspect, 8, and thus also 63, with 65 only a short step on, are extremely close to 7)

9 Purposeful brooding

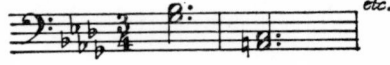

(An ingredient of 8)

10 The Norns' rope of destiny

(Derived from 2A but under the influence of 8)

11 Atonement as a force of destiny

(Related to 8)

12 Obligation as an expression of destiny

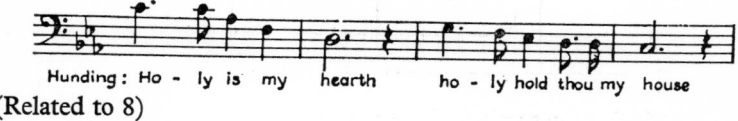

Hunding: Ho - ly is my hearth   ho - ly hold thou my house

(Related to 8)

13 Alberich's curse as a force making for transformation

Alberich : As by curse it come to me, ac - curs - ed be the ring!

(Basically an inversion of 8)

14 Wotan's treaties as part of his destiny

Wotan :

Ho - li - est trea - ties, trus - ty runes

(Related to the opening of 13)

15 Alberich's obsessive will as a force of destiny

(Harmonic version of the opening notes of 13)

16 Magic sleep as the 'womb of the unconscious'

(N.B. the elusive fluctuation of the modulations, and the repeated progressions by mediant harmony. The perpetually falling semitone relates to 68, hence ultimately to 4)

17 Wotan the Wanderer as the wise old man in touch with the unconscious

(Related to 16 with its mediant progressions; compare 82. The ultimate source may be 4)

18 Tarnhelm as unconscious fantasy

(Related to 16 but more focused; N.B. the mediant progression and the final bare fifth. There is some relationship with 68. Hence also with 4)

19 The magic potion as unconscious repression

(A further concentration of 18)

20 Loge the god of fire as libido (primal energy welling up from the unconscious)

20a

20b

20c

(Harmonically related to 16; N.B. the extreme chromatic elusiveness and ambivalence combined with restless energy. An extremer chromaticism than 8, 13, etc., but in the same general category; hence eventually linked with 4)

21   Loge as the ambivalence of the libido (primal energy)

(Further aspects of 20; also related to 18, but more dynamic)

22   The Valkyries as libido (primal energy) in action

(N.B. the chromatically augmented fifth, G to D sharp; related at the third bar to 20C; at the fourth bar an inversion of 20B. In the same group as 20 and 21; hence linked—especially in view of the augmented fifth—with 8, 13 and also 16; ultimately with 4)

23 The knowledge deep in the unconscious (here represented by the Norns)

(In one aspect a retardation of 22. N.B. the chromatically augmented fifth, G flat to D natural, as in 22, the Norns being another aspect of the Valkyries. Also indirectly linked with 16, i.e. ultimately with 4)

24 The unconscious as the matrix of consciousness

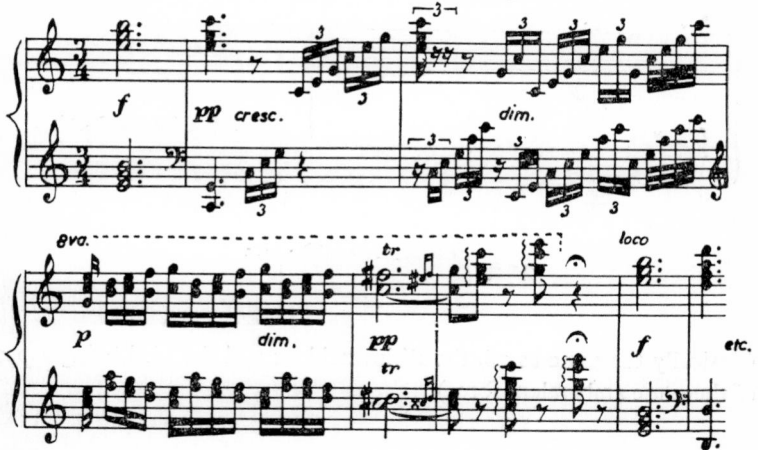

(N.B. the mediant progression from E flat minor to C flat major: a bright modulation in a dark tonality. *See* 25)

25 The light of 'psychic consciousness' dawning out of the unconscious

(N.B. the same mediant progression as 24, but from E minor to C major: a bright modulation in a bright tonality. The progressions are perceptibly reminiscent of 17, even of 16, hence ultimately of 4)

26 The song of the Rhinemaidens as tempters back to immature innocence

(Essentially a transformation of 1. N.B. the F as the added sixth to the tonic triad of A flat. There is a certain similarity to 7 to hint at the positive aspect of the Rhinemaidens as embodiments of the delight in nature. The forest bird's song, 27, is basically the same as this)

27 The song of the forest bird as initiator out of immature innocence

(Basically the same as 26, the Rhinemaidens and the bird being aspects of the same ambivalent force)

28   The glitter of the sun's light playing with the gold under the water, as childhood's innocent delight

(28)

(44)

(Related to 26 by the play between the fifth D and the sixth E; has its roots in 2, as its derivative 29 shows clearly)

29   The forest murmurs as Siegfried's childlike innocence and playful thoughts

(A version of 28; also related to 20C; rooted in 2)

30   Brynhilde sinking into the innocent sleep from which she will be woken into womanhood

(Same as the opening of 26 and 27)

31 'Rhinegold! Rhinegold!' (lower two staves)

(Harmonic modification of the added sixth of 26; occurs also with minor harmony)

32 The Rhinemaidens' song as developed in *Götterdämmerung*

(An extension of 31; N.B. the added sixth and the 6-3 chords)

33 The Rhinemaidens' deceptive delight

(Related to 31, with a hint of 28; also 21A, hence back to 16 and 4)

34 Truly innocent delight

(Related to 33; but ultimately derived from 26)

35 Siegmund as hero schooled in misfortune

(N.B. the implied diminished seventh harmony. Related melodically to 70, 73 and 74, hence ultimately to 4)

36 Sieglinde as heroine schooled in misfortune (at bar 2)

(35)

(Linked to 35 by a disposition towards diminished seventh harmony, and by extreme contrapuntal compatibility; but has a direct resemblance to 1 and 4 combined)

37 Love of Siegmund and Sieglinde (at bar 4)

(Goes back ultimately to 4. The suspended 4 B flat over the flat 7–5 at bar four conveys the pull of longing; but the notes are identical with 69, which in various rhythms may convey almost any sort of 'involvement' from fearful agitation, through urgent passion, to profound compassion)

38 Bliss, and the longing for bliss

38a (version of 6) (see 37)

38b *etc.*

(All linked with 6; hence with 2; the chromatic yearning rise is the complementary opposite to 37, 68, etc.)

39 The drink which unites the destinies of Siegmund and Sieglinde

(A symphonic extension of 35 and 36; but the bass shows the connection of 35 with 73, near which stands 79, and behind them 4)

40 Gutrune as foredoomed heroine

(40 feels related to 37, but also carries a subliminal reference to 8; 40A is certainly related to 37A. The common element expressed is the heart-rending combination of foredoomed vulnerability with sweetness and beauty. The ultimate source of 40 is 2)

41 The Gibichung brother and sister as foredoomed pair

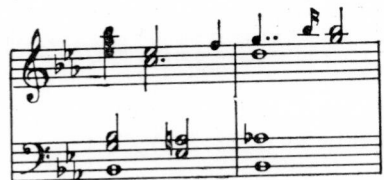

(A variant of 40, ultimately deriving from 2; but carrying a further reference to 7, the pathos of this reference lying in the irony of radiant hope foredoomed)

42 Honourable intentions; the appearance of honour and good faith; the keeping of promises, at least in outward seeming; the longing for normality

(Connected with 40 and 41; also with 43; the common source seems to be 45, thence directly from 1)

43   Nothung as the promised or longed-for sword

(Connected with 42A; probably the source is 45, thence directly from 1)

44   The gold as true worth

(Directly related to 1; closely connected with 45)

45   The sword as true manhood

(Directly related to 1, and also to 44)

46   The thunder as masculine spirit

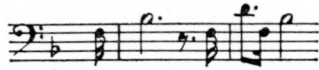

(Related to 44 and 45; thence directly to 1)

47   The Valkyries as the masculine element in women (Ride of the Valkyries)

(A variant of 46, hence closely related to 1)

48   Siegfried's horn call expressing his free spirit

(Related to 46, and directly to 1; *see* 65, which is a grander version of 48)

49 The dawn of Hagen's day

(Directly allied to 1 and 2)

50 Mime as smith (and forging generally)

(Directly represents the tapping of hammer on anvil: linked with 1 by the major third)

51 Mime as obsessive persistence

(Variant of 50)

52 Siegfried's heroic forging as his youthful impetuosity

(The heroic counterpart to 50, and more distantly to 58; the bass relates to 73; the ultimate connection with 1 passes through 70, 5 and 2)

53 Siegfried's youthful strength

(A further heroic counterpart to 58; slightly reminiscent of 46; decidedly reminiscent of 52, hence ultimately of 5, 2 and 1)

54 The vassals as the strong world of men

(A modified inversion of 53)

55 Siegfried's infectious impetuosity in love

(A brighter development of 53)

56 Siegfried's heroic freedom from entanglements

56a

(Still brighter developments of 52; but linked with 70, 73, and behind them 4. *See* also 72)

57 Fafner as the enormous backward pull (or inertia or resistance to change) of the unconscious

(Seems to be connected with 18, and perhaps with the opening of 70 inverted; but the first two notes are the same as 38 in a very different harmonic context. There is therefore a link through 6 with 2)

58   The giants as brute strength

(The dark counterpart to 53; related to 70 and 73, hence ultimately 4)

59   The giants as the brutal aspect of parental authority

(Development of 58, with particular insistence on 73)

60   Hunding as Siegmund's dark shadow

(Related to 58 and 62; and there is a certain dark parallelism with 63, hence also with 8. But the falling semitones C to B natural and A flat to G make a subterranean connection with 68, hence with 70, 73, etc. and therefore with 4)

61   Hagen as Siegfried's dark shadow, and the Gibichung race generally in this negative aspect

(The dark counterpart to 42. The first bar is distortedly reminiscent of 63, more directly reminiscent of 8. The bass comes from 3 by way of 5)

62 The darkness of death itself (Siegfried's funeral march)

(Related to 58 and 60)

63 Valhalla as genuine achievement; also as Wotan's genuinely creative thoughts

(A stable, diatonic version of 8)

64 The rainbow bridge to Valhalla

(A development of 1 under the influence of 63)

65 Siegfried's heroic deeds as the ever reborn spirit of youth

(A stronger version of 48)

66 The tragic but heroic destiny of the entire Volsung race

(A minor variant of 44 with some influence from 3 and perhaps 76)

67 Gunther's illusory appearance of heroism, hinting at the weakness in the 'shadow' aspect of the Volsung race itself, esp. Siegfried, since Gunther stands for part of Siegfried's shadow

(Related to 63, hence to 8; also to 66, with a reminiscence of 18 owing to the bare fifths)

68   Woe or grief, whether accepted or not

(N.B. the expressive falling semitone; related to 4; a complementary opposite of 38)

69   Agitation, but including both passion and compassion (at bar 2)

(An extension of 68; made up of the same notes as 37, of which it is the source)

70 Wotan's will frustrated

(Incorporates 68, hence distantly related to 4; also related very closely indeed to 73 and, in a striking parallelism of opposites, to 79)

71 Mime's will frustrated

(Version of 68; virtually the same as the opening of 70)

72 Mime's complaint

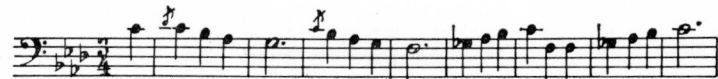

(Reminiscent of 68 and 70; a dark counterpart to 56, following much the same melodic sequence of notes, but in the minor)

73 The spear as Wotan's wilful authority, but also his entanglements and inhibitions

(A very close relative of 70, hence also of 68, but equally of 79 by a relation of opposites behind all of which lies 4: see also 90c)

74 The storm which opens the Valkyrie, as Wotan's resistance to destiny

(Derived from 73)

75 Restless plotting

(Connected with 70 and more directly with 68; thence 4)

76 Renunciation; often amounting to acceptance of destiny, and perhaps better labelled 'acceptance'

(Related to 68; but the rising minor sixth and the subsequent fall to the tonic are distinguishing characteristics. Basically derived from 4)

77 The Volsung race as instruments of destiny

(Related to the end of 70, and more distantly to the end of 35, and esp. of 35A; strongly reminiscent of the third bar of 66; decidedly reminiscent of 76 on account of the leap of the minor sixth; and there is also a distinct foretaste both of 88 and of 91. The first two notes perceptibly recall 68, even though here the falling semitone of grief is at once cancelled by the following rise, first of the semitone, then of the minor sixth. There is thus an ultimate connection with 4)

78 Siegfried's heroism as acceptance of his destiny

(The beginning is reminiscent of 76, 79 and 83; but the direct links with 1 and 4 are also clear)

79 Destiny accepted

(Directly related to 4; extremely close to 76, hence also to 68; a complementary opposite of 73)

80 Devotion, especially Siegfried's to Brynhilde, as part of the binding power of destiny

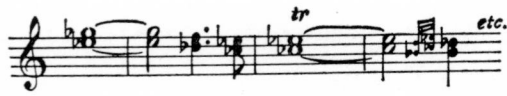

(Variant of 79)

81 Grief as acceptance of unavoidable suffering

(The semitone fall between D flat in bar one and C in bar three carries a subliminal reminiscence of 68; the last four bars are a variant of 76)

82   Wotan's grief at parting from Brynhilde

(Reminiscent of 81; but essentially related to 17, of which the ultimate source is perhaps 4)

83   Relinquishment

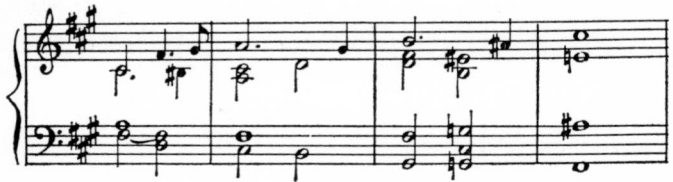

(Reminiscent of 76, by inversion of the first few notes; hence ultimately of 4; but the last two bars are shared with 84)

84   Destiny as the power to which all men must in the end surrender

(A version of the last two bars of 83, but used independently with great frequency and significance. Seems to be a modification of the beginning of 79, hence related to 76, the ultimate source being 4. There are links with the beginning of 77 and the end of 35, esp. as 35A; also with 68 and 69, and with the end of 70)

85   The inevitability of destiny

(Variant of 84; the connection with 79 and therefore with 4 being clearer in this variant, though almost certainly present in both cases)

86 Siegmund's love song of the coming of spring, as his experience of fulfilment with Sieglinde

(Related to 26, with a further suggestion of 7, and (at the third bar) of 69 and 37; but stands out somewhat from the general texture of the *Ring* as a lyrical interlude, almost an old-fashioned operatic aria—perhaps a slight misjudgment on Wagner's part, and comparable in this respect to 87 and 87A)

87 Brynhilde's holy love

87a

(87 suggests a triumphant counterpart to 40; and 87A has a touch of 6 and of 38; but strictly they both stand out from the real texture of the *Ring*, having been brought in from pre-existing sources)

88 Brynhilde as loving woman

(The first bar is a glorious transformation of 77, with the leap of the minor sixth changed to major; there is also a slight reminiscence of 76, on account of this same sixth, there minor, here major. The sequence C, G, B flat comprises the same notes as the start of the third bar of 86, itself reminiscent of 69 and 37. The falling minor seventh in the second bar is the bright counterpart of the harsh minor seventh in the second bar of 61. This falling minor seventh is also found between the fourth and fifth bars of 87; in the second bar of 90A; in the second bar of 90B into which 88 there merges; between the second and third bars of 90C (inverted); and in the third bar of 91A, of which 88 is an intermediate source)

89 Siegfried's tender love for Brynhilde, and hers for him

(There are slight resemblances to 32, 34, 65, 80, 87 and 87A; the falling major sixth at the start is somewhat reminiscent of the rising major sixth at the start of 88; but the main connection seems to be directly with 2, under a certain influence from 63, which itself is the diatonic aspect of 8, and perhaps from 7)

90 Love as fulfilment

and **90a**

88   **90b**

90c

(Connected with 87, 88 and 89, more distantly with 86; but 90C is a direct modification of 73)

91 Transformation

91a

(A sublimated modification of 88, with influences, especially in 91A, from 26, 32, 33 and 34. There is also in the first two bars a strong reminiscence of the melodic outline of 84, as if to recall that the transformation here suggested comes only when destiny has somehow not only been accepted, but accepted as part of the character concerned, which indeed on the inner view is essentially what destiny is. Hence the superb appropriateness of 91A as the last motive to make its appearance in the *Ring*)

NOTE

The headings given above are not put forward as titles for general reference. They are mostly meant as brief reminders of the lines of interpretation suggested in the context of the present book.

Numerical Index of Motives in the 'Ring'

Bibliography

In view of the fact that over 10,000 books and articles are known to have been evoked by Wagner in his own lifetime alone, and that the flow has not even yet altogether abated, I need not perhaps unduly stress that the following list, so far from being in any sense comprehensive, is the merest sample of the available literature. It is, however, intended to be a fairly representative sample, and it may serve to give the reader a start upon the vast field, in so far as he wants to get himself started on it. In addition, I have included a number of entries which do not belong to the Wagnerian literature, but which have some direct or indirect bearing upon my particular approach to Wagner's poetry and music in the present book. I have indicated with an asterisk those entries of which in my opinion the bearing is closest or the value or importance *in the present context* greatest.

* Highly recommended in the context of the present book

*Abraham, Gerald, *A Hundred Years of Music*, London, 1938: has a valuable chapter on Wagner, throwing light on the sources of his musical style.

Adolf, Helen, *Visio Pacis. Holy City and Grail. An Attempt at an Inner History of the Grail Legend*, Pennsylvania: The Penns. State Univ. Press, 1960: very relevant to Wagner's *Parsifal*.

Barford, Philip T., 'Mahler: a thematic Archetype', *Music Review*, XII, 4, Nov. 1960, pp. 297–316: traces a note-series through many transformations—an original and valuable study.

Barford, Philip T., 'The Way of Unity: a Study of *Tristan and Isolde*', *Music Review*, XX, 3–7, Aug.–Nov., 1959: an extremely interesting and perceptive approach.

*Barth, Herbert, *Internationale Wagner-Bibliographie*, 1945–1955, Bayreuth, 1956: contd. Henrik Barth for 1956–1960, Bayreuth, 1961.

Baynes, H. G., *Mythology of the Soul*, London, 1940: a minute examination of dream and pictorial material, with mythological associations.

Bayreuth, *Festival Programmes: see* Barth, *Internationale Wagner-Bibliographie*, for lists of articles by many important authorities; *also* Grunksy, Jacobi, Joachim, Viviar, Volkmann, Westernhagen.

*Bekker, Paul, *Richard Wagner*, tr. M. M. Boyman, London, 1931: a most serious and elaborate study, taking into account the relationship between Wagner's life and his art.

*Bertram, Johannes, *Mythos, Symbol, Idee im Richard Wagners Musik-Dramen*, Hamburg, 1957: in touch with Jungian thought; a perceptive and valuable study at a moderately deep level.

*Blissett, William, 'Ernest Newman and English Wagnerism', *Music and Letters*, Vol. 40, No. 4, London, Oct., 1959, p. 331: a most valuable and informative article.

Bodkin, Maud, *Archetypal Patterns in Poetry*, London, 1934: a pioneer study in its day, and still worth reading, though inevitably a little inconclusive by comparison with later work.

Branston, Brian, *Gods of the North*, London, 1955: a recent and very good account in all respects except that a few imaginative passages touching on the underlying psychological significance rouse hopes which are not fulfilled.

*Brink, Louise, *Women Characters in Richard Wagner*, New York, 1924: an extremely interesting essay on strictly Freudian lines up to the point at which they had then developed. Bound to seem old-fashioned now; but not to be despised.

Buesset, Aylmer, *The Nibelung's Ring*, London, n.d.: a brief survey on conventional lines, useful chiefly for its brevity.

Campbell, Joseph, *The Hero with a Thousand Faces*, New York, 1949: good material not very tautly organized or thought out. Almost too much grist for the mill to grind: next entry is a better book.

*Campbell, Joseph, *The Masks of God*, London, 1960: a fascinating book with a wealth of comparative material, anthropological and mythological; a little inconclusive; but full of suggestive ideas.

Clarke, R. T. Rundle, *Myth and Symbol in Ancient Egypt*, London, 1959: uncommonly insightful on this most basic of mythologies.

*Cooke, Deryck, *The Language of Music*, London, 1959: breaks new ground with regard to the fundamental reasons why music can express such definite emotional and intuitive contents; gets a very complex subject between his teeth like a bulldog and shakes it till it comes out simple—oversimple in parts, but an impressive achievement.

Cooper, Martin, 'Wagner as Christian or Jungian Myth', *The Listener*, 2 Jan., 1959; brief but important.

Corbett-Smith, A., *The Ring of the Nibelung: an Introduction*, London, n.d.: the conventional line at its most superficial.

Dale-Green, Patricia, 'Bufo Bufo; a study in the symbolism of the Common Toad', *Brit. Homoeopathic Journal*, XLIX, No. 1, Jan., 1960; and 'The Symbolism of the Toad: a Study in Ambivalence', Guild of Pastoral Psychology, Lecture No. 110, London, n.d. Two unusual and uncommonly insightful studies.

Dickinson, A. E. F., *The Musical Design of the Ring*, London, 1926: brief, clear, but with some doubtful ideas about what the motives mean.

Edda, The Elder or Poetic, tr. Olive Bray, London, 1908; tr. Henry Adams Bellows, New York, 1923: one of the world's great works of literature, and the fountain-head for most of the legends used by Wagner.

Edda, The Younger or Prose: see Sturluson, Snorri.

Ehrenzweig, Anton, *The Psycho-Analysis of Artistic Vision and Hearing*, London, 1953: a conscientiously Freudian study not cross-fertilized by Jungian influence, and consequently leaving the crucial effect of the archetypes out of the picture.

Ferguson, Donald N., *Music as Metaphor*, Minneapolis, 1960 and London, 1961: important on how meaning gets into music.

*Fordham, Frieda, *An Introduction to Jung's Psychology* (Pelican), London, 1953: a splendid piece of concise and lucid exposition.

*Fordham, Michael, *New Developments in Analytical Psychology*, London, 1957: subjects certain Jungian concepts to very searching critical examination and has also new things of importance to say.

*Fordham, Michael, *The Objective Psyche*, London, 1958: further essays similar to the above.

*Freud, Sigmund, 'On Narcissism—an Introduction' (1914), in *Coll. Papers*, Vol. IV; *Group Psychology and the Analysis of Ego* (1921), London, 1922; *The Ego and the Id* (1923), tr. Joan Riviere, London, 1927, Ch. III: relevant here with regard to the super-ego. The general relevance and importance of Freud's work cannot be overestimated.

*Freud, Sigmund, *Three Essays on the Theory of Sexuality* (1905), tr. James Strachey, London, 1949: a crucial early classic of psycho-analysis, still of fundamental importance, and relevant here with regard to the crucial influence of infantile sexual adjustments and maladjustments on the formation of the 'hero' personality—as indeed of everyone else's.

*Freud, Sigmund, *Totem and Taboo*, tr. A. A. Brill, London, 1919 (Pelican ed. 1938): a revolutionary research into the relationship of anthropology and depth psychology, and still to be taken very seriously indeed, in spite of one important error where Freud mistook what is truly the archetype of the ruler of the primal horde and his overthrow by jealous sons as a literal piece of prehistory, which as such is (also truly) rejected by reputable anthropologists.

*Ghiselin, Brewster (ed. and contr.), *The Creative Process*, New York, 1955: selections from writings by Einstein, Roger Sessions (particularly good), van Gogh, D. H. Lawrence, Cocteau, Yeats, Wordsworth, Coleridge, Stephen Spender, Henry James, Nietzsche, Jung, etc. etc., with an outstanding introduction by the editor. Not known to me till after I had finished my own book, but highly recommended.

Gregor, Martin, *Wagner und kein Ende. Richard Wagner im Spiegel von Thomas Manns Prosawerk*, Bayreuth [1958].

Grimm, Jacob, *Fairy Tales*, tr. J. Scharl, London, 1948: those of us who were brought up on this marvellous collection can count ourselves lucky; the few who were not can remedy the deficiency with this excellent recent translation.

Grimm, Jacob, *Teutonic Mythology*, tr. J. S. Stallybrass, London, 1882 ff.: this vast and complex work marked a turning-point in the systematic study of mythology and is still indispensable for specialists, though too involved and cumbersome for average readers.

Grotjahn, Martin, *Psychoanalysis and the Family Neurosis*, New York, 1960: very much in the forefront of post-Freudian writing, an original contribution of interest and value.

*Grunksy, H., 'Feuer, Tarnhelm und Zaubertrank als Symbole der Wandlung', *Festival Programme*, Bayreuth, 1957; 'Totem und Tabu im Lohengrinmythos', 1958; 'Mann und Weib in Wagners Werken vom Holländer bis Parsifal', 1960.

Guénon, René, *Man and his Becoming According to the Vedanta*, tr. R. C. Nicholson, London, 1945: an almost too compact but very exact account of this aspect of Indian metaphysical doctrine, of which the subtlety and the comprehensiveness exceed any Western formulation.

Hanslick, Eduard, *The Beautiful in Music*, Vienna, 1854, tr. G. Cohen, intr. M. Weitz, New York, 1957: the best book by Wagner's celebrated critic and opponent, this should be read with care and respect by Wagnerians. Hanslick did not understand Wagner's work or aims, but his opposition was far more intelligent and substantial than is often supposed. His prose is lucid and well written and his thinking on the principles of musical aesthetics is often perceptive.

Hartmann, Otto Julius, *Die Esoteric im Werk Richard Wagners*, Frieburg/ Br., 1960.

Hollinrake, Roger, 'Nietzsche, Wagner and Ernest Newman', *Music and Letters*, Vol. XLI, No. 3, July, 1960: an excellent article on the famous quarrel and on Newman's view of it; defends Nietzsche ably and with partial success (and after all, Nietzsche was a genius too).

Hutcheson, Ernest, *A musical guide to the Ring of the Nibelung*, New York, 1940: a fairly ambitious study, but does not contribute much new illumination.

Jacobi, Iolande, 'Archetypisches im Ring des Nibelungen', *Festival Programme (Rheingold)*, Bayreuth, 1958.

*Jacobi, Iolande, *Complex, Archetype, Symbol*, tr. R. Manheim, London, 1942, revised ed. 1959: a most illuminating summary and discussion of these three central concepts of Jung's psychology.

James, Burnett, *Beethoven and Human Destiny*, London, 1960.

Joachim, H., 'Elsa and Lohengrin. A psychological Study', *Festival Programme*, Bayreuth, 1959.

Jung, C. G., *Aion*, tr. R. F. C. Hull, London, 1959: a far-ranging study relevant here at many points; touches on the alchemists' partial awareness that they were projecting inner realities on to the outer matter of their experiments (*see* next entry).

*Jung, C. G., *Archetypes and the Collective Unconscious*, tr. R. F. C. Hull, being Vol. 9 of the *Coll. Ed.*, London, 1959, parts 1 and 2, of which part 2 includes *Aion: Contributions to the Symbolism of the Self*.

*Jung, C. G., *Psychology and Alchemy* (1944), tr. R. F. C. Hull, *Coll. Ed.*, Vol. 12, London, 1953: detailed and far-ranging, a rich source for mythological symbols.

*Jung, C. G., *The Psychology of the Transference* (1946), tr. R. F. C. Hull, *Coll. Ed.*, Vol. 16, London, 1954: an outstanding study containing alchemical parallels of particular relevance to the present book.

Jung, C. G., *Symbols of Transformation*, tr. R. F. C. Hull, *Coll. Ed.*, Vol. 5, London, 1956: a revision of *The Psychology of the Unconscious*, the early work by which Jung made his independent reputation; full of material relevant to the present book, though not quite so richly interpreted as in Jung's subsequent work.

*Jung, C. G., *Two Essays on Analytical Psychology*, tr. R. F. C. Hull, *Coll. Ed.*, Vol. 7, London, 1953: two classics of Jung's earlier period, since repeatedly and extensively revised; the second, in particular, gives one of the best general statements of his views on the aspects of the psyche most relevant to the present book.

Jung, C. G., 'Wotan', in *Essays on Contemporary Events*, tr. Barbara Hannah, *Coll. Ed.*, Vol. 10, London, 1947: not important from the Wagnerian angle, being mainly an exposure of Nazi mentality, and treating the Norse Wotan (and Wagner's Wotan) only in a somewhat incidental and superficial manner.

*Jung, C. G., and Kerényi, C., *Essays on a Science of Mythology*, tr. R. F. C. Hull, New York, 1949; also as *Introduction to a Science of Mythology*, London, 1950: an important and characteristic study in terms of analytical psychology, mainly dealing with the archetype of the divine (boy) child and that of the divine maiden (Kore). (*Coll. Ed.*, Vol. 9, part 1.)

Jung, Emma, *The Grail Legend*, tr. Elizabeth Welsh, in private circulation (copy available in the library of the Analytical Psychology Club, London): an inconclusive but extremely interesting study relevant to, though not concerned with, Wagner's *Parsifal*.

Kapp, Julius, *The Loves of Richard Wagner*, London, 1951 (based on a previous book, 1931): well done in general, but brings out very little new factual information on this biographically and psychologically important subject.

*Kerényi, C.; *see* Jung, C. G., and Kerényi, C.

Kerman, Joseph, *Opera as Drama*, London, 1957: general, but done with intelligence and insight.

*Kerman, Joseph, 'Wagner: Thoughts in Season', *The Score*, London, Jan., 1961: a suggestive article on Wagner's musical style, with an interesting comparison from our present standpoint in regard to serial (twelve-tone) technique.

Kündig, Alice, *Das Musikerlebnis in psychologischer und psychothera-peutischer Sicht mit besonderer Berücksichtigung seiner kompensatorischen Funktion*, Wintherthur, 1961.

*Kurth, Dr. Ernst, *Romantische Harmonik und ihre Krise in Wagners 'Tristan'*, Berlin, 1920: an important study.

Larousse Encyclopedia of Mythology, various authors, tr. R. Aldington and Delano Ames, London, 1959: a useful work of reference, excellently compiled within the limits of space available.

Layard, John, 'Boar-Sacrifice and Schizophrenia', *Journal of Analytical Psychology*, Vol. I, No. 1, 1955: a very penetrating study of some deep aspects of the problem of combating and transforming the terrible Mother by means of sacrifice and incest-symbolism.

Bibliography

*Layard, John, 'Homo-eroticism in Primitive Society as a Function of the Self', *Journal of Analytical Psychology*, Vol. IV, No. 2, July, 1959, p. 101: brief but important on the 'kinship-mandala', on sister-exchange marriage, on incest, and on the homosexual component of the psyche as a positive spiritual element.

Layard, John, 'Identification with the Sacrificial Animal', *Eranos-Jahrbuch*, Vol. XXIV, Zurich, 1956: valuable on transformed incest-longings as a source of energy for the early stages in building civilization.

*Layard, John, 'The Incest Taboo and the Virgin Archetype', *Eranos-Jahrbuch*, Vol. XII, Zurich, 1945: new insight into a topic highly relevant to the present book.

*Layard, John, 'On Psychic Consciousness', *Eranos-Jahrbuch*, Vol. XXVIII, Zurich, 1960: an extremely subtle piece of psychological thinking which advances the borders of our knowledge; contains an exposition by its inventor of the term 'psychic consciousness' used freely in the present book.

Layard, John, *Stone Men of Malekula*, Vol. I, *Vao*, London, 1942: a dramatic, readable and very thorough account of an existing stone-age society, its ritual, its mythology, its kinship system, its music and its everyday life. The material is of fascinating interest, and its interpretation penetrating and original. Bears only indirectly on the subject of the present book for the most part, but includes a charming Malekulan parallel (valuably interpreted) to Siegmund and Sieglinde in the brother-sister love-story of Erets and Lerets.

Layton, K. A. W., 'The Nibelungen of Wagner', *University of Illinois Bulletin*, 7 Jan., 1909: a carefully thoughtful and critical study on mainly conventional lines.

*Leighton, A. L. and Crump, B., *The Ring of the Nibelung: An Interpretation Embodying Wagner's own Explanation*, London, 1909: an excellent example of a conventional interpretation along the orthodox lines.

Leroy, L. Archier, *Wagner's Music Drama of the Ring*, London, 1925: ambitious but unoriginal.

Loomis, Gertrude, *Tristan and Isolt: a Study of the Sources of the Romance*, New York, 1960: invaluable for those wishing to trace the background of Wagner's *Tristan*.

*Lorenz, A., *Das Geheimnis der Form bei Richard Wagner*, Munich, 1924–33: a classic.

Mann, Thomas, *Essays of Three Decades*, tr. H. T. Lowe-Porter, New

York, 1947: includes two essays on Wagner which are among the most penetrating to have been written, and also an essay on Freud which is excellent on the real meaning and importance of myth and the mythological attitude. (*See* Gregor, Martin.)

Meinertz, Josef, *Richard Wagner und Bayreuth: zur Psychologie des Schaffens und des Erlebens von Wagners Werken*, Berlin, Wunsiedel [1961].

Michel, André, *Psychanalyse de la Musique*, Paris, 1951.

Michel, Paul, *Über musikalische Fähigkeiten und Fertigkeiten: Ein Beitrag zur Musikpsychologie*, Leipzig, 1960.

*Neumann, Erich, *The Great Mother*, tr. R. Manheim, London, 1955: a magnificent work of research and interpretation; not easy reading, but one of the most rewarding of recent studies of a mythological image as interpreted in the light of analytical psychology.

*Neumann, Erich, *The Origins of History of Consciousness* (1949), tr. R. F. C. Hull, London, 1954: not easy reading, but one of the most fundamental contributions to the theory of analytical psychology, and particularly with regard to the light thrown by mythology on the nature of consciousness.

*Newman, Ernest, *The Life of Richard Wagner*, 4 vols., London, 1933–47.

Newman, Ernest, *Wagner as Man and Artist*, New York, 1914.

Nibelungen Lied, The, tr. A. G. Foster-Barham, London, 1887: a very important and impressive version of the saga.

Ninck, Martin, *Wodan und germanische Schicksalglaube*, Jena, 1935: an important study including a wealth of material relevant to the background of Wagner's *Ring*.

Overhoff, Kurt, *The German-Christian Myth of Richard Wagner*, tr. R. Chapin, Bayreuth, 1955: imaginative, but lacks psychological substantiation and is somewhat behind the times.

Radin, Paul, with commentary by C. G. Jung, *The Trickster: a Study in American Indian Mythology*, London, 1956: a fascinating and important study of a typical Trickster-God myth, throwing light incidentally on Wagner's Loge.

Rank, Otto, *The Myth of the Birth of the Hero*, tr. F. Robins and S. E. Jeliffe, New York, 1941: a most illuminating study by this distinguished colleague of Freud.

*Read, Herbert, *Icon and Idea: the Function of Art in the Development of Human Consciousness*, London, 1955.

*Read, Herbert, *The Forms of Things Unknown: Essays Towards an*

Aesthetic Philosophy, London, 1960. This and the foregoing are important philosophically.

Read, Herbert, *The Meaning of Art*, London, 1931: a justly celebrated discussion which retains its value.

*Read, Sir Herbert, 'Poetic Consciousness and Creative Experience', *Eranos Jahrbuch*, Vol. XXV, Zurich, 1956, p. 357: an invaluable essay because of its rare combination of artistic understanding and psychological insight.

*Roeke, S., *What does Richard Wagner relate concerning the Origin of his Nibelungen Poem?* tr. C. Parish, London, 1907; and *What does Richard Wagner relate concerning the Origin of his Musical Composition of the Ring of the Nibelungs?* tr. C. Parish, London, 1908: important source material.

Rosenfeld, V. V., *see* 'Viviar'.

Rydberg, Viktor, *Teutonic Mythology*, tr. R. B. Anderson, London, 1889: a learned successor to (and in some ways challenger of) Grimm; now more valuable for material than interpretation.

Shaw, Bernard, *The Perfect Wagnerite*, London, 1898: vastly readable; had the great merit of drawing early attention to the fact that a topical human reality lies behind the fairy-tale surface of the *Ring*; but exaggerates the allegorical references to the outer world of politics and economics; overlooks the inner symbolism; and with regard to the music, mingles great sense and great silliness in about equal proportions.

Smith, G. Elliot, *The Evolution of the Dragon*, Manchester, 1919: a distinguished contribution by the famous 'diffusionist' anthropologist.

Stein, Jack, *Richard Wagner: the Synthesis of the Arts*, Detroit, 1960: a valuable and to some extent novel study of this aspect of Wagner's theory and practice.

Sterba, Editha and Richard, *Beethoven and his Nephew*, New York, 1954, London, 1957: a mainly Freudian angle.

*Sturluson, Snorri, *The Younger or Prose Edda*, tr. A. G. Brodeur, New York, 1916: the most detailed source of much of the mythology used or adapted by Wagner, and a mine of fascinating narrative and information.

Sullivan, J. W. N., *Beethoven*, London, 1927: an uneven but highly intuitive study which brings out the connection between an artist's life-problems and his work, although written before most psychological writings on this subject.

Taylor, G. R., *Sex in History*, London, 1953: too preoccupied with the more sensational aberrations to be quite as valuable as it might be.

Not a word about Parsifal or the chaste knighthood of the Holy Grail!

Tippett, Michael, *Moving into Aquarius*, London, 1959: a characteristically rich and imperfectly sorted flow of ideas bearing on music and life from the angles of hermetic philosophy, astrology and other unexpected quarters, but chiefly from the author's own original turn of mind.

*'Viviar' (V. V. Rosenfeld), 'A genius and his Parents', *Festival Programme (Walkyrie)*, Bayreuth, 1958: concentrates on the Oedipal problem to the exclusion of other aspects, but discusses it well; 'Images and Pictures' (*Fliegende Holländer*, 1959): excellent on Wagner's image of the eternal feminine; 'The Inexpressible; an Essay on Wagner's Leitmotifs' (*Parsifal*, 1960): illuminating.

Volkmann-Schluck, K. H., 'The Ring of the Nibelung. Crisis of Consciousness', *Festival Programme*, Bayreuth, 1956.

Völsunga Saga, The, tr. E. Magnússon and Wm. Morris, London, n.d.: perhaps the most moving of all the sagas relating the story of the Volsung race, and a most important source for Wagner's material.

Wagner, Richard, *Collected Prose Works*, 8 vols., tr. W. A. Ellis, London, 1892–99.

*Wagner, Richard, *The Nibelung's Ring*, tr. F. Jameson, London, 1896: an English translation of very high merit in view of the difficulties involved.

Westernhagen, Curt von, 'Die Symbolik des Todes', *Festival Programme*, Bayreuth, 1960.

Westernhagen, Curt von, *Gesprach um Wagner. Discussion on Wagner. Entretiens sur Wagner*, Bayreuth, 1961.

*Westernhagen, Curt von, *Richard Wagner. Sein Werk, sein Wesen, seine Welt*, Zurich, 1956.

*Winnicott, D. W., *Collected Papers*, London, 1958: adds up to one of the very best and most original studies of the formation of personality during infancy and afterwards.

Zuckerkandl, Victor, *Sound and Symbol: Music and the External World*, Bollingen Series, XVIV, New York, 1959: a most interesting attempt to account for the symbolism of musical imagery, but not altogether successful, nor in any decisive respect novel.

Index

---❈---

The main page references are in bold type.
There is a numerical index of motives on page 308.

Index

Index

323

Index

Index